RELATIONSHIP ENHANCEMENT
FAMILY THERAPY

WILEY SERIES IN COUPLES AND FAMILY DYNAMICS AND TREATMENT

Florence W. Kaslow, Series Editor

Relationship Enhancement Family Therapy

Barry G. Ginsberg, PhD

John Wiley & Sons, Inc.

New York • Chichester • Weinheim • Brisbane • Singapore • Toronto

All names in this book are fictitious.

This text is printed on acid-free paper.

This publication is designed to provide accurate and authoritative
information in regard to the subject matter covered. It is sold
with the understanding that the publisher is not engaged in
rendering professional services. If legal, accounting, medical,
psychological, or other expert assistance is required, the
services of a competent professional person should be sought.

Library of Congress Cataloging-in-Publication Data:

Ginsberg, Barry G., 1936–
    Relationship enhancement family therapy / by Barry G. Ginsberg.
        p.   cm. — (Wiley series in couples and family dynamics and
    treatment)
    ISBN 0-471-04955-7 (cloth : alk. paper)
    1. Family psychotherapy.   I. Title.   II. Series.
    RC488.5.G53   1997
    616.89'156—dc20   96-46033

Printed in the United States of America

10   9   8   7   6   5   4   3   2   1

I dedicate this book to my wife, Mindi, with deepest love and acknowledgment of the profound meaning our relationship has had in my life. Her faith in me continues to sustain me and motivate me to be the best I can. Without her part in my life, this book could not have been written.

Series Preface

Our ability to form strong interpersonal bonds with romantic partners, children, parents, siblings, and other relations is one of the key qualities that defines our humanity. These relationships shape who we are and what we become—they can be a source of great gratification or tremendous pain. Yet only in the mid-twentieth century did behavioral and social scientists really begin focusing on couples and family dynamics, and only in the past several decades have the theory and findings that emerged from those studies been used to develop effective therapeutic interventions for troubled couples and families.

We have made great progress in understanding the structure, function, and interactional patterns of couples and families—and have made tremendous strides in treatment. However, as we stand poised on the beginning of a new millennium, it seems quite clear that both intimate partnerships and family relationships are in a period of tremendous flux. Economic factors are changing work patterns, parenting responsibilities, and relational dynamics. Modern medicine has helped lengthen the life span, giving rise to the need for transgenerational caretaking. Cohabitation, divorce, and remarriage are quite commonplace, and these social changes make it necessary for us to rethink and broaden our definition of what constitutes a family.

Thus, it is no longer enough simply to embrace the concept of the family as a system. In order to understand and effectively treat the evolving family, our theoretical formulations and clinical interventions must be informed by an understanding of ethnicity, culture, religion, gender, sexual preference, family life cycle, socioeconomic status, education, physical and mental health, values, and belief systems.

The purpose of the *Wiley Series in Couples and Family Dynamics and Treatment* is to provide a forum for cutting-edge relational and family theory, practice, and research. Its scope is intended to be broad, diverse, and international, but all books published in this series share a common mission: to reflect on the past, offer state-of-the-art information on the present, and speculate on, as well as attempt to shape, the future of the field.

FLORENCE W. KASLOW
Florida Couples and Family Institute

Preface

When I entered the doctoral program at the Pennsylvania State University in September 1969, I was unprepared for what I found. I had just received a master's degree in clinical school psychology from the College of the City of New York. The program was dominated by teachers from the William Allison White Institute. I had been strongly influenced by the existential psychoanalytic movement and particularly by the interpersonal approach of Harry Stack Sullivan. I was also trained in a diagnostic treatment model that assessed clients along a sickness–health continuum.

What I found at Penn State was dramatically different. A group of researchers led by Bernard G. Guerney and Louise Guerney had recently moved from Rutgers University to the College of Human Development at Penn State, and they were generating much excitement. They had developed an innovative approach to psychotherapy that was educational and involved family members with each other.

Today, it is hard to imagine how difficult their work must have been in the early years, and how much courage they needed to persevere. In the 1950s, when they began their research, therapy was largely conducted on an individual basis and emphasized intrapsychic factors. The Guerneys, however, began to explore ways of doing psychotherapy that featured joint sessions with family members (parents and children, husbands and wives), bringing family members together rather than separating them into their own individual therapies. They believed that therapy should be interpersonal and emphasized the primary relationship of the family. They, too, had been strongly influenced by Harry Stack Sullivan. This exploration led to the development of filial therapy, in which parents are taught to conduct weekly play sessions with their own children at home.

The Guerneys received funding for a large, three-year (National Institute of Mental Health) grant to assess the effectiveness of filial therapy. The results demonstrated the value of this approach. (Stover & Guerney, 1967) and led them to apply their ideas and methods to other relationships (B. G. Guerney, 1977).

The Guerney's approach to therapy introduced an educational model of psychotherapy, which directly challenged the prevailing medical model. Unless clients had a clear organic problem, the Guerneys felt that people would be helped by learning skills to cope with the realities of their everyday lives and emotional experiences. Their new vision of therapy dramatically altered the role of the therapist, who became less of a diagnostician and more of an educator.

This idea—that the therapist is less someone who understands and diagnoses a problem and more someone who educates people in the skills they need to cope with their difficulties—had a very strong impact on me. I was struck by the respect inherent in this approach, which placed my clients and me in a more equivalent relationship, a concept drawn from Rogers's principles of client-centered therapy (1951). This resonated with my own reading of Jay Haley's work (1969), which cleverly challenged the use of power in traditional models of therapy.

As I began to learn the Relationship Enhancement (RE) approach to therapy, I became increasingly excited about how it empowered clients. As a therapist, I also felt empowered by its structured, systematic, and time-designated methodology. At the same time, I appreciated RE's emphasis on using, as the agents of change, the clients' own primary and significant relationships rather than the therapist–client relationship. I was particularly impressed with the dramatic changes in people that occurred in surprisingly short periods of time.

Ironically, the core concepts of RE—training family members as helpers for one another; making efficient use of community resources (i.e., training nonprofessionals and other professionals in these skills); recognizing the cost-effectiveness of groups; integrating the best from psychodynamic, client-centered, interpersonal, behavioral, communications, and systems approaches—are precisely those demanded by today's healthcare marketplace with its emphasis on efficiency and effective managed care treatments. In this sense, the Guerneys were years ahead of their time.

Following the completion of my doctoral studies, and while practicing as a psychologist in a mental health center, I took additional training in family therapy and a variety of other therapies. Over the years, I've found many of these approaches useful, but, in retrospect, I recognize that I regularly turn back to the RE approach as my primary method of intervention. I have been most satisfied with the outcomes that have been elicited by directly applying the RE approach to the issues and problems that people have brought to my attention. My enthusiasm from this experience sparked my decision to write this book. I have adopted RE's developmental perspective. The issues and needs that clients struggle with evolve over time. With this in mind, I have structured this book to show how the principles and methods of RE are applicable at all stages of development and are beneficial across the life span.

BARRY GINSBERG

Acknowledgments

My deepest appreciation to Louise and Bernard G. Guerney, Jr., who had the wisdom to be innovative and creative and the courage to stick with their beliefs and principles all these years. I appreciate the guidance, support, encouragement, and friendship that have characterized my relationship with Bernard Guerney for more than a quarter century. His creation played a significant part in the direction I took in my life. I could not have had a better mentor. Louise Guerney epitomizes what Carl Rogers meant when he developed his concept of "acceptance." She has been the best model, teacher, and friend. I am grateful for her guidance and our friendship.

I am grateful to have known Lillian Stover, the person who introduced me to Relationship Enhancement and encouraged me. Her warmth, friendship, supervision, and insight helped me see the values and power of RE. Her guidance helped form the basis of how I understand and use RE.

Roberta Israeloff has been my consultant in writing this book. She has engaged with me on each sentence, paragraph, and chapter. She understood my meaning and helped me find the words to describe it. Her warmth, insight, and sensitive feedback helped me learn more about myself. I value the friendship that we have developed.

Cassie Hosier, my administrative assistant, typist, and friend, has been instrumental in the completion of this book. Her competence, and my confidence in her, have allowed me to focus on writing. I can't thank her enough.

I am very grateful to Florence Kaslow, who invited me to write this book and who could see its potential.

Kelly Franklin, my editor at John Wiley & Sons, had confidence that there was "a good book here." I appreciate her support and guidance.

To my sons, Joshua, Daniel, and Jeremy, and their families I owe much gratitude. What I have learned from them over the years as a father and grandfather is beyond acknowledgment. The friendship that has evolved between us gives me tremendous satisfaction and fulfillment at this stage of my life.

B.G.G.

Contents

CHAPTER 1

Basic Principles

Clients bring a number of presenting problems to therapy. But often, once their initial concerns are relieved, new problems surface. A crisis arises and is attended to, action is taken, change occurs, and a new understanding emerges. But this new understanding spawns new problems, issues, and concerns. Thus, the cycle repeats itself. This is the nature of life.

According to common psychiatric belief, clients' problems are a product of a central underlying mental disorder that can be systematically labeled and treated. This approach, however, does not hold true for most of the issues couples and family therapists confront in practice. The effort to objectify and systematize the process that brings people to treatment, though admirable, flies in the face of the broad variability of human experience and behavior. In spite of the attempt to systematize the diagnostic and treatment process, our ability to predict how people will think and act remains imprecise. Instead of just struggling to uncover the "truth" underlying psychological problems, it makes more sense to try to teach people the skills they need to effect ongoing change and gain the means to care for themselves.

RELATIONSHIP ENHANCEMENT THERAPY

Relationship Enhancement (RE), an approach to therapy that integrates psychodynamic, behavioral, communications, and family systems perspectives, emphasizes the importance of identifying beliefs about how problems arise and helping clients learn skills that will enable them to address these problems. In short, the therapist first helps clients to feel understood, to recognize their problem more clearly, and to understand how learning specific skills will help *them* deal with the problem. Together,

1

therapists and clients then agree on a time-limited course of action. This "contract" directs the course of the therapeutic relationship until a new "contract" is agreed on. All the while, clients are fully informed about the principles, methods, and applications of the therapy. As a result, they are inclined to more fully collaborate with the therapist. By emphasizing collaboration between therapist and client, a skill-training approach such as Relationship Enhancement therapy fosters greater equivalence between therapist and client, empowers the client, and allows the client to draw on his or her own resources in the process.

THE EDUCATIONAL VERSUS THE MEDICAL MODEL OF THERAPY

Relationship Enhancement therapy is based on education rather than treatment. It emphasizes the importance of learning certain skills—how to cope with and enhance relationships, improve self-concept, and thereby achieve personal and interpersonal satisfaction—rather than curing or solving a particular problem. The problem's solution is not ignored; rather, the client is taught to solve problems as part of the therapy. The intent is less to help people change than to help them learn to create a context in which constructive change is more likely to occur. Once this context is established, clients become more autonomous and differentiated and, ultimately, more intimate with significant people in their lives. Having learned these skills, and trusting that they can solve their own problems, clients are in a better position to deal with life's crises on their own.

Bernard G. Guerney, Jr. (1982b, pp. 484–485) has described the assumptions underlying the rationale for skill training as therapy:

1. Personality—defined here as the relatively enduring, preferred ways of dealing with emotions, people, and self-concept-related thoughts—is based on the interplay, over time, of one's biochemistry (including genetic components) and the environment.
2. The effects of all nonbiochemical interventions depend on the individual's interaction with the environment—that is, on learning.
3. The best models for therapy come not from clinics and the practices and procedures of physicians (medical model), but from schools and the practices and procedures of teachers (educational

Table 1.1   Educational Model versus Medical Model

Educational Model	Medical Model
• Emphasizes developmental processes, psychosocial needs, and life stresses.	• Emphasizes sickness (maladaption/pathology).
• De-emphasizes insight and etiology.	• Emphasizes insight and etiology.
• Problem lies within individual's control.	• Problem lies outside the individual's control.
• Client agrees to learn from the practitioner (teacher).	• Client depends on the expertise of the practitioner for change.
• Best healing and change come from the client's own efforts.	• Healing is dependent on the practitioner's skill.
• Clients are encouraged to seek the knowledge and resources they need.	• Generally, clients under the exclusive care of the provider.
• Methods include: setting goal(s), understanding rationale and methods of skill, skill practice and learning, generalizing the problems of everyday life, and maintaining skills.	• Methods include: diagnosis, treatment, and cure.
• No distinction between prevention and amelioration.	• Methods are skewed more toward treatment than prevention.

model). Only the latter model efficiently and effectively produces the learning and relearning required for personality change (see Table 1.1).

4. Compared to the medical model, the educational model of intervention is more accessible for greater numbers of people because the public more readily accepts educational procedures. In addition, the educational model can be more widely disseminated by employing paraprofessionals and using mass-produced media aids, such as audio and video training tapes.

5. Significant and enduring personality change is achieved most effectively through an educational program that combines cognitive instruction—which concerns such issues as principles, attitudes, and values—and behavioral instruction—which concerns emotional self-reconditioning and guided practice or rehearsal of new ways of handling emotions, interpersonal

interactions, and self-concept-related thoughts. This dual approach is defined here as skills training.

In addition to Guerney's five assumptions, two others can be emphasized:

6. The medical model focuses on individualized intervention. In the educational model, a structured and systematic program is developed to address the psychosocial needs and problems common to many individuals.

7. The educational model helps clients to achieve goals, a positive approach, rather than to eliminate underlying pathology, a negative approach that often elicits resistance. In the educational model, the practitioner shares the planning and decision making with the client. An agreement (informal contract) is then established between the parties. In addition, there is no expectation that the client is under the exclusive care of the practitioner, as is implied in the physician–patient relationship. The practitioner using the educational model encourages clients to seek out whatever knowledge and resources they need.

Practitioners using the educational model assume that the best healing or change arises from the client's own efforts. The outcome is not dependent on the expertise of the practitioner, but on the expertise clients gain to deal with their concerns. The practitioner of the educational model believes that skill building is the most effective way to help the client.

Aaron T. Beck (Beck, Emery, & Greenberg, 1985) has indicated that cognitive therapy is based on an educational model. According to Beck, problems arise when people learn inappropriate ways to cope with life experience, and the best approach the therapist can take is as a teacher of skills (in this case, anxiety-management skills). Beck incorporates didactic techniques such as providing information, assigning reading, listening to audiotapes, and homework—all of which are part of the RE approach. Since the beginning of RE therapy in the 1960s, educational approaches have become more accepted and popular. The therapist-as-teacher is a concept favored in many recent therapeutic approaches, particularly behavioral family and marital therapies (Falloon, 1991; Holtzworth-Monroe & Jacobson, 1991).

In the psychosocial educational model, the practitioner's values are made explicit so the client can choose to participate. Because the skills that practitioners emphasize are based on their own values, these beliefs (values) must be made apparent to clients.

Another advantage of the educational model is that the same or similar methods can be used to prevent as well as ameliorate problems. There is no distinction between sick and not sick. Furthermore, it is easier to assess the benefit of a pragmatic approach that is designed to teach psychosocial skills than to assess treatment and cure.

HOW RE THERAPY BUILDS ON FAMILY SYSTEMS THEORY

RE therapy recognizes that we all enter the world as members of a relationship system, usually called "family." As we develop, we seek to perpetuate this type of relationship system. Thus, RE therapy holds that the family is the primary context within which to work. Even in individual therapy, RE therapy recognizes (as do most family therapies) that we are working within the family context.

An early influence on RE therapy was Leary's interpersonal theory of personality (1957), based on the theories of Harry Stack Sullivan (1947). In this view, the individual's personality is shaped by his or her early relationships, which in turn shape relationships over the life span. The individual is seen as developing "interpersonal reflexes" (Leary, 1957; Shannon & Guerney, 1973), which trigger the same kind of response in others. This is a reciprocal process that operates outside of our awareness. Shannon and Guerney (1973) have determined that these interpersonal reflexes elicit like responses: Positive statements elicit positive responses and negative statements elicit negative responses. Out of this framework evolved the notion of training people to learn constructive relationship skills.

Over the years, RE therapy has been subtly influenced by other family therapies and therapists. The family system is different when it includes the therapist (Minuchin & Fishman, 1981) and is engaged in a process over time (Carter & McGoldrick, 1980, 1988). Thus, to enable the family to change its functions outside of the therapeutic arena, the family members need to be trained in adaptive skills. This supports RE's psychoeducational approach.

The RE approach to family therapy evolved independently from the groundbreaking work of Bowen (1976, 1978a), Bateson (1972, 1979), and Minuchin (1974), yet RE incorporates many of their principles, including these notions:

- Circular processes that are reciprocally contingent influence the behavior of the family and its members in a complex manner and facilitate family stability or instability.
- The triangle is the basic building block of the relationship system, and emotion motivates its functioning.
- The more one is differentiated, the more autonomously one functions emotionally and intellectually.
- Clear boundaries for individuals, subsystems, the family, and the external environment lead to better functioning.
- Functional boundaries, particularly those between generations, depend on communication.
- Naturally occurring alliances and coalitions within relationship systems become dysfunctional as they become rigid.
- When boundaries are not clear, relationships become enmeshed.

A recent study (Griffin & Apostal, 1993) considered the effectiveness of the RE program (B. G. Guerney, 1987a, 1987b) in increasing the functional and basic levels of differentiation of self (Bowen, 1978a). In the study, 20 married couples were trained in RE skills over six two-and-a-half-hour sessions. Researchers took measures of differentiation of self, the quality of the relationship, and anxiety levels before and after training, and then repeated the measurement of these variables one year following treatment. Their data found significant increases in functional and basic levels of differentiation of self and in the quality of the relationship, and significant negative correlations between differentiation of self and anxiety. These results confirm that the educational approach of RE positively influences important individual and family systems' variables.

RE skills also incorporate the values and beliefs that have been enunciated by the contextual therapy of Boszormenyi-Nagy (1966, 1972; see also Boszormenyi-Nagy, Grunbaum, & Ulrich, 1991; Boszormenyi-Nagy & Krasner, 1986; Boszormenyi-Nagy & Spark, 1973). These include:

- *Family loyalty:* the internalized expectations, injunctions, and obligations in relation to one's family of origin, which have powerful and significant interpersonal influence, particularly on the development of trust and responsibility.
- *Relational ethics (fairness):* the belief that the basic life interests of each person need to be taken into account by others in the relationship system. This approximates the concept of equivalence in RE therapy.

- *Multigenerational perspective:* the use of a three-generation perspective to understanding the individual's development and the family's functioning.
- *Multidirectional partiality:* emphasizes empathy and respect for all family members.

Like contextual therapy, RE emphasizes the responsibility of the therapist to be humble, respectful, and fair to all family members. This helps to foster the essential collaboration between client families and the RE therapist.

Olson, Russell, and Sprenkle (1983) have identified and researched three dimensions of family behavior—(a) cohesion, (b) adaptability, and (c) communication—in his circumplex model of marital and family systems. All three dimensions are important in RE.

Family cohesion is defined as the "emotional bonding that family members have toward one another" (Olson et al., 1983, p. 70). This dimension considers issues of coalitions and boundaries and assesses levels of cohesion from disengaged to enmeshed. RE's emphasis on emotional expression and acknowledgment in a nonjudgmental, accepting environment enhances family cohesion. The structured nature of the RE approach, particularly its emphasis on self-ownership, helps family members to differentiate, and, consequently, to define boundaries more clearly.

Family adaptability is defined as "the ability of a marital or family system to change its power structure, role relationships, and relationship rules in response to situational and developmental stress" (Olson et al., 1983, p. 70). This is particularly relevant as the family develops over time: as children are born, grow up, and leave home. This measure ranges from rigid to structured to flexible to chaotic. Olson et al. hypothesize that the central levels ("structured" and "flexible") are more functional than the levels at the extremes of the range. RE therapy directly addresses this dimension of adaptability; its concepts of acceptance and equivalence are directly related to family adaptability. The more we can accept ourselves and others, the more flexible we can be. If we take a position that we are basically equivalent to each other, it changes the way we use power as well as the way we establish roles and rules in the family. It is easier to accept the natural or agreed-on hierarchical roles necessary to relationship functioning under these conditions of acceptance and equivalence. Further, learning the skills that enhance secure and trustful relationships fosters greater flexibility.

The third dimension, family communication, is defined as including constructive (positive) communication skills such as empathy, reflective listening, and supportive comments. RE skill training emphasizes these skills. Olson sees communication as the facilitating dimension for cohesion and adaptability. This view coincides with RE therapy's emphasis on communication as the primary focus of skill learning.

PRINCIPLES OF RE THERAPY

The following principles and methods form the basis of all RE therapy programs. RE therapy is an educationally based skill-training family therapy that is structured, systematic, and time-designated. As an educational approach, it is nondiagnostic; similar methods are used for prevention or amelioration. It is a collaborative approach in which the therapist openly describes to clients his or her own values, beliefs, and methods, in the interest of establishing a genuine collaboration. These values and methods emphasize the importance of relationships with others in all human development. Given this importance, language and communication are the essential ingredients of interpersonal functioning. Furthermore, RE therapy places strong emphasis on emotion and the communication of feeling in human interaction.

The specific methods of RE therapy are built on the importance of the following beliefs: (a) Healing or change is the outcome of the person's (client's) own efforts; (b) Understanding ourselves and others helps us cope; (c) Trust is essential to all relationships; it improves openness and vulnerability while reducing anxiety and defensiveness; (d) RE therapy is based on the fundamental equivalence of all human beings despite differences in age, stage of development, power, and hierarchical position.

THE RE THERAPEUTIC PROCESS

Education does not have to occur in a formal and didactic context. It can occur in a tutorial with one person or in a small group. In fact, the tutorial approach of RE approximates the traditional treatment approach: Clients under stress consult with a practitioner. After understanding the clients' stress and concerns, the practitioner identifies the rationale for how certain skills can ameliorate these concerns. He or she then proposes a systematic program to help clients learn the skills and apply them in everyday life. The clients agree to this program after understanding the benefit of learning these skills, which are taught in a structured, systematic, and time-designated process. This process operates in an intimate and secure tutorial context. When coaching and modeling the skills, the practitioner is didactic. Once the clients learn the basic skills, they then practice on their own, and the practitioner shifts from tutor to consultant. With the practitioner's guidance, clients determine how often they feel they need consultation to help generalize and maintain the skills. This empowering, positive process reduces the dependence of the clients on the practitioner. The clients "own" the problem—and its solution.

How a Typical Interaction Works

John and May have come into the therapist's office because John has moved out of their bedroom recently, complaining that he "can't take it anymore." The conflicts between them have become increasingly difficult and frequent. May is very upset and "can't understand why he is doing this."

A review of the problem history seems to suggest that a change in May's family-of-origin (an inheritance) has precipitated these difficulties. The therapist informs John and May that the couple's difficulties likely will be eased once they improve their communication skills. John is unsure how this skill-learning approach will address what he believes to be an impossible situation. The therapist acknowledges these feelings and identifies how a recent conflict arose from difficulties in communication. The therapist points out the importance of improving speaking and listening skills and constructively integrating them into a relationship. The therapist explains, "It's hard because neither of you seems to listen to the other. As a result, you both get defensive, and that makes it harder for you to resolve your difficulties. When you're defensive, you're sure to be accusative, judgmental, or questioning. This only leads to more defensiveness and more difficulty. I think it would be helpful to slow down the process, and help you both improve your speaking and listening skills so that you will feel better and be more able to resolve things."

May and John agree, and the therapist encourages them to try practicing these new skills under the therapist's guidance. They are supervised in a short trial around a less sensitive or more positive issue. They both see the value of doing this. John reports, "I even feel a little better." They agree to practice this way under the therapist's supervision for four sessions. At the end of this period, all agree that John and May are ready to practice on their own at home. In the meantime, John has moved back into the bedroom. After a taped practice session at home that is reviewed during therapy, both May and John agree to continue practicing once a week. They also agree to meet with the therapist in four weeks to review their progress.

BASIC BELIEFS OF RE THERAPY

A primary belief of RE therapy is that a lack of understanding or a misunderstanding of ourselves and our intimates undermines our functioning. Conversely, understanding helps us cope and function better. A basic goal of RE therapy is to increase that understanding. According to this approach, *enhanced relationships are those in which individuals have developed a greater capacity to better understand themselves and each other and are able to communicate that understanding.*

The goal is not simply to increase the capacity for understanding, but to use it to resolve past hurts, act more effectively in the present, and cope with life's disruptions in the future. These skills become a permanent part of the individual's repertoire; they are ready to be used when needed. In this way, RE therapy helps people do more than change a condition that is causing a problem; it reinforces their capability to do things differently. Habitual patterns can then be altered and possibly replaced by more functional methods.

VALUES IN RE THERAPY

Doherty and Boss (1991) emphasize that "values and ethics underlie everything we do in family therapy" (p. 634). According to Spiegel (1971), values "have an evaluative component—that is, they serve as principles for making selections between alternative courses of action; an existential component, which means that the value orientations help to define the nature of reality for those who hold the given values; and finally they have an affective component, which means that people not only prefer and believe in their own values but are also ready to bleed and die for them. For this reason, values, once formed, can be changed only with the greatest difficulty" (p. 190).

Spiegel (1971) further states that values are beliefs that help guide us to make choices between different courses of action. This is particularly important in RE therapy because one of the therapist's responsibilities is to inform clients of the beliefs that underlie the therapeutic approach so that they can genuinely choose to participate and collaborate in it. In essence, making the therapist's values explicit helps clients genuinely grant permission for the therapist to proceed. According to Aponte (1985), the negotiation of values is central to the process of therapy. The therapist must understand the link between the therapist's values and family assessment and intervention. The RE therapist works hard to maintain the values inherent in RE's foundation.

THE FOUR PILLARS OF RE

RE therapy stands on four important pillars:

1. Empathy.
2. Language and relationship.
3. Emotional expression.
4. Acceptance (including being nonjudgmental and embracing the notion of equivalence).

These principles are consistent throughout all the applications of RE and provide a cohesive core.

Empathy

The RE rationale states that people learn to become more honest and compassionate when they understand their own needs, desires, preferences, aspirations, and values, and those of others. In such an empathic relationship, people can see and express issues and emotions more openly, without a great deal of defensiveness, guilt, and blame. When each person is more sensitive and aware of his or her own values, needs, and feelings regarding a relationship, the person engages in fewer psychological defense ploys. We relate to one another more clearly and directly so as to lessen the other's emotional pain and the common tendency to respond with defensiveness or to counterattack. This philosophy also supports the idea that an empathic and open relationship promotes a feeling of well-being and confidence and helps to raise a person's self-esteem and ego strength. This affirmation of self in turn makes it easier for a person to acknowledge and affirm another.

Through the RE principles, individuals are more able to create an interpersonal climate that allows them to more calmly confront their honest thoughts and feelings. It enables them to problem-solve effectively and to maximize their potential for happiness and satisfaction with self and others. This helps ensure positive, healthy growth.

Adhering to and practicing the RE principles can also lead to the development of more egalitarian relationships with people who are important to us. Individuals then resolve conflicts by using negotiation and compromise rather than coercion and power. Each individual has a better chance of experiencing a sense of strength and importance because each one's thoughts and feelings are being heard, acknowledged, and viewed as having value and worth.

Language and Relationship

RE therapists believe that relationship systems are meaning-generating systems that are dependent on language, and that a therapeutic relationship system is a "problem-organizing, problem-dissolving system" (Anderson & Goolishian, 1988). In essence, problems are mutually determined in the conversation between parties; in turn, problem change or resolution is mutually determined between client(s) and therapist. Anderson and Goolishian (1988) believe: "The goal of therapy is to participate in a conversation that continually loosens and opens up, rather than constructs or closes down" (p. 380). In such a context, meanings are changed, thus creating more choices for change. However, the RE therapist takes responsibility for the conversational context that promotes this loosening or opening up, and tries to help clients create such contexts in their own lives.

Each therapist derives his or her own epistemology regarding therapy. We all have a worldview that naturally will influence the choices we make as clinicians. Nevertheless, the RE therapist assumes a position of humility with regard to the problem that clients present. We cannot fully understand or know how a problem came to be, nor can we be sure we know how to help solve it. For Anderson and Goolishian (1988), the process of change requires communicative action: "This capacity for change is in the ability we have to be in language with each other," and "through this process . . . we reorganize our mutual living and our self descriptions" (p. 387).

In effect, this is done in RE therapy. We emphasize the importance of maintaining conversation between the clients rather than between the therapist and client(s). Therapeutic change occurs primarily in the context of one's significant others and one's living system. The primary focus of therapy is having clients converse with each other using RE principles and skills. When conversations continue over time, genuine change can occur. The therapist needs to help clients understand the rationale underlying the conversational rules so that they can agree to collaborate. With their understanding, the therapist is given permission to maintain a safe context for such conversations as long as the agreement between clients and therapist continues. These methods of communication are necessary to develop constructive and empowering conversations that will help people conduct more satisfying and fulfilling lives.

Emotional Expression

Clear expression and acknowledgment of feeling is essential to the kinds of conversation that RE therapy fosters. Mahoney (1985) believes that "emotional changes are bound up with significant personal changes, and that emotion is seen as both expression and driving force (motivation)" (p. 27). If we are to be truly understood, we need to understand how we "feel" in relation to what we're saying. When we don't understand our feelings or motivation, we can't communicate what we mean, and others must infer our meaning. Emotion underlies all human action. Words (feeling expression) come closest to recognizing and acknowledging what we experience in our bodies. Without emotional language, we could not understand our actions or their motivations and would be helpless to regulate those actions and/or convey an understanding of our actions to others. That is why expression of feelings is so central to the skills that clients learn in RE therapy.

Without language we would be unable to represent or change our understanding of our experience. An important objective in RE therapy is to help clients improve the coherence between understanding their experience and the experience itself. Finding the words that come closest to our direct emotional experience helps us understand our own meanings. Personal meaning essentially depends on affect. "Conscious self experience, which does incorporate this emotion-based information, is created by the process of attending inwardly to and symbolizing one's emotional responses to situations" (L. S. Greenberg, Rice, & Elliott, 1993, p. 57). Emotion is symbolized through feelings, which Rogers (1959) defines as "emotionally tinged experience, together with its personal meaning. Thus, it includes the emotion in its experiential context. It thus refers to the unity of emotion and cognition as they are experienced in the moment" (p. 158). RE therapy insists on acknowledging the feeling that pertains to the expression of one's meaning, that is, finding the words that best describe the feeling that pertains to the meaning. Because of this emphasis, RE therapy elicits a unity of emotion and cognition. When this meaning is shared with and understood by a significant other, as is encouraged by RE therapy, one's sense of self in the world is more secure. A person who is more true to self can then act more assertively and confidently. Talking about emotions can elicit many different conceptions, definitions, and descriptions; nevertheless, we all seem to agree that emotion—how we "feel"—is important to how we function. Specifically, emotional regulation is important to childhood development and influences the quality of social relationships. Social relationships in turn have a regulatory effect on each individual's expression of emotion (Fox, 1994). Fox (1994) suggests that emotional regulation organizes cognitive processes and helps the individual adjust to the complexities of a particular situation. In turn, these emotional regulation functions build social relationships, which continue to be modified by the interactions that take place within those relationships. "Thus, the context (e.g., the care-taking environment) should be seen as playing an integral part in shaping the strategies and patterns of the emotion response that the child develops as he or she meets different developmental challenges" (p. 5).

Emotions help people adapt to changing circumstances. "In living systems, the purpose of affectivity is to select perceptions, ideas and actions" (Brown, 1991, p. 8). This is done through what Brown characterizes as "thermodynamic ideas" (p. 8), which are, in essence, physiologically determined. Efran, Lukens, and Lukens (1990) define emotions as "the bodily predispositions that underlie, support and create readiness for action" (p. 157). They believe that emotion is always with us in our bodyhood, and that "every rational act rides piggyback on an underlying emotional predisposition even when that disposition is not being noticed or made explicit in language" (pp. 157–158). That is, even if we don't notice our feelings or don't acknowledge them, they are behind every rational act. Bretherton, Fritz, Zahn-Walker, and Ridgeway (1986) have emphasized a functional view of human emotion. They believe that emotions are adaptive, providing survival-promoting processes, but that they have a major intrapsychic regulatory function as well as an interpersonal one. Essentially, they believe that emotions are "organizers of personal and interpersonal life and development itself" (p. 530). That is why RE therapy emphasizes the importance of people's recognizing and taking responsibility for their feelings.

Rogers (1990) states, "As material is given by the client, it is the therapists' function to help him recognize and clarify the emotion he feels" (p. 162). Rogers (1959) stresses that therapeutic change involves becoming aware of those feelings that have been denied or distorted. In RE therapy, becoming aware of feelings and having them acknowledged and processed constructively in important relationships is an essential skill. Meaning can only be understood when the feeling is connected to the content of one's interpersonal perception. In fact, Campos, Mumme, Kermoian, and Campos (1994) describe emotion as contextually bounded. Helping people be more skillful in conducting conversations that emphasize feeling helps them to better understand the meaning of their relationships and ultimately themselves. The skill training and other methods used by RE therapy primarily emphasize increasing a client's ability to improve shared meanings through conversation about emotion. Emotion is the thread that fosters shared meaning.

Steve Duck (1994) depicts human beings as striving to understand and being driven to find meaning. Understanding meaning implies a relationship in context with others in one's world. Meaning is driven by emotion. Without the presence of emotion, meaning could not be determined. Lazarus (1993) believes that emotion is always a response to relational meaning. The way we make sense of our world is through the use of language, and this is derived from and out of our relationships with others.

It would be hard to talk about RE therapy without emphasizing the role of emotion and feeling expression. Because language emerges long after the child has developed understanding and meaning, the words and sentences we use can be only an approximate representation of our meaning. Language has developed from our need to communicate with each other and from our capacity to develop and use language. Thus, it is possible to assume that we recognize our own meaning only through our interactions with each other. The more we are able to find language that conveys our meaning, the more we can recognize and understand ourselves and therefore act according to our motivations. Through language, we are able to represent the meaning of our world; what motivates this is emotion.

Acceptance

Perhaps the most important value at the core of RE therapy is derived from Rogers (1951): Each of us has the capacity to master our own experience and resolve our own interpersonal conflicts. This is best done in an interpersonal context that feels safe and secure. Certain values are a necessary part of any interpersonal context. In RE therapy, these contextual values are *an atmosphere of nonjudgment, acceptance, and the inherent equivalence among all human beings* no matter what their role relationship or place in any hierarchy might be. Maturana (1992) emphasizes "objectivity in parenthesis," which is similar to the values of nonjudgment and acceptance. This is a recognition that all conversations have a relative meaning, depending on who's talking. Even though there may be naturally occurring role relationships in which one person has more power than another, mutual respect for the inherent equivalence among all parties is essential to creating an environment that fosters optimum personal and interpersonal functioning and development. Furthermore, deviation from these values often creates personal and interpersonal difficulties.

RE therapy emphasizes the acknowledgment of feeling in relation to the content of what one is saying. It also couples acknowledgment with "acceptance"; that is, we must go beyond recognizing and acknowledging the feelings that pertain to our own experience and accept the other person's experience.

Neil Jacobson (1992) has stimulated a renewed interest in the clinical literature regarding the importance of acceptance. With his colleague, Andrew Christensen, he has introduced the notion that we can foster acceptance while promoting change. "Whereas 'change' refers to compromising with and accommodating to a partner, 'acceptance' refers to letting go of the struggle to change and in some cases even [embracing] those aspects of a partner which have traditionally been precipitants of conflict" (Jacobson, 1992, p. 497). He further states that " 'acceptance' work implies that some conflicts cannot be resolved and it attempts to turn areas of conflict into sources of intimacy and closeness" (p. 497). This is consonant with RE therapy in that problem resolution is fostered when one recognizes that the power to solve problems can occur only by accepting each person's perspective, experience, and feelings. In one of his propositions (XVIII), Rogers (1951) integrates the ideas of self-acceptance with acceptance of others: "When the individual perceives and accepts into one consistent and integrated system all his sensory and visceral experiences, then he is necessarily more understanding of others and is more accepting of others as separate individuals" (p. 520). Note that this statement implies that the ability to perceive one's own experiences is a prerequisite for acceptance. Denial of one's experience elicits defenses against symbolizing these experiences. It fosters a view of experience as potentially threatening and sets up a response pattern in interpersonal relations such that "words or behaviors are experienced and perceived as threatening, which were not so intended" (p. 520). As in RE therapy, the more one recognizes and accepts one's reactions, the more functional one becomes and the more one can recognize and accept others. This enables people to differentiate while maintaining an intimate connection. RE therapy teaches and reinforces the specific skills of self-recognition and acceptance, and the recognition and acceptance of others, while maintaining intimacy and engagement between people. Kathy Weingarten (1992) believes that meaning in intimate interactions is cocreated and shared. The ultimate objective in RE therapy is to improve the ability of clients to cocreate and share meaning with each other while respecting that they are separate and distinct entities. This level of engagement elicits optimal functioning.

THE RELATIONSHIP AS CLIENT

Each individual is important in the family, and yet any action by a family member impacts relationships among other family members. One of family therapy's most important contributions was to recognize the importance of relationship systems and how they can function to elicit the problems that an individual, or "identified patient," might represent. This understanding shifts the focus of the intervention to the *process between people* rather than the people themselves; in other words, the *relationship* is the patient.

Yet the internal framework of an individual's experience and functioning is built out of relationships with primary and significant others. As the ongoing process in these relationships evolves over time, the meaning of one's life is forged. The strength of each person's ability to confront the larger world depends on what has happened and what continues to happen in his or her relationships. This pattern can be seen in young children, who are dependent on their parents and other family members for their security and well-being. It is less easily seen in adults, who have relationships with primary and significant others. However, the more engaged, intimate, and positive these relationships are, the more one is able to cope with stress.

The degree to which people are engaged in a mutually empathic, supportive, intimate, yet differentiated way will determine their ability to cope with these pressures. Learning skills that improve and maintain this mutual engagement will enable clients to cope more effectively with the stresses that make functioning difficult.

Writing about the normative development of women, Jordan and his associates (Jordan, Kaplan, Miller, Stiver, & Surrey, 1991) suggest that women's primary motivation is to grow within relationships, a quality termed "self-in-relations." "What we are emphasizing . . . are the key aspects of attaining a capacity to be attuned to the affect of others, understanding and being understood by the other and thus participating in the development of others" (Kaplan, 1991, p. 208). These are the very skills that are systematically taught in RE therapy. And though men's development seems to emphasize separateness and independence, Gilligan (1982) suggests that each perspective is valid and can contribute to the other's. In fact, the skills learned in RE therapy help people integrate both perspectives, fostering self-in-relation as well as increased independence and autonomy.

This goal is achieved when all members of the system learn and practice skills. Listening skills foster becoming attuned to the affect of others and being able to convey understanding to others. Speaking skills stress assertion of one's own perspective, thereby improving independence and autonomy. When practiced together in a safe and secure context that clients themselves create, the relationship is strengthened. Concurrently, understanding of others is increased and integrated with a burgeoning sense of independence. This emphasis on using the relationship as the vehicle or context for change makes the relationship between client and therapist less important; the primary significant relationships are mostly responsible for improvement. Meeting with the therapist becomes less and less important.

Empathy, language and relationships, emotional expression, and acceptance are the four pillars on which RE therapy is based. The following chapters, in which the skills of RE therapy are explored and the various types of RE therapy—with children, adolescents, young adults, couples, and families of origin—are explained, will keep circling back to these foundational principles.

CHAPTER 2

Skills Clients Are Taught

Relationship Enhancement therapy begins as soon as a client and an RE therapist begin talking. Each of the basic skills RE therapy emphasizes is learned through conversation. During therapy sessions, conversations are slowed down so that people can understand, learn, and practice each of the basic skills.

Essentially, there are only one of two positions that a person can take in an interpersonal encounter: *expressive speaking* or *receptive listening*. These terms are broad and may include other actions that convey information between parties. But the important thing is that information is exchanged between parties. Without this exchange of information, there is no relationship. In each of these information exchanges, one participant has to be expressive and the other receptive vis-à-vis information being conveyed. If both are expressive or receptive at the same time, there can be no conversation or relationship. The relationship is dependent on a sequence of "speaking" and "listening" back and forth over time.

A third component that emerges from the interaction is the *conversive* skill, and it has two components. The *interactive* principle designates, through negotiations, who is speaking and who is listening. The *engagement* principle of the conversive skill involves asking the participants to acknowledge how they feel (what it means) to understand the other person's feelings (meaning).

An important objective in RE therapy is to help clients use these skills in everyday life. At the same time, the client also strives to take more and more responsibility for practicing and implementing the relationship skills. To achieve these twin objectives, two additional skills are taught: *generalization* and *maintenance*. Generalization helps clients naturally integrate the relationship skills into their everyday lives. Maintenance helps

Table 2.1   Core Relationship Enhancement Skills

- Expressive (Speaking) Skill.
- Receptive (Listening) Skill.
- Conversive (Interactive/Engagement) Skill.
- Generalization Skill.
- Maintenance Skill.

clients understand that regression will occur if they don't practice the relationship skills.

These five components make up the core skills of RE therapy (see Table 2.1). The more skillful people are in using these methods and integrating them into their relationships, the more satisfying these relationships will be.

HOW RELATIONSHIP ENHANCEMENT SKILLS ARE TAUGHT

The RE therapist teaches the skills in a structured and systematic way within a context that is safe, secure, and trusting. The therapist both teaches and models RE skills. After some discussion of the presenting problem (or reasons for being interested) with clients, the therapist introduces the rationale and values of the RE approach. This is done in a didactic and explanatory manner. Clients are helped to understand the value of learning the skills and how these skills will address their particular concerns. The rationale and specific guidelines for each skill are described.

After clients have had a chance to ask questions, the therapist models the skills. Clients are asked to first practice the skills using subjects that are positive and/or less serious before moving on to more problematic subjects.

The therapist structures each session so that clients have time to practice each skill. Learning is enhanced through positive reinforcement and successive approximation. Clients are also taught generalization and maintenance skills in the early sessions. Home assignments are used to reinforce learning and to help clients assume increasing responsibility for the therapy. Homework also helps to maintain continuity from one session to the next.

As office meetings with the therapist become less frequent, home assignments become more important in the therapy. The RE therapist often will use home assignments in the beginning sessions as a vehicle

Table 2.2 Steps for Teaching RE Skills

- The therapist creates a context that is safe and secure and fosters learning.
- The therapist models the relationship enhancement skills to foster a safe, secure learning environment.
- The therapist clearly explains the values and rationale for learning the RE skills.
- The therapist explains how the RE skills apply to self-development and interpersonal functioning, and specifically to the presenting problem.
- The therapist demonstrates and models each skill before asking clients to do so.
- Clients first practice with less serious and/or positive topics before talking about the more difficult ones.
- The therapist is sensitive to the boundaries of each skill (e.g., no judgments, accusations, or questions) and helps clients keep the boundaries clear.
- The therapist structures the conversation so each person has sufficient opportunity to practice each skill.
- Positive reinforcement (verbal and nonverbal) helps motivate clients to practice and improve their skills.
- The therapist is sensitive to difficulties in learning the RE skills and systematically increases his or her expectations (successive approximation).
- The therapist begins to introduce generalization and maintenance from the first session through the use of homework assignments.
- After clients have had sufficient supervised practice in the therapist's office, they are asked to practice at home and audiotape these home sessions.
- The audiotaped home practice sessions are brought to the office sessions for supervision.
- As clients become more skillful, the therapist sees them less frequently and becomes more of a consultant.

Source: Drawn from B. G. Guerney (1987a, 1987b) and Preston and Guerney (1982).

for clients to begin learning problem/conflict resolution skills. Negotiating on the specifics of the homework assignment can be used to model this important skill (see the section below on problem/conflict resolution skill). As the clients improve their skills, they are encouraged to find a time to practice at home. Practice sessions are audiotaped for supervision in the therapist's office. Once clients are engaged in home practice, sessions become less frequent, and the therapist acts more as a consultant, encouraging clients to assume greater responsibility for the therapy (see Table 2.2).

CONFLICT IN RELATIONSHIPS

It's important to consider the role of stress and conflict in relationships. In fact, it is when families experience significant stress and conflict that they seek therapy. In general, though, stress and conflict are part of all relationships. According to Sayers, Baucom, Sher, Weiss, and Heyman (1991), "We refer to conflict and problem-solving behaviors as 'constructive engagement.' Constructive engagement is a process that potentially enhances couples' future satisfaction by increasing the likelihood that the spouses will discuss and solve conflicts in their relationships" (p. 27).

This process is also relevant to hierarchical relationships such as those between parents and children. Sayers et al. (1991) found in their research that increased marital satisfaction was associated with their concept of constructive engagement. Markman (1991) agrees:

> I believe that all couples will experience disagreements and conflicts. This essentially means that all people will experience negative emotions (anger, hostility, mistrust, fear, sadness, etc.), and that a major task for partners in close relationships is to be able to handle constructively these negative affects as they interact. Constructive handling of negative affect involves the ability to (a) express negative feelings about specific behavioral events, and (b) receive and respond constructively to (i.e., hear and validate) one's partner's expression of negative feelings. (p. 91)

In addition, in RE therapy one must not only hear and validate (acknowledgment) one's partner's expression of negative feelings, but also convey *what this means to the partner* (engagement) to understand those feelings.

Markman (1991) continues:

> Thus, high levels of the constructive expression of negative affect may be associated with future relationship success, but negative escalation (e.g., the listener is not able to handle the speaker's negative affect constructively and responds destructively by escalating or withdrawing) should be a sign of current distress and should predict future distress. (p. 91)

Teaching clients skills that will enable them to more effectively handle negative affect enhances the possibilities of future constructive engagement.

In their effort to promote acceptance, Koerner, Prince, and Jacobson (1994) claim that the *response* to differences—not the differences themselves—affect marital satisfaction. Boszormenyi-Nagy and Krasner (1986) state, "Interpersonal conflicts of interests between two partners are inevitable and unavoidable, and are not equated with failure in relationships" (p. 143). Furthermore, they extend this idea to all relationships: "The existential interests of parent and child, of man and woman, and of sibling and sibling converge and diverge, blend, collide and find resolution or fester and build" (p. 143). Thus it is not that we have conflicts, but how we engage around the conflict that is the important variable for the therapist's action. The content of the conflict is less relevant to the RE therapist than how clients can learn to relate more constructively to each other. With the development of these skills, many issues are resolved naturally and on their own.

How Conflict Is Handled in Relationship Enhancement

Fran and Stan are having a disagreement about one of their children. Here is a transcript of their conversation.

FRAN: I was angry and hurt when I depended upon you to take care of Allison and you didn't do what you said you would do.

STAN: You're angry with me and hurt by that.

FRAN: You're damn right. You know how exhausted I was, but I had to get up to take care of Allison.

STAN: You didn't like that.

FRAN: No, and particularly your coming in all the time to ask me what to do.

STAN: Well, I feel badly that you are angry with me about that and guilty and frustrated that I couldn't please you.

FRAN: You're upset that I'm angry with you.

STAN: Yes, I'm always afraid that you'll criticize me whenever I take care of Allison. That's why I came in to ask you what to do.

FRAN: You're afraid I'll criticize you.

STAN: I am afraid of that, but I also feel guilty and inadequate because of that.

FRAN: That makes you feel bad.

STAN: Real bad!

FRAN: I'm concerned you feel that way and feel guilty myself that you are afraid I'll be critical.

STAN: You feel guilty that I'm afraid you'll be critical.

FRAN: I do. I just worry you won't do the right thing, but I want to try to trust you more.

STAN: You'd like that.

FRAN: Yes!

STAN: That makes me feel good and I'll try harder the next time to take care of her and not bother you while you're resting.

FRAN: You'd like to try to do that.

STAN: Yes.

FRAN: That makes me feel good.

Fran and Stan were able to resolve this conflict because they took the time to listen to one another. They didn't accuse, judge, or question; rather, they acknowledged their feelings.

As a result, they were able to acknowledge a deeper issue: Stan's openness about his fear of Fran's criticism and his subsequent feelings of inadequacy helped Fran recognize the reality of Stan's feelings. This helped her acknowledge her difficulty in trusting him. As a result, Stan was encouraged to try harder the next time. It is very likely that this theme will pop up again, but more encounters like this one will gradually ease stress and improve the trust between them.

THE COMMUNICATION/RELATIONSHIP SKILLS THAT ARE TAUGHT TO THE CLIENT(S)

Markman and Notarius (1993) report that information they gathered in 1980 could predict in 1990, with over 90 percent accuracy, which couples would survive and which would end in divorce. They conclude, "It's how you handle differences when they arise that counts" (p. 20). Being able to resolve differences is crucial to maintain all close and intimate relationships, both hierarchical relationships (e.g., parent and child) and equivalent ones (intimate partners). Furthermore, Markman (1991) states that couples trained in his Prevention and Relationship Enhancement Program (PREP), a program that incorporates a speaker-listener model, have a 50 percent lower divorce rate, lower rates of marital violence after five years, and can more constructively handle conflict.

Embedded in the ability to handle constructive conflicts are issues of genuineness, trust, and acceptance. Handling constructive conflicts is an important component of constructive engagement, and requires the creation of a context in which people are able to stay engaged with each other either until the conflict is resolved or both (or all) parties agree that it can't be resolved. In either case the development of this relationship context will lead to other opportunities for handling constructive conflict. It is through our differences with each other and our efforts to find resolution that we create meaning in our relationships and our own existential selves.

This context of genuineness, trust, and acceptance can be built by applying the rules of speaking, listening, and conversive (interactive/engagement) skills discussed below. These skills are defined by the rules (limits or boundaries) that participants follow in order to promote intimacy, differentiation, and continuity. In other words, the context that is created is like a circle within which people conduct their conversations (interactions), and the boundaries are represented by the rules of these three basic skills. To the degree that people stay within these boundaries, they are free to be themselves yet conduct relationships that are intimate and engaged. When people are under stress, not coping well, or experiencing conditions that bring them to therapy, helping them to conduct themselves in such a context and to learn to generalize the skills necessary to create such a context in their everyday lives can help them improve their coping skills and foster change and enable them to live in a more satisfying way.

RELATIONSHIP ENHANCEMENT SKILLS

Expressive (Speaking) Skill

The expressive skill helps clients to recognize their own emotional, psychological, and interpersonal meaning and experience and to convey this meaning to others without projecting the responsibility for it onto them, thereby not engendering defensiveness, hostility, or conflict. This is done by acknowledging and asserting meaning ("owning" thoughts and feelings) without judging, accusing, or questioning others.

To accomplish this, the speaker makes no judgment or accusation that implies right or wrong and asks no questions. Furthermore, to adequately "own" this expression, the speaker must verbalize the feeling (motivation) that pertains to the statement. For example, if you are dissatisfied with the behavior of another person, you don't say, "That was foolish of you"; nor do you say, "You're always doing foolish things" or ask "Why did you do that?" All of these statements can make the other person defensive. What you do say is, "I don't understand why you did that" or, with more ownership (self-revelation), "I'm upset (angry, hurt, concerned, etc.) that you did that." The key here is to maintain this posture of "ownership" so that you can shoulder the responsibility for your own meaning or purpose.

After such a statement is acknowledged by the other person (the listener), it is up to the speaker to continue to express his or her thoughts and feelings. As you do this, the underlying nonconscious meanings begin to surface and your awareness of yourself becomes acute. For example, your dissatisfaction with the other person's behavior may represent your worry that the other person is rejecting you. You might not recognize this right away, but as you "own" your feelings more and more, this awareness surfaces. This increased awareness of yourself and your motivation will help you regulate your feelings and actions, helping the other person understand you better, thereby making it easier for you to understand the other person's perspective. With this understanding, there is a greater possibility that the outcome will be constructive. Concurrently you gain increasing insight into your own feelings, behavior, and thoughts. This in turn can enhance your feelings of security and self-acceptance.

The speaker determines what to say to the other person and how much to reveal. By avoiding accusation, judgment, and question, the speaker does not project responsibility for his or her thoughts and feelings onto others, making it easier for them to grasp his or her meaning (see Table 2.3).

The process by which the speaker takes such responsibility occurs in a context in which others are trying to be receptive, nonjudgmental, and accepting. As a result, the speaker might feel freer to express unexpressed

---

Table 2.3   Guidelines for Expressive (Speaker) Skill

- State things in a way that acknowledges the subjectivity of your perceptions and judgments. Use *I* statements rather than *you* statements (e.g., "I'm concerned about your being late" rather than "You're always late").
- Try to include feelings that underlie your statements (e.g., "You left me alone for an hour, and I didn't *like* that" or "You talked with him all night, and I was *hurt* by that").
- Try to avoid:
  —Accusations.
  —Questions.
  —Generalization.
  —Motivational analyses.
  —Characterizations of others.
- Be specific and behavioral (e.g., "It's important that you be home by 6:00 P.M., so I can be on time for the class").
- Temper any implied criticism with positive underlying feelings or expectations (e.g., "It really makes me feel good to be there before the teacher comes in").
- If appropriate, add a concrete suggestion to help resolve the issue or problem.
- Remember that the purpose of the expressive skill is to "own" (take responsibility for) what you mean to say without projecting it onto the other person.

---

or repressed thoughts and feelings that could help to open up the relationship. The idea here is not to promote the cathartic projection of these thoughts and feelings, but to help the speaker feel more ready to acknowledge these feelings and thoughts. Wile (1981) suggests that patterns in people and relationships are characterized by a sense of not being entitled to certain feelings, which lead to an inability to *acknowledge, accept,* or *express* these feelings. This effort to help speakers "own" their expressions increases the possibility that they might express unacceptable or unacknowledged feelings. Again, this is made possible by the safer context created by the structure and rules of RE therapy, particularly the receptivity of the listener.

B. G. Guerney (1982b) has emphasized that positive attitudes often underlie negative expressions. The importance of the relationship, anxiousness to be closer, and the need to be understood and/or avoid being hurt could underlie the negative expression. It is useful to encourage a client to consider the underlying positive attitude when owning his or her expression. It adds insight to the speaker's awareness and helps the listener be more receptive to the speaker. A simple example of this is when a parent's concern for a child gives rise to the parent's anger ("I was really worried about you and I'm angry with you"), or when one partner is critical of the other because of an underlying need for greater closeness or intimacy ("I resent your coming home late all the time. I really miss you"). Recognizing and expressing the concern for the child and the importance of intimacy with the other person (both positive attitudes) significantly changes what is being communicated. This important principle is part of both the expressive and receptive skills that are taught in RE therapy.

Receptive (Listening) Skill

The receptive skill implies openness to taking in, letting one's guard down, being more accepting—and conveying this receptivity to others. Originally, this skill was called empathic responder mode (B. G. Guerney, 1977), the word "responder" emphasizing that this is not a passive skill. B. G. Guerney states, "You must strive to put yourself in a receptive frame of mind" (p. 27). One also needs to be skillful in conveying that receptivity. For instance, when a person is feeling anxious it is not a receptive response to say, "You are a worry wart, always afraid of something. Why don't you do something about it?" This speaker has put aside *receptive* listening to become *expressive.* In other words, the person is not listening at all but using the feelings of the other person to express his or her own feelings. Perhaps the other person's anxiousness threatened him or her. In any case, this would make for a one-sided, unsafe conversation and represents a "fusion" (undifferentiated) response: One person's anxiety becomes an issue that the other person (the listener) acts upon. Relationships that proceed in this fashion are always struggling with enmeshment and disengagement issues (see Table 2.4).

Importance of Acceptance in Receptive Skill

Acceptance is a significant component of receptivity. Jacobson (1992), who has helped to restore this concept to the therapy literature, defines acceptance as the letting go of the struggle to change one's partner. In talking about how therapy helps clients change, Rogers (1957) says,

> One hypothesis is that the client moves from the experiencing of himself as an unworthy, unacceptable and unlovable person to the realization that he is accepted, respected, and loved in this limited relationship with the therapist. "Loved" here has perhaps its deepest and most general meaning—that of being deeply understood and deeply accepted. (p. 159)

Maturana and Varela (1987) concur:

> Biology shows us that we can expand our cognitive domain. This arises through a novel experience brought forth through reasoning, through the encounter with a stranger, or more directly, through the

Table 2.4 Guidelines for Receptive (Listening) Skill

- Provide the speaker with your full attention, both physically and mentally.
- Allow the speaker ample time to complete thoughts.
- Let the speaker know what you understand before you say what you think.
- Try to hear the feelings that underlie the speaker's statement and include this with your restatement of what was said.
- Avoid:
  —Asking questions.
  —Presenting your own opinion and perspective about what the other person is saying when you are listening.
  —Interpreting what the speaker says.
  —Suggesting how the speaker might alter the situation or solve a problem.
  —Judging what has been said.
- It's important that you try to let the speaker know that you understand what he or she means from his or her point of view.

expression of a biological interpersonal congruence that lets us see
the other person and open up for him room for existence beside us.
This act is called *love,* or, if we prefer a milder expression, the *acceptance* of the other person beside us in our daily living. This is the
biological foundation of social phenomena; without love, without
acceptance of others living beside us, there is no social process and
therefore, no humanness. (p. 246)

This idea of opening ourselves to make room for the existence of others
is a poignant way to define acceptance. Rogers (1951) has emphasized
respect for and acceptance of the other person's capacity and competence to direct himself or herself. Acceptance is an act in which we open
up to acknowledge the existence of others while respecting their presence and capacity to be responsible for themselves. This stance is essential if we are to respond in a receptive way to others.

Essentially, the receptive listener acknowledges the thoughts and
particularly the feelings of the other person without judgment, accusation, or question. This is not a simple reiteration of what the speaker is
saying but an acknowledgment that conveys respect and *acceptance* of the
other person's right to his or her own experience. The listener's own perspective does not enter into this response. Instead, the listener genuinely
attempts to grasp the other person's perspective and experience, and to
convey that understanding back.

Conversive (Interactive/Engagement) Skill

The difficult conversive skill, which includes the speaking and listening
skills already described, helps one recognize when to speak and when to
listen to the other person. It helps each person to acknowledge the relevance and importance of the other person's expression to one's own
meaning and to the meaning of the relationship, and to avoid digressing
from the conversation at hand, thus keeping the conversation (and thereby
the relationship) engaged. Although it is broken down into two component
skills, interactive and engagement, in practice these components are fully
integrated with each other and with the skills of speaking and listening.

In an atmosphere of trust, respect, and acceptance, knowing when
to speak and when to listen can be negotiated with few stresses. However, under stressful conditions we are likely to feel and act defensively.
Being able to achieve a constructive outcome when feeling defensive is an
objective of the conversive skill. In many ways it is like a dance where

Table 2.5   Guidelines for Conversive (Interactive/Engagement) Skill

- The person speaking is most vulnerable. Therefore, the speaker is primarily responsible for mode switching.
- Typically, the speaker requests mode switching and the listener agrees to it.
- A mode switch is accomplished only after the listener has satisfactorily acknowledged the last expression of the speaker.
- Following the mode switch, the first expression of the new speaker (the former listener) is to state how it feels to know the other person's (the former speaker's) feelings. This emphasizes the intimacy and meaning of the relationship.
- When the listener requests mode switching (because of his or her own feelings), it is important that the speaker is satisfied that the listener has adequately recognized the last expression of the speaker.
- It is ultimately up to the speaker to agree to the mode switch.

When to Mode Switch (Interactive Skill)

The speaker switches mode when:

- You are satisfied that you have already expressed your important thoughts and feelings, and feel "fairly" understood by the listener.
- You want to know the other person's views and feelings.

Note: Try to keep in mind that it might be hard for your partner to listen if you try to say everything or talk for too long. Try to keep it short.

The listener requests a mode switch when:

- You are satisfied that you have already acknowledged the other's feelings on an issue.
- Your own thoughts or feelings make it hard for you to continue listening.
- You think that what you have to say may help clarify the issue.

Note: It's important to try to listen longer if the speaker isn't ready to switch.

Speaker's Behavior When the Listener Requests a Mode Switch

- Don't state any new ideas or feelings.
- If you are satisfied that the listener understands what you are saying, switch. Make sure the listener has acknowledged you before switching.
- If you are not satisfied or are unsure that the listener understands, restate your point once (twice at the most), and then switch. You'll have a chance later to clarify what you mean.

Listener's Behavior after the Switch (Engagement Skill)

- As the new speaker, make sure the first statement that you make after the switch includes how you *feel* to know the other person's *feelings*.
- Keep to the same topic unless you believe the point has been made.
- You are free to choose any topic as the new speaker.

each partner coordinates movements in an integrated way, leading or following the other person while trying not to step on each other's toes—to keep engaged without withdrawing (see Table 2.5).

Interactive Skill

In RE therapy, participants practice the interactive skill within the boundaries of certain rules. These rules pertain to when a mode switch occurs (from speaker to listener and listener to speaker). Typically, clients say aloud the word "switch" to designate their willingness to switch modes. The switch occurs under the following conditions:

1. The speaker should switch when he or she feels understood by the other person. The speaker may not feel *completely* understood; perhaps he or she has spoken for so long that the other person can't be receptive anymore. However, since the speaker is likely to be open and vulnerable, the switch is best when the speaker takes responsibility for the switch. If the listener switches while the speaker is feeling too vulnerable, not understood, or misunderstood, the speaker will feel too defensive to listen. Having the speaker be responsible for the switch helps indicate a readiness to be receptive to the other person's expressions.

2. If the listener requests a switch, the speaker can try to respect this by switching within the next few interchanges. It is important that the speaker recognize that a request to switch represents that the listener is having difficulty being receptive and is feeling very defensive. Under these conditions, it is practical to switch and helpful for the speaker to realize that it may take time (a series of switches) before things can become clear or fully understood.

Before the switch occurs, the listener must acknowledge the last thing that the speaker has expressed. If this expression does not satisfy the speaker, the speaker needs to make one last attempt to clarify the expression, which then is acknowledged by the listener before he or she becomes the speaker.

At first, this process might feel clumsy and somewhat unsatisfying, but with practice participants are able to be more fluid and flexible. Practice helps participants learn to be sensitive to the negotiation of speaking and listening involved in everyday life.

The following transcript illustrates this process. Andy is upset because Ginny has subtly accused him of being irresponsible.

ANDY: My integrity is really, really important to me and feeling that my being a responsible person and you don't feel that way upsets me incredibly. It upsets me
because I don't feel I'm an irresponsible person and it upsets me that you don't
think I'm a responsible person and it upsets me to the point of total anger and
it's really important to me.

GINNY: You're really, really angry that I would think that you're not a responsible
person because being responsible is something that you see as central to your integrity and it is very, very important to you being responsible and it makes you
really, really upset and angry that I would think you were not responsible.

ANDY: It makes me angry to think that if because I have an image of you writing a
list of my characteristics down that near the top of the list would be irresponsible because I don't finish jobs or don't put my clothes away when—that ought
to be about fifteenth on the list after a whole slew of other things that I think are
important and it's real important for me to feel that. I am a responsible person
with you. Your feeling about me as an irresponsible person is real important to
me in a negative fashion.

GINNY: It's real important to you that I not think of you as an irresponsible person
and you're having a mental image of me making all that stuff characteristic
about you with irresponsibility at the top of the list and you're very upset because for me to label you irresponsible for not finishing jobs or picking up
clothes makes you really angry because I would do that and it upsets you.

THERAPIST: It's very important to him that you consider him responsible. That's
how important your view of him is (positive connotation).

GINNY: It's real important that I think of you as responsible because my opinion of
you is really important to you. Can I switch?

ANDY: Your opinion of me is extremely important to me and I want you to know it.

GINNY: My opinion of you is extremely important to you and you want me to know
it.

ANDY: It hurts my feelings incredibly to think that you would not respect my feelings or responsibilities. It's real important and I want you to know.

GINNY: It really hurts you to think that I wouldn't understand how strong your feelings of responsibility are and you want me to know that.

ANDY: Switch.

GINNY: It makes me feel happy to know that you care so much about my opinion of
you. It makes me feel a little afraid how important my opinion of you is in this
area, yet I'm surprised I didn't understand that you cared so deeply about my
opinion of you—it's hard for me to think about. I feel like a different species or
something because I don't think about listing your characteristics—I wasn't
wedded to the term "irresponsible."

THERAPIST: It makes you feel good how important you are and that's a wonderful
thing for you and at the same time you feel scared that your opinion affects him
so, and how he would put so much on you.

GINNY: It does make me feel wonderful that you care so much about what I think
about you, and it is kind of scary that your perception of my opinion of you
could cause you to be so upset and angry with me.

ANDY: You're happy to know that I care that much about what you think, but you are scared about the responsibility and the thought that I should care so deeply about what you're thinking that I might be so angry and upset with you.

Andy reacts strongly to his perception of being accused of irresponsibility, and Ginny feels defensive. The therapist then intervenes by modeling a succinct response that conveys the underlying positive messages to help reduce Andy's defensiveness. Ginny accepts the model, but wants to switch. Obviously, Andy is not as ready and seems to ignore her request. Ginny recognizes this and continues to acknowledge (listen to) Andy. However, Andy has heard her and after Ginny acknowledges him some more, he switches. Ginny expresses her good feelings about her importance to Andy, but also identifies her fear of this. The therapist intervenes again when she begins to become defensive, modeling her central message. Ginny responds to this and reiterates the central message.

This transcript demonstrates some of the variables surrounding the switch from speaker to listener. It also shows how the therapist uses modeling to reduce defensiveness, to keep couples engaged, and to elicit the underlying positive message. As couples practice these skills, they manage these issues themselves.

It's also important to recognize that when one person is particularly emotional, the other person can be most helpful by remaining receptive. After a while, the speaker will be more ready to listen to what the other person has to say. It still is important for the speaker to say "switch" or for the listener to check readiness for a switch by saying, "I wonder if I could talk now."

Engagement Skill

The second component of this skill, engagement is based on the fact that it is very helpful for the listener to be receptive—to acknowledge and accept feelings and thoughts without judgment. Engagement helps the speaker feel good about himself or herself and understand his or her own motivations.

There is another subtle variable at play here. When you are speaking and I am listening, we are not on an *equivalent* basis because I'm not equally sharing my feelings with you. The listener is hierarchically one up on the speaker. They only become equivalent when the listener expresses his or her thoughts and feelings. In this view, if the switch occurs without the new speaker acknowledging the meaning of the other person's feeling, one person would be hierarchically one up on the other. It is only at the switch when *the new speaker first says how he or she feels to know how the other person feels* that the parties achieve parity and the full relevance of their relationship is made clear. Furthermore, optimum engagement occurs when this is acknowledged at each switch throughout the conversation. With practice, participants learn more and more how to bring this acknowledgment of their equivalence and engagement into their conversations in real life.

The rule for the engagement skill is as follows: At the switch, the new speaker first expresses how he or she feels to know the other person's feelings before expressing his or her own issues. The therapist often assists this by cueing, "How does it make you feel to know that?" If the person does not indicate how he or she *feels* to know the other person's *feelings,* the therapist structures this further (e.g., "How do you feel to know that he feels good, bad, etc.?"). It is essential that this be expressed and acknowledged by the new listener before the new speaker can continue.

For example, Marie has been talking, expressing her feelings, and then says "Switch."

ED (NEW SPEAKER): It makes me *feel awful* that you were *hurt* when I did that!

MARIE (LISTENER): You feel really badly that I was hurt.

ED (SPEAKER): Yes, I would never *want* to do that. I only came late because I thought you were busy and wouldn't mind my lateness.

MARIE (LISTENER): It's *important* that I know that.

ED: Switch.

MARIE (NEW SPEAKER): It makes me *feel good* that you're *concerned* about how I was feeling, but it's *important* that you at least call me if you're going to be late.

ED (NEW LISTENER): You're glad I'm concerned about your feelings, but it would make you feel good if I called when I might be late.

This conversation clearly illustrates the rule that the new speaker has to acknowledge how he or she feels to know the other person's feelings. By following the rule, Marie and Ed stay engaged, and the potentially adversarial, disengaged conversation changes to one that is closer, more intimate, and engaged.

The skills of speaking (owning one's thoughts and feelings without judgment) and listening (acknowledging the other person's thoughts and feelings without judgment and with acceptance) are evident in this vignette as well. These three essential skills compose an integrative whole. In real life, one doesn't formally wait in one position or the other as the conversation spontaneously proceeds. Yet these essential elements of nonjudgment, acceptance, acknowledgment, ownership of feelings, and engagement are present in the ongoing conversations of people who have learned and practiced these skills. The value of the formal structure that RE therapy promotes is to provide a safe context in which these elements can be learned, practiced, generalized, and maintained in real-life relationships.

FOSTERING A SECURE CONTEXT

When people begin therapy at times of crisis and stress, it is very comforting for them to have the safety of the formal context that therapy offers. Having rules reduces their anxiety and defensiveness. Once clients are engaged in the RE therapy context several therapeutic outcomes emerge. First, when people slow down the conversation to express and acknowledge their feelings and issues, their understanding of each other and thereby the meaning of the conversation changes. When they begin to truly listen to each other and convey that understanding to each other, they feel relieved. The RE process also reduces conflict by helping people understand each other better and feel understood. They become increasingly engaged and more open to an intimate encounter, which not only helps to heal their present hurt, but also incrementally heals the inner hurt built up during years of judgment and accusation from present and past relationships.

GENERALIZATION AND MAINTENANCE OF RELATIONSHIP ENHANCEMENT SKILLS

Two additional components of the core skills are *generalization* and *maintenance*. Generalization and maintenance skills are important because RE therapy conversations need to extend beyond the therapist's office. The therapeutic situation is like a laboratory setting, clearly distinct from everyday life. If clients were to confine their use of these skills only to the therapeutic setting, they would be less likely to use the skills in everyday life. In addition, there is the danger that clients will become dependent on the therapist to work out their difficulties. Emphasizing the importance of generalizing and maintaining skills helps clients become aware of their increasing responsibilities for their own issues, relationships, and change.

Generalization and maintenance skills are taught concurrently. Once clients begin the process of generalization and maintenance, they usually meet with their therapist less frequently, thereby reducing dependence on the therapist. Generalization and maintenance are first tried at home sessions that are taped (audio or video) and brought to subsequent sessions for supervision. Clients listen to these tapes together with the therapist, who provides supervision for future home practice. Practicing generalization and maintenance in this way also helps clients shift into an observational position related to their own conversations and relationship. This observational position enables them to better observe their own interactions and behavior, which in turn enhances their learning and strengthens their responsibility for their own change.

The importance of generalization and maintenance are discussed from the beginning of therapy. Early on, RE therapists explain their belief that nonconscious, reflexive, and habitual behavior is responsible for most of the difficulties that bring people to therapy, and that a structured, systematic approach based upon skill learning and practice can help people to develop more constructive habits. In the early phases of therapy, clients are encouraged to observe their behaviors and that of others to see how the skills can make a difference.

Another benefit of these observations is that clients become sensitive to the skills and their value. This consciousness-raising period helps make clients aware of the skills and motivates them to learn and practice them. Once people get excited about the value of learning and applying the skills, they frequently and spontaneously relate circumstances at work or with friends or other family members when they tried the skills and found them useful. Even if the skills weren't useful, talking about their experience enhances their understanding of the process. These early efforts to teach generalization are informal and may include having clients observe themselves and others, setting aside a "talking time," and continually assessing client readiness for home practice.

Formal efforts at instituting generalization begin when the clients are able to conduct structured conversations that remain within the confines of the rules with little therapist involvement. It also occurs when clients feel comfortable practicing at home, usually between the fifth and ninth session. This can vary with the sophistication of the client, degree of stress in the relationship, or psychosocial functioning.

Often, a good portion of a session is devoted to structuring the home practice. A handout, *Instruction for Home Practice* (see Table 2.6), is given to clients at this time. Clients are then asked to devote 30 to 60 minutes for home practice and to determine the best time for this practice session. For example, a couple with young children may not want to practice at a time when their children might need them. Furthermore, clients are asked to turn off their telephones during this time. They are also encouraged to use the most conducive space in the home for this purpose. Sometimes they

Table 2.6 Relationship Enhancement Therapy
Instructions for Home Practice

A. Set aside one hour to one and a half hours at the same time each week. An alternative time should also be chosen in case an emergency prevents the conversation from occurring.
B. Make sure that you meet in a comfortable place at home. Also, make sure that you will not be interrupted (by children or phone) during this time.
C. Each week one of you is designated as the first SPEAKER. It is your responsibility to think of a topic and begin the conversation. This responsibility alternates from week to week.
D. It is the responsibility of the partner who is first listener for that week to remind the first speaker shortly before the designated time. Also, it is the listener's responsibility to prepare the tape recorder and tape. (All sessions are recorded and then reviewed in office sessions.)

The Basic Rules

A. Speaker
   1. Make no judgments or accusations, and ask no questions.
   2. Own your statement and feelings.
   3. State the feeling that is the basis (motivation) for your statements.
   4. State your message in a few sentences so that your listener can grasp your meaning. Remember that you can continue until you are satisfied that your partner understands your meaning.
   5. Remember that it may be hard for your partner to continue to listen if you speak for a long time before switching.
   6. You, as speaker, control the switch. Say "Switch" to indicate that you are willing to give up the speaker position and become a listener. Say "Switch" only after your partner has reflected your last statement.
B. Listener
   1. Make no judgments or accusations, and ask no questions.
   2. Remember not to give your point of view at all until you are speaker.
   3. Reflect back (acknowledge) what the speaker has just said, and include the feeling that pertains to the message.
   4. When listening, remember that you are *accepting* what the speaker is saying and feeling, *not agreeing*.
   5. Also, remember that even though you have restated what the speaker has said exactly, the speaker may not mean that and may want to restate it. It is important to accept that and try to reflect the new statement by the speaker.
   6. If you feel accused or judged by what the speaker is saying, you can state that ("I feel judged or accused"). The speaker then tries to restate it without judgment.
   7. If the speaker fails to state the feeling that pertains to the statement, you can say, "I'm not sure what you are feeling." The speaker then will state the feeling. You as listener can identify the feeling yourself, if you are comfortable doing that. For example: The speaker says, "It's hot outside." You as listener say, "You're uncomfortable" or "You like that," whichever the speaker seems to imply.

(Continued)

Table 2.6   (Continued)

C. Switching
  1. The speaker is always responsible for the switch.
  2. The listener can request the switch, but the speaker can say a little more to be sure the listener understands before switching.
  3. The listener must reflect the last thing the speaker says before the switch can occur.
  4. After the switch, the new speaker must state how he or she *feels* to know the feelings of the former speaker. After that, the new speaker can talk about anything important to that person.
D. Home Practice
  1. Remember not to direct the other person. If you have to state your discomfort, *own your feelings.*
  2. If either party feels uncomfortable and wants to stop at any time, that person says, "I'd like to stop now." The other person says "Okay" and stops. The conversation ends at that point. The person requesting the stop is free to be alone. It is that person's responsibility to indicate when he or she is ready to resume contact. The other person respects that and trusts that the first person will make contact again when ready.
  3. When contact is renewed, there is no obligation to continue talking about the issue discussed at the time of stopping.

prefer to practice in their cars, while taking a walk, or at a park. The therapist often will question these specifics of the practice session to enhance the structure and consistency of their home practice. Underlying the teaching of generalization and maintenance skills is learning the importance of structure and its implementation.

Early in the therapy, clients are asked to establish this home practice time. In the early stages, before they are ready to practice RE therapy skills on their own, they are encouraged to avoid stressful or conflictual topics, and instead to discuss positive issues or those not pertinent to the relationship. Even when formal home practice begins, they are still encouraged to use the structure to talk about positive issues first before turning to the more difficult ones.

Clients are encouraged, if they have the time, to review the tape and choose the relevant or important sections for supervision. Otherwise, the therapist randomly picks portions of the tape for supervision. As therapy sessions become less frequent, it is important to bring tapes to therapy sessions to reinforce the value of skill practice. This helps the therapist positively reinforce the client's improvement. In addition to the formal home practice, additional client guidelines are suggested (see Tables 2.7 and 2.8).

Table 2.7   Client Guidelines for Generalization Skill

- Pay attention to how you and others are communicating and assess your changes over time.
- Recognize that communication and relationship problems arise from responses that are reflexive and nonconscious (habitual). These responses are elicited by cues in our environment (and by others) and have a tendency to be repeated.
- These skills must be practiced to maintain your skills and improve your mastery of them.
- *To improve generalization formally:*
  —Pick a consistent time to practice the skills at home.
  —Choose a time and place that allows for the optimum opportunity to practice skills, that is, a time when you anticipate no outside interruptions.
  —If an emergency supersedes the practice time, have an agreed upon alternative time in place.
  —Keep to the formal RE structure during these practice times to improve skill mastery (see Table 2.6).
  —Maintain weekly practice sessions for at least six months. Gradually reduce the frequency thereafter (e.g., every two weeks, then once a month).
- Don't expect a definite outcome each time the skills are practiced. These are *skills,* not *solutions.*
- Under stressful and conflictual conditions, request a formal RE conversation held only when both (or all) parties agree to it.
- *To improve generalization informally:*
  —After the structured and formal home practice has become comfortable, try practicing the skills with others in an informal way.
  —Review your interactions with others in relation to the RE skill guidelines.
  —Try to understand the other person's feelings before responding. Often, not understanding the feelings of the other person leads to misunderstanding.
  —Be aware of the cues (of judgment, accusation, and question) that elicit your defensiveness.
  —Review your interactions with others at the end of the day.
  —Imagine using the skills in those interactions that left you feeling unhappy.
  —Imagine what you might encounter each new day and practice using RE skills.
- MOST OF ALL: *Practice, practice, practice.*

Source: Drawn from B. G. Guerney (1987a, 1987b) and Preston and Guerney (1982).

Regression

Clients' motivation to continue practicing the skills will change as life presents them with new and different issues. Taking therapy time to talk about the likelihood of regression and to plan for ways to maintain the skills in their lives is useful. This effort also helps clients acknowledge the importance of taking responsibility for their own change.

Table 2.8 Guidelines for Maintenance Skill

- Keep the skills in mind; review and practice using them monthly if possible (see Table 2.7). There is a natural tendency to regress if skills are not used regularly.
- Review the skill guidelines at least once a month.
- Maintain a formal practice time at least once a month.
- Save special issues or difficulties for these conversations, in order to enhance their outcomes.
- When you observe some regression, practice more frequently.
- Regularly review your interactions with others to see if the skills can be used to enhance your relationships.
- Every six months, find a time with your partner and/or other family members to review these relationships. Use RE skills during these discussions.

Source: Drawn from B. G. Guerney (1987a, 1987b) and Preston and Guerney (1982).

The first step is to help them accept that some regression is bound to occur, particularly when practice is stopped. Clients are encouraged to maintain weekly home practice for six months to achieve the optimum outcome. Advise clients that it is helpful to review the skills when things become difficult and to use them more consciously at these times. After that, clients should be encouraged to establish a maintenance pattern by structuring less frequent practice sessions, for example, practicing every other week for a month, then every third week for six weeks, then once a month, and ultimately only when necessary. Clients should be urged to maintain this regular time as support to their relationships, as a family meeting time, as talk time, or just time to be together without interruption. When time is so precious (see Ritterman, 1995; Ventura, 1995), it is useful to have an established time to be together without interruption. Structuring this time in a more formal way can be helpful when conflict or impasse occurs; however, it is essential that both parties agree to choose this option.

Clients should also understand that they can return to the therapist for future sessions to help them through these impasses and to reinforce their skills. Knowing that they are free to consult with the therapist even after these formal sessions have stopped helps clients cope with their stress for longer periods of time, which often allows them to achieve resolution on their own. When they do return to the therapist, only a session or two is commonly needed to help clients move on.

A face-to-face visit can also be useful when new developmental or relationship issues emerge that were not addressed in the earlier therapy.

For example, when families who have benefited from filial therapy (child-centered relationship enhancement therapy) reach the adolescent state of development, they often return for a few sessions. Because family members are already familiar with the skill-learning approach, RE therapy works as a comprehensive family therapy.

Generalization and maintenance skills help clients create a context that is increasingly trustworthy and intimate. This context is one in which individual needs can be respected and the sense of equivalence can be fostered. Under these conditions, families and their members are in optimum conditions to cope with life and meet their needs. Meeting with the therapist becomes less important but can continue over time as the therapist's resources are needed.

SUMMING UP

These five core skills—expressive, receptive, conversive (interactive/engagement), generalization, and maintenance—form the basis of RE therapy. Using the core skills alone can help to further self-improvement. In fact, practicing the core skills elicits a gradual shift to greater ownership of one's feelings without projecting them onto others. Increasing one's receptive skills further helps the differentiation process, and the increasing acceptance of others helps foster self-change. Being more proficient in the conversive (interactive/engagement) skill fosters increased closeness with others and greater self-esteem.

SECONDARY (RELATED) SKILLS

Secondary (related) skills, which are drawn from and use the core skills, include problem/conflict resolution skill, self-change skill, helping others change skill, and facilitative skill. Each of these is modified from the core skills to help clients more effectively use their relationship skills. Whereas the core skills are generic relationship skills, the secondary skills have specific objectives and are used to help accomplish these objectives.

The secondary RE skills can be taught in several ways, ranging from a more structured and systematic to a spontaneous approach (i.e., when the need surfaces). The skills are best taught in a structured and systematic way (see Table 2.9).

Table 2.9   Skills Are Taught in a Consistent and Systematic Fashion

- The principles, methods, and guidelines of the skill are thoroughly explained to clients.
- The therapist demonstrates the skill.
- Clients practice the skill under therapist supervision.
- Clients practice at home.
- The therapist supervises home practice sessions through taped practice and/or self-report methods.
- Generalization and maintenance of skills are reinforced.
- The therapist becomes a consultant to clients.

However, given economic pressures and the increasing emphasis on time-limited therapy, it may be necessary to focus on core skills and introduce the secondary skills only to help particular clients.

These secondary (related) skills are commonly taught and practiced after clients have learned the core skills and are engaged in formal home practice. Usually, this is done when the need arises or clients request them.

Secondary skills are typically introduced once clients are practicing the core skills at home and are generally taught in the following order: problem/conflict resolution skill, facilitative skill, self-change skill, and helping others change skill.

Problem/Conflict Resolution Skill

This skill helps clients work out agreements and understandings that take into account each person's purpose and have the best chance for lasting success. Many conflicts arise out of misunderstandings and miscommunications. Often, when people feel better understood or understand each other better, problems and differences disappear. Using the core skills can help remove differences arising from misunderstandings and lack of acknowledgment. Often this alleviates the need for problem solution, and the problem/conflict resolution skill can then be used for more intractable issues. The principles of this skill provide a structure or framework that people can use to help resolve their differences and come to an agreement even if only agreeing to disagree.

The problem/conflict resolution skill is modeled early in the therapy in conjunction with homework assignments. If, for example, clients are asked to read introductory material about the RE approach, the therapist can help clients agree on a time to discuss this reading assignment. In the next session, when clients relate the outcome of this home assignment, the therapist can positively reinforce the clients' responsibility and their ability to come to agreement about this homework. If clients are unable to do the home assignment, the next session can explore some of the factors that undermined their ability to read and discuss it with each other. The therapist may discuss with clients what needs to be changed so that they can complete their next homework assignment. Working on issues of home assignments from session to session prepares clients to learn the problem/conflict resolution skill.

It seems most natural to formally introduce, model, and practice the problem/conflict resolution skill when clients are already practicing the core skills. Most likely, clients have already incorporated aspects of this skill while practicing the core skills. Many opportunities arise to introduce this skill when the therapist is supervising clients' core skills. Informally, the therapist can suggest to the speaker (after the speaker's feelings have been expressed and acknowledged clearly), "Start a sentence with 'It would make me feel good if . . . ,' or 'I'd like it if . . . ,' or 'It's important that . . .' " The speaker is also encouraged to complete the sentence as specifically as possible. For example, during practice between partners, one partner may look at the therapist, not knowing what to do next.

THERAPIST: You could switch now or start a sentence with "It would make me feel good if . . ."

FIRST PARTNER: It would make me feel good to know you understood my feelings.

SECOND PARTNER: That would make you feel good.

FIRST PARTNER: Yes.

THERAPIST: What could your partner do specifically so you would know that your feelings are understood? Tell your partner.

FIRST PARTNER: It would make me feel good if you would say things to me like "You're pissed off," "You feel awful about that," or "You're really angry at Jason (son)." It would make me feel better to know that you understand how I was feeling—it would really make me happy if you could do that.

FIRST PARTNER *(after Second Partner acknowledges First Partner's feelings)*:   Switch.

SECOND PARTNER: It really makes me feel happy to know what you want and understand what I can do that would please you. I'll try to do it.

The therapist can easily include this approach in the office training and practice. When clients are practicing at home, the therapist can introduce the more formal steps of problem/conflict resolution skill for home practice (see Table 2.10).

Table 2.10   Client Guidelines for Problem/Conflict Resolution Skill

Things to Keep in Mind

- Differences and conflicts are inevitable in all relationships because we *are* different.
- The resolution of the problem/conflict is less important than how we go about resolving it.
- In all close relationships, positive feelings always underlie problems and conflicts.
- If we understand each other's feelings, the problem changes.
- Sometimes the resolution is to accept that we can't find a resolution. This also can lead to compromise.
- Deeper, more significant problems may not be solved in a single conversation.
- Some problems take years to change and pop up periodically, becoming less and less frequent as things improve.
- Choose an appropriate time and place for problem resolution. If one of the parties is not ready, take more time before beginning.

Steps to Problem/Conflict Resolution

- Review your own feelings and perceptions to more clearly understand your position.
- Own your feelings.
- Take the time to understand each other's feelings (use speaking, listening, interactive/engagement skills).
- Make sure that you understand each other's feelings before attempting a solution. Check with the other person to be sure of his or her feelings (e.g., "You feel . . . about . . . It's important that I understand . . .").
- As you understand each other's feelings, acknowledge the underlying positive feelings (e.g., "What upsets me is that you are so *important* to me that when you don't kiss me when you leave, I get really hurt").
- Be behaviorally specific (e.g., "When you leave your socks on the floor, it really makes me mad. It would please me if you would put them in the hamper instead.").
- Try to talk about one issue at a time.
- Admit to your partner when you can't think of a solution, and state that it would make you feel good if he or she could suggest one.
- Shake hands or select some other mutual action to indicate agreement.
- Write down what you agreed on in very specific terms.
- Agree on a specific time to meet to review the success of the agreement (e.g., in a week or a month).
- Agree on ways to reinforce the other person when he or she responds to the agreement.
- Be flexible when discussing how the agreement can be changed if it doesn't work.
- *Above all, remember to use your RE skills.*

Source: Drawn from B. G. Guerney (1987a, 1987b) and Preston and Guerney (1982).

Facilitative Skill

This skill helps clients learn how to convey RE principles and skills to others who want to learn them for themselves and in their relationships with the client. This skill, which uses the basic skills and reinforcement principles employed in RE, is useful in family meetings, at work, and in other group contexts. Since the facilitative skill occurs under conditions in which all parties agree, it enables one member to take the role of teacher. When this is done formally the "facilitator" can also use modeling and prompting to help facilitate skill practice and learning. (See Chapter 3 for therapist skills.)

The facilitative skill is typically taught with generalization and maintenance. It is especially useful for family meetings when one member of the family is designated as leader and is responsible for maintaining the structure of RE.

Informal facilitation is a useful skill when clients are conversing with each other and one person is uncomfortable with another's response. For example, if one client recognizes that the other is not staying within the guidelines of the skills, the first person communicates this to the other by saying, "I feel judged." It is important that the speaker stop speaking and listen to the other person's concern. Then, the speaker should try to restate the message according to expressive skill guidelines. Finding ways to do this is part of facilitation skill. Alternatively, the listener could stay in the receptive (listener) mode until the other person is ready to listen, and then use expressive (speaking) skills to convey his or her feelings about the issue (see Table 2.11).

Self-Change Skill

This skill helps clients use the core skills in a way that fosters constructive personal change while reducing the possibility for relapse. It also helps them take greater responsibility for making these changes.

Primarily, self changes come from the core skills and their practice. The more one can "own" one's issues and feelings and the less one projects responsibility onto others, the better able one is to change an issue in oneself. Practicing the RE skills helps one come to accept one's actions and feelings more. Self-acceptance, the first step to self-change, is more likely if people also set realistic goals for themselves and are patient waiting for change. The guidelines in Table 2.12 can be given to clients who request help and self-change.

Table 2.11   Client Guidelines for Facilitative Skill

Informal Facilitation: Informal facilitation is part of a two-person conversation in which each partner tries to help the other person apply the RE skills.

* Agree on a signal to convey concern that the other person is not staying within the guidelines of the RE skills.
* After signaling your partner, try to own your concerns that your partner is not staying within the RE guidelines.
* Give your partner time to restate his or her response.

Formal Facilitation: Formal facilitation occurs when there are more than two persons practicing together and a third person is asked to *facilitate.* When RE therapy is conducted in family or multiple-family groups, a family member takes on a role similar to therapist and facilitates conversations that follow the basic RE structure and guidelines.

* Reinforce and maintain principles of both speaker and listener.
* Recognize and acknowledge when judgments, accusations, or questions emerge.
* Emphasize feeling statements.
* At the switch, make sure that the new speaker states how it makes him or her feel to know the other's feelings.
* Encourage switching if:
  —The conversation is going on too long.
  —The listener has adequately acknowledged the speaker.
  —The listener's emotions seem too strong.
* Make sure everyone gets a chance to speak and listen.

Source: Drawn from B. G. Guerney (1987a, 1987b) and Preston and Guerney (1982).

Helping Others Change Skill

This skill helps clients remain independent (differentiated) from others while responding in a manner that helps others change. Based primarily on the core skills, this skill also includes using positive reinforcement (within the boundaries of the speaking skill). One of the components of this skill is accepting that change takes time and that each person is responsible for his or her own change (see Table 2.13).

GOAL HIERARCHY LIST

Although goal hierarchy (Preston & Guerney, 1982, pp. 158–173) is not designated as a skill, it is an important element of RE therapy throughout

Table 2.12   Client Guidelines for Self-Changing Skill

- Review the issue and make sure you are motivated to change this aspect of yourself.
- *Own your feelings.* Keep the responsibility for the issue on your shoulders.
- Talk with your partner using RE skills to help you clarify your thoughts and feelings. Be behaviorally specific and set realistic goals.
- If you would like your partner's help to cue you beforehand or when you forget to do what you have decided to practice, make sure to request this as specifically as possible.
- Drop this agreement if reminders frustrate you. Acknowledge your appreciation if your partner is helping you.
- Remind yourself of the specific issue you'd like to change (e.g., put a note in a strategic place, carry something with you to remind yourself).
- Be realistic about self-change. It requires practice, practice, and more practice. Set specific short-term goals (e.g., once a day at first, then twice a day, etc.).
- When your method for change is not achieving results, review your progress and make your objectives and actions more realistic.
- Reward yourself for reaching specific goals.
- Be patient. Change takes time.

Source: Drawn from B. G. Guerney (1987a, 1987b) and Preston and Guerney (1982).

Table 2.13   Client Guidelines for the Helping Others Change Skill

- Remember, no one can directly change another. It is best to offer help when the other requests it.
- Use your RE skills to help the other person clarify his or her objectives.
- Make sure that your agreement to help is clear and behaviorally specific. Use your RE skills to clarify any misunderstandings.
- Social reinforcement (acknowledgment of your own feelings) of positive behaviors is most useful in helping another change (e.g., "It made me feel *good* when you did that").
- The less you can be invested in the outcome, the greater chance of success it has.
- Try to ignore negative behaviors.
- When you want another person to change a behavior, make sure to own your feelings.
- Be patient. Genuine change takes time.

Source: Drawn from B. G. Guerney (1987a, 1987b) and Preston and Guerney (1982).

Table 2.14   Client Guidelines for the Goal Hierarchy List

- This exercise is to help you consider more deeply what your goals are for yourself and in your relationships.
- These goals will be used as topics for skill-learning practice.
- The goal hierarchy list should be updated regularly and used in home practice.
- Choose ten goals for your list.
- This is to be done on your own. You are not to share your list with each other until the next session. This is to make sure that your list is not influenced by any other person's list. Later, it will be fun to see which goals you share and which are different.
- Rank the goals from 1 to 10 in difficulty, with 1 being the easiest and 10 being the hardest.
- The goals should deal with initiating something new, improving something, and working through a problem or conflict.
- The goals should be important to you, not just negative or positive.
- Try to balance positive and negative goals.
- Try to include feelings in each goal statement (e.g., "It's important to me," "I'd like that," "I'm unhappy about that," "I'm hurt by that," "That would make me feel good").
- Try to include the underlying positive message in each statement (e.g., "Because you're important to me," "I love you," "I feel good when you do that," "I like to please you").
- Try to make these statements as specific as you can without accusation or judgment.
- It's important to choose goals that you want to share with the other person.
- Make sure that your goals are realistic, that you have control over them, that you'll be able to carry them out, and that you will have the opportunity to work on and accomplish them.
- Review your goals weekly and update them.
- Bring the list to each session.

Source: Drawn from Preston and Guerney (1982).

all sessions. It is particularly useful in the initial sessions, but clients are encouraged to continue to update this list as the sessions continue.

The goal hierarchy is important, for it helps clients focus on their specific issues and make them more behaviorally specific. Because these issues are formed as goals, a more positive, future-oriented perspective is promoted (see Table 2.14).

The goal hierarchy list provides a continuity throughout the course of the therapy. As issues change in the relationship, the list can acknowledge and accommodate those changes. In the early stages of RE therapy it is helpful for clients to work toward the least difficult goals first until they become more skillful. The more difficult goals are best left until the clients have some rudimentary RE skills.

FLEXIBILITY OF RE SKILL TRAINING

A therapist can structure therapy programs to fit client needs. Relationship Enhancement therapy can be quite flexible, teaching the core skills alone or with any or all secondary skills. Possible combinations include the core skills with the problem/conflict resolution skill; core skills, self-change skill, and other changing skills; and, for family meetings, the facilitative skill with the core skills.

An advantage of the skill-learning emphasis of RE is that other skill-learning approaches can be integrated with it. Some examples of these skill-learning approaches are stress-management skills, self-hypnosis, relaxation training, and anxiety management.

Learning the secondary RE skills is significantly facilitated by using the core skills, thus reducing the amount of office time required; typically, they can be taught in one to three sessions. Clients then can include these skills in their home practice activities. The core skills and secondary skills together create a comprehensive approach that helps people deal with the difficulties they experience in themselves and their relationships. With sensitive and skilled therapist leadership, clients can learn these skills and use them to help them change, deal with problems, and enhance their lives.

CHAPTER 3

Relationship Enhancement Therapist and Leadership Skills

Early in the development of RE therapy, Guerney and his colleagues worried that the dynamic elements of good therapy would become subsumed in a more didactic, educational approach (Andronico, Fidler, Guerney, & Guerney, 1967). They emphasized that a therapist, as any good teacher, needs to develop trust, confidence, and a good working relationship with clients while taking a more directive and didactic stance.

The outcome of any therapy is dependent on the client-therapist relationship. Therapists need to have good interpersonal skills, including those identified by Rogers (1957, 1959): genuineness, empathic understanding, and acceptance—the very skills that clients are taught. Therefore, there is a coherence between the way the therapist acts (models) and what he or she is teaching. Two attitudes of the RE therapist have an especially important impact on the outcome of therapy:

1. *Humility* regarding one's ability to understand and directly influence or solve clients' problems.
2. *Respect and trust* in clients' ability to understand themselves and others and to handle their own personal and interpersonal problems.

These are not the only traits of successful RE therapists. They must also be receptive to their clients and able to own their position and feelings when expressing and acknowledging the relevance of their clients' concerns. Therapists should also be able to create a context in which clients feel safe. They should own their responsibility to create such a context, which in turn helps to establish their competence. This then helps therapist and client learn to trust each other. Therapists need to be fair and impartial while being free to form coalitions to help balance power. They need to know how to remain free of the triangles that naturally occur in families. Finally, it is critical for therapists to have good teaching skills: to motivate people to learn the skills; help them change their attitudes and behaviors; help them see the relationship between their problem issues and the value of learning the RE therapy skills and attitudes; and foster clients' confidence that they can learn the skills and change.

A short dialogue illustrates how RE therapists can merge their therapeutic and didactic roles:

CLIENT W: He never listens to what I say. He either ignores me or yells at me.

THERAPIST: You're upset about that. *(Receptive)*

CLIENT W: Yes, I don't think he cares.

CLIENT H: Well if she would stop demanding things from me, maybe she'd get more of what she wants.

THERAPIST: You're pretty frustrated. *(Receptive)*

CLIENT H: You're GD right. You can't talk with her.

CLIENT W: Well, if you'd only talk to me more.

CLIENT H: You'd never listen.

THERAPIST: I think you are both hurt and frustrated with each other. *(Receptive)*

CLIENTS H & W *(Both nod affirmatively.)*

THERAPIST *(switching to didactic mode)*:   That's why slowing down your conversation and avoiding accusation could help a lot. *(Didactic)*

CLIENT W: I don't think he's willing!

CLIENT H: Well, I don't think she is!

THERAPIST: Sounds like you're both afraid of that, but I sense that you both might be willing to try if the other person would. *(Receptive, structuring)*

CLIENTS H & W *(hesitantly)*:   O.K.

THERAPIST: I'm glad, because I believe this has a chance to help you. *(Conversive, expressive)*

Notice that the therapist is using all three of the basic skills—expressive, receptive, conversive—that are taught to clients in this interaction. Modeling is an essential part of this approach.

RELATIONSHIP ENHANCEMENT THERAPIST RESPONSES/SKILLS

Relationship Enhancement therapists need to develop certain skills just as clients do. Ten specific skills are outlined in Table 3.1 (B. G. Guerney, 1977, 1984, 1987b, 1994b).

The *administering* skill enables the therapist to manage the entire course of therapy. The therapist must pay attention to the structured, systematic, and time-designated nature of RE. Keeping the therapy moving; taking breaks; and dealing with homework assignments, intake procedures, insurance, fees, and so on are also part of this skill.

The *instructing/structuring* skill enables the therapist to introduce and explain the structure of this approach and to identify and/or remind clients of the guidelines and principles. Structuring the home practices, as well as any other assignments, are included here. Follow-up is essential

---

Table 3.1   Relationship Enhancement Therapist/Leadership Skills

1. *Administering* (directive).
   • Managing the therapy in a directive way.
2. *Instructing/structuring* (didactic).
   • Structuring the therapy.
   • Guiding home assignments.
3. *Demonstrating* (didactic).
   • Providing examples.
   • Expressing guidelines.
   • Indicating how skills can be used.
4. *Reinforcing.*
   • Applying principles of operant conditioning.
5. *Modeling.*
   • Expressing skills and feelings in a way that is consonant with RE principles.
6. *Prompting/encouraging.*
   • Encouraging clients to express thoughts and feelings.
   • Encouraging client participation.
7. *Supervising home assignments.*
   • Structuring and reviewing homework.
8. *Troubleshooting for client.*
   • Helping clients resolve their difficulty or anxiety using RE skills.
9. *Becoming/doubling.*
   • Helping clients who feel too overwhelmed or upset to respond.
10. *Troubleshooting for self.*
   • Using RE skills when difficulties arise in the therapist-client relationship.

Source: Drawn from B. G. Guerney (1987a, 1987b) and Preston and Guerney (1982).

---

to improve the consistency of response and to promote generalization and maintenance.

The *demonstrating* skill enables the therapist to help clients understand the specific guidelines, principles, and skills of RE. The therapist demonstrates how the skills can be used in real life. Role-play methods are used extensively to elicit understanding.

The *reinforcing* skill fosters learning. Overt methods of reinforcement include informing clients about RE's uses and value. Primarily, social reinforcement methods based on operant principles (positive reinforcement) are used. Reinforcement techniques are best done spontaneously but can be used deliberately. Shaping (graded learning) is an important component of reinforcement; in fact, graded learning (skill learning in successive steps) is probably the most effective teaching method. Therefore, therapists keep in mind the various skill levels of their clients and reinforce them accordingly. These responses help to improve performance and promote learning. Therapists use a variety of verbal and nonverbal responses to connote positive attitudes toward client responses, avoid making judgments, and help clients stay on course. Therapist need to be aware of the importance of the proximity and frequency of reinforcement and of the value of vicarious reinforcement.

The *modeling* skill is used extensively throughout RE therapy sessions. At the outset, it is important that therapists model the relationship skills that they would like clients to learn. In this way, what is being taught is congruent and coherent with the therapist's own action, which in turn conveys the essential attitudes of acceptance and nonjudgment. Modeling is also used specifically to help clients recognize how to respond according to the guidelines. Therapists can do this by asking speakers to express what they want to say in their own fashion, modeling this according to the guidelines, and then asking the speakers to say it in that way to the listeners. The therapist might identify the feeling that the listener may have trouble identifying, state it as acknowledgment, and ask the listener to respond in that way. This process helps clients internalize skills.

The *prompting/encouraging* skill is related to structuring, but differs in that the therapist does not specifically review the guidelines. This response may arise when a client is reluctant to express a thought or feeling or needs to be encouraged to become more explicit. The therapist uses RE skills in the response (e.g., "I would appreciate it if you would restate that"; "It's hard to be sure, try again"). This response should only be used in a receptive way, first making sure the client is ready. If the client is not ready, other responses such as modeling should be used.

Supervision of home assignments is another important therapist skill. Home assignments begin after the first client session. The supervision of home assignments establishes the structure that supports generalization and maintenance. Emphasizing home assignments helps clients learn to take responsibility and transfer what they've learned in the office sessions to their everyday lives. Each session should include sufficient time for supervision of home assignments. This supervision is structured very carefully and includes a great deal of therapist involvement to assure that clients follow through with their assignments. Once homework becomes a regular part of the client's daily life, the therapist can begin to decrease his or her involvement with the home activities.

Consistent use of either audio- or videotaped home practice sessions helps the therapist reinforce clients' efforts. The direct supervision of home practice tapes or reports is also an important component of home assignment supervision. Here the therapist's objective is to support the client's efforts to be responsible for continued practice, generalization, and maintenance. The therapist focuses on improving skills and helping to smooth out particular problems or stresses that might impede these home assignments and practice.

Troubleshooting for the client is a process ongoing throughout the therapy. Essentially, troubleshooting occurs whenever the skill-learning interactions are disrupted. Often the disruption arises from anxiety and defensiveness on the part of one or more family members. RE therapists expect that clients will have difficulty with the learning process, especially due to the emotional nature of their presenting issues. People in relationships have long-standing habits that may impede progress or cause the learning process to be undermined. RE therapists use all their skills to help smooth these disruptions and keep clients motivated. When therapists have to engage themselves in the process more directly or personally, they are troubleshooting. As clients get into deeper and more relevant issues skill practice usually becomes more difficult. At these stressful times, the therapist often engages with the client more directly by modeling the RE skills to get the process back on track.

When clients aren't ready to engage in the RE process, face an emerging issue, or become defensive, the therapist can explore these difficulties more directly or engage with clients directly to keep the interaction safe for them. Home assignments—picking a special time to be together, having a date with each other, taking time for oneself, doing something special with a child, bibliotherapy (develop a reading list and then read a book together) on communication relationships, and problem solving—can help clients become more comfortable and safe with the therapy process. Reviewing family history and developing a genogram (a format for drawing a family tree that records information about family members and their relationships over at least three generations; McGoldrick & Gerson, 1985) can also help clients feel more at ease. Occasionally, the therapist engages directly in problem solving to keep the therapy safe for the clients. However, the therapist's prime objective remains returning to and/or maintaining RE skill practice.

Becoming/doubling occurs when the client is unwilling or unable to speak or respond. In this case, the therapist asks permission to take the role of that person, frequently checking to see if the response is consistent with the client's purpose or meaning. Then, the therapist encourages the client to try the response.

This therapist skill response, playing the role of one of the clients, can also be elicited when the therapist seeks to restore the security of the session after an emotional breakdown occurs. This is also a good modeling technique when the relationship is tense, upset, or conflictual. In these cases, the therapist tries to assess the most appropriate time to encourage the client to resume taking the role, first checking with the client to see if he or she is ready.

Becoming/doubling can also be used to balance power inequalities and to break through impasses. The therapist accomplishes this by modeling for the client how to assert oneself instead of expressing oneself defensively. When a client who relates to family members by exercising direct power observes the therapist modeling the same meaning in an assertive (nonjudgmental) way, the power orientation is often diffused. RE therapists also use becoming/doubling to model the receptive skill when a power-oriented person disrupts the communication by his or her inability to be receptive.

Snyder and Guerney (1993; Snyder, 1995) emphasize becoming as a method that deepens and enhances empathic accuracy. They often teach clients the becoming skill to improve receptivity of clients to each other.

Troubleshooting for self occurs when difficulties arise not between clients but between a client or clients and the therapist. Here the therapist engages directly as himself or herself in relation to the client. Often, it is useful to use or model the RE format to talk about this. Troubleshooting for self often occurs when a client is not cooperative, when clients become upset with the therapist, when there is an emotional breakdown with which other clients (family members) have difficulty, and during outbursts of uncontrolled emotion when the therapist is unable to help another client use appropriate skills to engage the emotional client. Under these conditions, the therapist engages directly with clients as himself or herself until the interaction can be returned to the clients.

The RE therapist keeps these leadership/therapist skills/responses in mind as the therapy proceeds and uses them concurrently to help keep the process structured, bounded, and focused on skill practice. This tension between process and didactic elements employed by the RE therapist creates a context in which clients can learn and change.

RELATIONSHIP ENHANCEMENT THERAPY SHORT-TERM MODEL FOR COUPLES AND FAMILIES

With managed care influencing mental health services, many clients find a short-term approach very attractive. Relationship Enhancement therapy can be offered in a ten-session program lasting over a period of six months to a year. The advantage of the RE skill-training approach is that therapist involvement can be kept to a minimum while clients continue to practice at home on their own.

After the initial introductory session, clients are asked to agree on an additional four (weekly) sessions focusing on practicing communication with each other under therapist supervision. At the end of this agreement (fifth session), the clients and therapist review the progress of therapy and decide to continue or discontinue. Most clients who discontinue feel satisfied with what they have learned and prefer to continue on their own. The majority of clients choose to continue for a second four-session period. At this time, it is important to assess clients' ability to conduct practice home sessions on their own. When clients decide to practice at home, the frequency of sessions with the therapist shifts from weekly to biweekly. At the end of this second four-session period, (four to eight weeks) clients usually decide to meet in two or three months to assess their progress derived from the weekly home practice sessions.

The Initial Call

The RE therapist can respond in several ways when called for an appointment. During the initial call, the therapist should elicit certain information to help structure the first session: the nature of the problem, the identified patient(s), the composition of the family, referral source, and time availability. As part of this telephone conversation, the therapist identifies the importance of including significant others and helps clients decide who should accompany them to the first session. Taking time for this initial telephone contact helps to begin the structuring of the therapy. It also provides an opportunity for therapists to convey their orientation and to prepare clients for the initial office session by informing them about the location of the office, what it looks like, any special precautions (particularly important when young children and adolescents are included), and how to address the therapist (by Dr., first name, etc.).

The 10-Session Relationship Enhancement Format

Session 1

The therapist introduces himself or herself, discusses the presenting problem with clients, reviews the family histories of the clients, identifies the value of the RE therapy approach, provides a description of the principles and methods of RE therapy, and allows time for clients to experience a conversation in an RE format (see Session 1 of the basic program on pp. 78–79 for filial therapy). After clients are motivated, the therapist suggests they agree to continue for four additional sessions. As homework, clients are instructed to complete and bring the goal hierarchy list (Table 2.14) to the next session and to not discuss this homework with each other.

It is helpful to emphasize the agreement that all clients not discuss or share this homework assignment until the next session. It is important that these topics are perceived as genuinely coming from that person, in a way owned by that person and not directly influenced by others. It is common in relationships for one person to consistently be the initiator, with the other person being dependent on that and acquiescing to the first person's issues. Often, this action on the part of the dependent person is to constantly please the other and avoid conflict. The goal hierarchy exercise promotes greater equivalence between parties. It also establishes a more independent stance between them and has the potential to elicit more often the control themes and underlying issues.

This exercise can be done more informally with couples exchanging their lists at the next session and being encouraged to update them and keep bringing them to the sessions. The items can be used as topics for discussion, particularly at times the speaker feels "blank" about what to talk about. A more formal approach can be taken that helps to structure the interaction supporting the more anxious clients.

Session 2

Client and therapist review the initial session and discuss any questions or concerns. Clients exchange their lists and discuss them. One person volunteers to speak first and the therapist reviews the principles, skills, and rules, after which clients begin practicing under therapist supervision. For homework, clients decide on a time that can be regularly set aside to practice skills.

Session 3

This and each subsequent session begins with a review of the previous session and a discussion of any thoughts or concerns that have arisen in the interim. The therapist inquires if the clients have decided on a time for home practice and asks them to try to use that time to share with each other. The therapist advises them to bring up positive issues first as a means of avoiding conflict. The rest of the therapy session is devoted to therapist-supervised skill practice.

Session 4

As in Session 3, supervised practice continues. Clients are reminded that the next session includes a progress review and planning for the future.

Session 5

In this review and planning session, progress is measured by reviewing the clients' presenting problems and objectives. With the agreement of the clients, the therapist determines whether the clients are ready to practice at home. If so, they are asked to practice at the appointed time and to audiotape their interaction, which will be reviewed at the next session. They also receive the home practice handout (Table 2.6). The frequency of sessions with the therapist is reduced to biweekly.

　　If clients are not ready for home practice, weekly meetings continue until they are ready to practice at home.

Sessions 6–9

Home practice continues. A portion of the therapy session is devoted to reviewing the home tape; the balance could include more practice or discussion leading to a deeper understanding of their own dynamics and other separate but related issues (work, children, family of origin, etc.).

Session 10

This session is conducted one to three months after the last session. The clients are asked to bring their most recent home practice tape for supervision. Parts of the tape are reviewed, and clients and therapist discuss how clients can continue generalizing their skills. Continued home practice is strongly encouraged. Clients are asked to contact the therapist in a few months for a follow-up session; however, the therapist should indicate willingness to be available if needed before then.

This 10-session model can be applied to an individual, group, or whole family. Depending on the nature of the problem, family dynamics, and outside factors (involvement of social agencies, job stresses, traumatic event, etc.), the number of sessions can be reduced or increased. In other words, each session can be expanded to two sessions or two sessions can be efficiently combined into one. In any case, the structured, systematic, and time-designated nature of this approach is retained.

Other Session Formats

The exigencies of modern life—financial difficulties, demands on everyone's time—often require different RE therapy formats, such as biweekly rather than weekly sessions and intensive weekend sessions (3 to 12 hours), which can be repeated as needed. With highly structured home activities and periodic meetings, RE can be quite flexible. In all formats, maintaining the structured, systematic, and time-designated design is essential. After the problem is discussed and clients become motivated, the therapist models the RE skills. The therapist then supervises as clients practice the skills. Finally, the therapist supervises home practice to support generalization and maintenance skills. At this point the therapist shifts to a more consultative role. Examples of other formats include intensive, single-session, and periodic sessions.

Intensive Format

In this format, RE therapy is conducted for longer periods of time, such as a half day, over a weekend, or weeklong. This intensive format promotes the most learning in a short period of time.

Rappaport (1976) described an intensive format for a couples group that consisted of two 8-hour and two 4-hour sessions on alternating Saturdays and Sundays over a two-month period. The first 8-hour session included an introduction, rationale, and method. This was followed by demonstration, role playing, and supervised practice. Homework, which included readings and role-play practice at home, was assigned. Couples were instructed to complete homework forms and bring audiotapes of the practice session to the next meeting.

The second session (four hours) emphasized role-play practice with more threatening topics. First, the homework assignment was reviewed, then group members listened to several tapes of the home practice. After this, couples continued in supervised practice. The homework included completing a reading assignment, audiotaping home practice, and preparing a list of the two most serious or conflictual areas in the relationship.

The third session (eight hours) was devoted to specific areas of conflict in the relationship. Again, homework included role-play practice at home and audiotaping of these conversations. In addition, each member prepared possible solutions to problems that had emerged.

The fourth session (four hours) emphasized conflict resolution using the RE skills. Couples were encouraged to continue practice following this program.

Family-of-origin therapy generally necessitates an intensive format. It is difficult and often costly to get far-flung family members together except for weekends and holidays. An intensive weekend format that can be repeated after a period of time works best in these situations (see Chapter 8).

Often couples who live far away from the therapist prefer to come for an intensive weekend and to follow up at another time for a shorter period (e.g., a half day or one day).

Single-Session Format

In this format, clients come to the therapist only once. This session, designed to meet the particular interests and needs of the client, can last from an hour and a half to all day (eight hours): the longer the session, the more intensive it becomes. Therapists need to provide clients with a packet of materials to use at home. These can be drawn from the *Relationship Enhancement Manual* (B.G. Guerney, 1989). It is also important to help clients agree on a time to practice RE skills at home on a weekly basis.

Periodic Format

If clients are unable to come to therapy on a regular basis due to difficulties with time or money, the periodic format can be used. In this model, an initial session is devoted to introducing the RE skills and programs; very little attention is devoted to "problems." Instead, the therapist emphasizes how learning and practicing the skills will alleviate problems. At the end of the initial session, clients are given homework and a packet of reading materials such as "Instructions for Home Practice" (Table 2.6) and B.G. Guerney's *Relationship Enhancement Manual* (1989).

Clients should understand that they need to set aside a specific time each week—an hour at 9:00 P.M. Sundays, for example—during the month between therapy sessions. This hour can be used to talk about positive things, discuss the readings that have been assigned to them, and to practice RE skills and tape these sessions. Each subsequent session with the therapist includes follow-up and reinforcement of the home activities.

Booster Sessions

Once the therapy sessions end, it is helpful to develop a booster program to encourage clients to continue to practice the skills and principles of RE. Booster sessions with the therapist can be scheduled at varying intervals (e.g., every 3, 6, 9, or 12 months). Clients are asked to continue RE practice on a consistent basis and bring in audiotaped samples or written reports of these sessions. Vogelsong (1975) demonstrated that a booster program was effective in enhancing the gains of a mother-daughter group Parent-Adolescent Relationship Development (PARD) program. In his booster program, mother-daughter pairs were asked to set aside weekly times for discussion. Each pair was given six weekly logs and stamped envelopes addressed to the therapist. These logs were to be completed and sent to the therapist each week for the six-week period between each of the four booster sessions (24 weeks in all). The therapist also called each pair at the end of the first, second, and fourth weeks to reinforce their home practice and return of the weekly logs. The number of calls gradually decreased, with the hope that the pairs would progressively incorporate these patterns in their relationship. During the booster sessions with the therapist, the group members were encouraged to discuss any difficulties. Obviously, this program was highly structured to enhance the research. Nevertheless, a booster program to foster generalization and maintenance skills is implicit in all RE therapies.

STRUCTURE AND PROCESS IN RE THERAPY

The didactic elements of RE provide opportunities whereby important emotional and dynamic processes emerge (Andronico et al., 1967). In other words, the structured, systematic, and time-designated (didactic) elements provide a consistent framework so that the dynamic processes can emerge in a safe and secure context. In fact, these didactic elements often elicit dynamic processes because of the increasing security they promote. By keeping to the structure, clients feel less need to become defensive and are better able to recognize what they mean in their conversations and relationships with each other. The RE therapist needs to help clients handle this dynamic material without losing the structure that helps to keep it safe.

In the following vignette, a couple who has just begun to practice at home bring up their sex life for the first time. They have, however, spent a great deal of time in the therapist's office using RE to talk about anger in their relationship. She begins:

WIFE: I feel real upset with myself and with you too that the only way that I knew to control your anger, irritability, was to have this sex with you and I feel terrible about it now and angry with you—the whole thing makes me disgusted with it, and I'm really upset about it.

HUSBAND: *(Quiet, not responding.)*

THERAPIST: She is really upset about that. I wonder if you could tell her?

HUSBAND: You're really disgusted and sad and you're angry with yourself that all this joyless sex was used to control my irritation and anger and you're angry with me and it upsets you.

WIFE: I feel better now—having talked about it and it makes me feel better, but it's still upsetting to me.

HUSBAND: It makes you feel better that we've talked about it, but you're still upset.

WIFE: Because a part of me is a little despairing that we're not going to get beyond this, and I'm worried.

HUSBAND: Part of you is worried that we're not going to get beyond this.

WIFE: Switch.

HUSBAND: *(Quiet again. Therapist motions to wife to wait.)* It angers me, too, to think about all those years of joyless sex, because it was pretty joyless for me too. It makes me sad to know how worried and concerned you are. I don't share your concern about the future because I feel comfortable about the way we talk and the way we are working anger out and my own lack of anger through our discussions that I can't see us doing joyless, mechanical sex, and I don't think it's just for myself and that makes me feel happy and hopeful.

WIFE: You feel happy and hopeful because our combination of talking about anger and you're sad that I'm concerned about it, but you're hopeful because you're looking forward to it.

HUSBAND: Yes. Switch.

WIFE: I'm relieved to know how you're feeling and glad we're talking about it. I'm beginning to feel hopeful myself.

HUSBAND: You are beginning to feel better about this.

Of course, this is only the beginning of their conversation. It is note-worthy that this sensitive topic emerges out of the process of previous conversations and within the safety and security of the RE structure. Sex arose as a topic because the clients were ready to deal with it. This happened following a number of difficult but productive sessions discussing anger.

Nevertheless, it is still a hot topic and needs skillful guidance by the therapist. In this case, the RE therapist intervenes minimally, trusting that the structure and guidelines of RE will allow both people to feel safe. The therapist facilitates the process by encouraging the husband to acknowledge his wife. This in turn helps the husband feel more at ease and he responds. At the switch, the therapist motions to the wife to wait for the husband's expression, which helps them both feel more at ease. The husband then begins by being open with his wife about this sensitive and difficult topic. Because this conversation occurred at a later stage in the therapy, the therapist guides and facilitates in a very limited way. Early in the therapy, the RE therapist is considerably more active.

At the heart of RE therapy is a paradox: It promotes a highly structured and didactic format, and the therapist can be quite directive. Yet, as a result, a deep and spontaneous process emerges that very closely approaches the essence of the difficulties people have. Once people express, acknowledge, and accept their underlying hurt, anger, and distrust, they become much less defensive and naturally find ways to understand themselves and their partners and resolve their conflicts.

CHAPTER 4

The Young Child in Family Therapy

FILIAL RELATIONSHIP ENHANCEMENT

At the 1990 biennial meeting of the International Council for Children's Play in Adreasberg, Germany, the participants advocated that parents and children spend more time playing together. This recommendation was based on concerns regarding accelerating alienation within families and between generations. Television, divorce, and the complexity of society were cited as factors contributing to this growing alienation. The council emphasized the need for new unifying forces within the family (Sutton-Smith, 1994). Filial therapy, a family therapy program developed during the 1960s (B. G. Guerney, 1964; B. G. Guerney, Guerney, & Andronico, 1966; B. G. Guerney & Stover, 1971; L. Guerney, 1976), does just that.

Filial therapy is the RE therapy program that addresses the needs of young children and their families. This form of RE therapy is primarily developmental, that is, play is the preferred mode of working with children since this is their primary mode of self expression. They are dependent on their parents and tend to follow parents' lead. Because of this, parent expressiveness is limited to that which improves the initiative and freedom of expression of the child. A greater sense of equivalence between child and parent is emphasized, fostering more understanding and intimacy. Obviously, this can't be done unless the context is secure and safe. Parents create a safe context by providing structure, setting limits, and clearly applying limits. Parents express themselves when the child requests it; otherwise, the interaction remains child-centered.

From infancy, play is the preferred mode for self-expression and self-development (Singer, 1994). Playing is doing; play is universal; play is fun; play has everything in it (Winnicot, 1982). Playing is pleasurable, intrinsically motivated, spontaneous, and involves some active engagement by the person who is playing (Garvey, 1990). It is the child's way of life, aids growth, is voluntary, provides freedom of action, offers opportunity for trial-and-error learning, is imaginary, provides a basis for language building, promotes interpersonal skills, provides opportunities for self-mastery, and is a dynamic way of learning about oneself and the world. In essence, it is essential to human survival (Caplan & Caplan, 1974, pp. xi–xviii).

Given play's centrality, how could we not include play in our therapeutic work with children? And what better strategy than to involve children in play with the truly important people in their lives? Helping parents learn to conduct weekly home play therapy sessions enhances the child's development and fosters greater trust and intimacy in the parent-child relationship and family life. It also strengthens parenting skills and improves the parents' relationship with each other.

Filial therapy, also called child-centered relationship enhancement therapy, is based on the same values, principles, and methods as the other RE programs. In fact, it was the first RE therapy program, conceptualized in the early 1960s by Louise and Bernard Guerney (B. G. Guerney, 1964; L. Guerney, 1976). Contributing to the development of filial therapy was the concern that mental health needs would overwhelm the number of professionals available to meet these needs. Involving natural family members as psychotherapeutic agents with each other (B. G. Guerney, 1969) seemed to be a viable alternative. It also seemed useful to consider helping parents become direct change agents for their own children. A great deal of therapist time and resources could be saved by teaching parents to do what therapists do. Also, parents could be taught in groups, further extending the therapist's expertise.

CLIENT-CENTERED PLAY THERAPY

The play therapy approach emphasized in filial therapy is based on client-centered play therapy (Rogers, 1951) developed by Virginia Axline (1947, 1969), which she called "self-directed play." Presently, the term *child-centered play therapy* is used to identify play based on the child's own direction and initiation. Rogers's (1951) belief in the capacity of each of us to be responsible for ourselves and able to master the difficulties that life presents underlies this approach. The child-centered play therapist creates a context within which the child feels safe and secure and which optimally enables the child to direct what happens in these play sessions. In this context, the child experiences acknowledgment, acceptance, and nonjudgment from the adult. As a result, the child learns mastery, self-concept, and trust. Training parents to conduct these play sessions is the essence of filial therapy.

The Research Program

A three-year pilot program and study investigated the effect of filial therapy on children, four to eight years of age, who had serious emotional difficulties (B. G. Guerney, 1964; B. G. Guerney & Stover, 1971). Measures were completed by parents and therapists. In addition, therapists observed the children in play sessions, worked with the parents, and spoke with teachers and other school staff. All the children evidenced significant improvement on all measures. A follow-up measure by Oxman (1971) found significant improvement in the experimental group over the control group, which clearly was due to treatment effects. In the filial therapy study (B. G. Guerney & Stover, 1971), one important observation regarding behavior during play sessions was particularly meaningful. At first, the children escalated their aggressive behaviors. In later sessions with their mothers, however, these children engaged in more game playing, real-life conversations, and cooperative-sharing behavior.

> As the children experienced the permissiveness and acceptance of their mothers in the playroom, they worked out their aggressive feelings, cut out affectional displays (which probably were a defense against the aggressive feelings that had previously gone unexpressed) and dealt with their mothers more realistically—shared with them, conversed with them, etc. (L. Guerney, 1976)

A companion outcome from this study indicated a low dropout rate (17 from a sample of 71), further suggesting the power of this approach. B. G. Guerney and Stover (1971) concluded that parents can learn the skills to reflect feelings, to allow their children self-direction, and to involve themselves in their children's expression of emotion and behavior.

The outcome of this study and subsequent ones (Sensue, 1981; Sywulak, 1977) demonstrated the effectiveness of filial therapy. Initial gains were maintained several years later (Oxman, 1971; Sensue, 1981).

Filial therapy has been found to be useful with a wide range of problems and populations (Andronico, 1983; Ginsberg, 1976, 1984a, 1984b, 1989; L. Guerney, 1979; VanFleet, 1992).

THE BASICS OF FILIAL THERAPY

The essential ingredient that gives filial therapy its power is the context that is created by weekly play sessions. Parents establish a special time with the child for these play sessions, finding a place at home that allows the child optimum freedom of movement and lets the child know that he or she is acknowledged and accepted. The parent also is sure about the few limits that remain and states these clearly to the child *only* when a limit is broken. Furthermore, the parent applies consequences in a step-by-step fashion that helps the child take responsibility for the limits. Under these conditions, a context is created for both child and parent that is safe and secure and fosters intimacy and understanding. Ultimately, this relationship-based therapy model is built on the power that our primary and significant relationships have on our functioning.

GOALS OF FILIAL THERAPY

Filial therapy was developed to help children having emotional, behavioral, or developmental problems improve their functioning, facilitate their development, improve their self-concept, and generally feel more secure in their lives. At the same time, filial therapy improves the parent-child relationship, enhances the skills of the parent, and improves the general climate of the family (see Table 4.1).

The process of learning how to conduct these home play sessions and continuing them over time changes children, parents, and family. The shift in the family's interactional processes arises from the structured and systematic application of these home play therapy sessions. In filial therapy, the therapist needs to emphasize the centrality of the home play sessions to achieve these objectives.

SKILLS PARENTS ARE TAUGHT

Parents learn a number of skills while being taught to conduct play sessions (see Table 4.2).

Table 4.1   Objectives of Filial Therapy

The child is able to:

- Better understand and communicate feelings.
- Accept himself or herself more completely.
- Feel more secure.
- Solve problems.
- Gain mastery.
- Be responsible for his or her own actions.
- Change maladaptive behaviors to more proactive ones.
- Become more interpersonally competent.

Parents are able to:

- Improve their understanding of children's development.
- Develop more realistic expectations.
- Become more receptive to children's feelings and experience.
- Better accept children and their behavior.
- More skillfully communicate to children their understanding and acceptance.
- More effectively communicate their own expectations and needs.
- Generally improve their parenting skills and functioning.

The family is able to:

- Feel more secure and comfortable with each other.
- Have better relationships with each other.
- Trust, accept, respect, and be open to others.
- Be more intimate with each other.
- Be more independent while acknowledging the importance of the family relationships.
- Reduce stress and conflict.
- Shift the family interactional system to a more positive, functional, and proactive system.

Table 4.2   Filial Therapy Parent Skills

- Structuring Skill.
- Receptive Skill.
- Acknowledging Skill.
- Limit-Setting Skill.
- Facilitating Child Initiation/Self-Direction Skill.
- Self-Awareness Skill.
- Generalization Skill.
- Maintenance Skill.

Most parents learn these skills when they are taught how to conduct play therapy sessions. These skills are reinforced when clients and therapists generalize them to everyday life. Commonly, these skills are taught together and practiced each time the parent conducts a play session. However, it is useful to delineate each skill separately.

Structuring Skill

The structuring skill is essential in helping parents create a play context that is free, open, safe, and intimate. Parents learn methods that promote positive outcomes in their everyday lives with their children. They are better able to recognize the child's needs and development, and to develop more realistic expectations. And parents learn to recognize how much the child's environment and relationships influence his or her behavior and development.

Parents are taught to structure the play session by:

- Picking an area of the house that will be most conducive to conducting these special sessions.
- Removing as many objects as they can to reduce danger and the need for unnecessary limits.
- Establishing the best time (after consultation with the child) to conduct these weekly play sessions.
- Creating a special kit of toys for these sessions that foster children's creativity, responsibility, and initiative.
- Clearly identifying the few limits that remain, such as not being hit, remaining within the play area, ending sessions properly, and so on.
- Clearly informing children that they can do almost anything they want, and if there is anything they can't do, the parent will let them know.
- Expressing limits (and consequences) in a fashion that helps children be responsible for them (see limit-setting skill).
- Setting time limits and clearly informing the child of the beginning and ending of the play session, including indicating periodically how much time is left (e.g., "We have fifteen minutes left to play").

Receptive Skill

The receptive skill helps parents be more sensitive and efficiently responsive to their children. Being realistic regarding their child's development, being able to accept the child and his or her feelings in the present, and being able to wait for the child to initiate play are all important components. Using this skill, parents enter the child's field of experience, suspending their judgment and needs in order to experience the child more fully. This is the beginning of a process during which parents learn to accept children as they are; to appreciate and respect children's capacity and resourcefulness; and to trust in children's ability to resolve many of their own difficulties. Parents learn this skill during play sessions when they practice waiting for the child to initiate before responding.

Acknowledging Skill

Also called the empathic responding skill, the acknowledging skill allows parents to recognize their children's actions and feelings (meaning) in such a way that the children can feel good about themselves and can use this acknowledgment to gain greater self-mastery. The acknowledgment skill includes conveying an understanding and acceptance of the child without judgment. This skill is very close to and dependent upon the receptive skill.

Limit-Setting Skill

This skill helps children learn to become responsible. It fosters independence and self-reliance and enables children to take responsibility for their actions and feelings. In the play session, parents learn this skill by reducing the number of limits to a manageable few; by stating limits clearly so that the child can understand and be responsible for them; by establishing consequences that are related to the limits. Parents state limits and consequences in a step-by-step fashion to help children become responsible for their actions and feelings.

Facilitating Child Initiation/Self-Direction Skill

The integration of the receptive and limit-setting skills is worthy of its own category. Parents who learn this skill are able to help children freely express themselves and direct the play session any way they choose while being responsible for the rules that make it safe for the child and parent to interact in this way. Parents also handle limits in a way that fosters child self-direction. Mastering this skill is a process of gradually learning to wait for and accept increasing levels of child initiation and responsibility, being more confident of the child and context, and being able to keep both child and parent safe when the need for limits arises. An increasing interactive component of this skill comes into play: As the child becomes more responsible, the parent trusts the child more and has fewer concerns about limits.

Self-Awareness Skill

This skill enables parents to better understand their own feelings and needs in a way that does not undermine the child's freedom to initiate and direct what happens in these sessions. Parents taught to conduct these play sessions are asked to explore their feelings and needs in relation to what they are being asked to do. They are encouraged to accept these feelings and needs and to structure the play session so that they don't compromise the child's freedom of self-expression.

Generalization and Maintenance Skills

These skills are very close to those described in Chapter 2. After learning to conduct these play therapy sessions, parents are helped to conduct sessions at home. Once regular weekly play sessions are established, office sessions focus on reinforcing and strengthening parents' play therapy skills. Additionally, the therapist continues to use play session principles and skills to foster parent effectiveness. In other words, RE therapists often respond to a parent's concern about child behavior by asking, "How would you respond if you were in a play session?" It is also useful to use *Parenting: A Skill Training Approach* by Louise Guerney (1995) to reinforce these skills. This is an excellent parent education manual that is drawn from the principles and skills of filial therapy.

Parents are requested to continue weekly play sessions for at least six months and thereafter for as long as the child requests them. After play sessions have become an established routine, parents are encouraged to introduce "special times" as a method to continue meeting with the child at a special time that is less structured and more like everyday interactions. The therapist encourages parents to apply the skills more naturally during special times. This transition to special times helps to generalize and maintain skill practice.

TRAINING MANUAL FOR PARENTS: INSTRUCTION IN FILIAL THERAPY

As part of the introduction to filial therapy, parents are given a training manual that includes a description of filial therapy, its rationale, its principles, and how to structure and conduct home play sessions. A copy of this manual (adapted from the manual by L. Guerney, Stover, & Guerney, 1972, 1976) appears in the Appendix.

This parent's manual is useful to inform parents about the value, principles, and methods of filial therapy. Parents typically receive a copy of this handout in the first session and are asked to read it between sessions. During the subsequent sessions, it is used to answer parent questions in office sessions, and parents are asked to refer to it when conducting home play sessions.

Play Therapy Vignette

The best way to understand the value of child-centered play therapy is to "join" a play therapy session. Five-year-old Alan, whose parents are in the process of separation, is presently living with his mother at his grandmother's house with half-siblings of his mother. He has been kicked out of every child care program in which he has been enrolled for aggressively acting out. These behaviors have escalated significantly since his parents separated. The following play therapy vignette between a male therapist and Alan occurs during a group filial therapy session in which Alan's mother and the other parents watch behind a two-way mirror.

The therapist instructs Alan that he can do almost anything he wants to do and if there is anything he can't, the therapist will tell him so.

ALAN: What do we need that water for?

THERAPIST: You're wondering about that. You're curious about those things. You have a gun—you want me to have one.

ALAN: I like the gun.

THERAPIST: You like those guns a lot.

ALAN: Give the gun to me.

THERAPIST: You want me to give the gun to you. You want this gun back. You're getting all the guns.

ALAN: I need all these targets.

THERAPIST: That's important to you.

ALAN: Yeah, I can do whatever I want to do.

THERAPIST: And you're happy about that.

ALAN: *(Says something about target.)*

THERAPIST: You know that. You don't like that one. That bothers you.

ALAN: I'm taking that.

THERAPIST: You know that, you gave me that.

ALAN: Yeah, I need these.

THERAPIST: You need these, those are important to you.

ALAN: This is all I need. *(Says something about taking something else out.)*

THERAPIST: You're giving me those.

ALAN: I have these.

THERAPIST: You wanted to do that, you liked that.

ALAN: Where are the targets? . . .

THERAPIST: You want to know where the targets are?

ALAN: Aaargh . . .

> *(Laughter going on—child and therapist.)*
> *(He was able to shoot the dart.)*

THERAPIST: That's hard, you were surprised, you liked that, you liked that a lot, that pleased you.

ALAN: Yeah. *(Still laughing hard.)*

THERAPIST: You're really happy about that. That makes you feel really good. You enjoyed that. That's hard to do.

ALAN: I can do it.

THERAPIST: You can do it, you know that. It's hard, you're going to do it with your teeth. Oooh, oooh, that's hard. You're really frustrated with that.

ALAN: Just . . . *(Unclear)*

THERAPIST: Yes, you're mad. Seems really hard to get that thing to go, you really tried hard, and you're trying hard again. That's really hard to do. You're really frustrated with that.

ALAN: I just need red.

THERAPIST: You think a red one will make a difference.

ALAN: Yeah.

THERAPIST: Yeah, that will make a difference. You're really frustrated and mad about that and it bothers you a lot.

> *(Both therapist and child making sounds of how hard it is to do something with the gun.)*

ALAN: Can you do this?

THERAPIST: You want me to do it for you. *(Therapist making sounds of how hard it is to do.)*

ALAN: I can't get it down.

THERAPIST: You're really frustrated with that.

ALAN: You have to try it. *(Hands it to the therapist.)*

THERAPIST: You want me to do it for you. I don't think I can do it either.

ALAN: I'll get this.

THERAPIST: You want to get that gun to work.

ALAN: Put the target in and you're all set.

THERAPIST: You're happy about that.

ALAN: This won't work either.

THERAPIST: That upsets you.

ALAN: Dammit!

THERAPIST: It makes you mad.

Clearly Alan is trying desperately to gain some sense of mastery in his life. His effort is as strong and focused as his aggressiveness in the outside world. The therapist and child are very highly engaged with each other, the therapist following the child's initiatives and affect.

ALAN: This is a weapon.

THERAPIST: That's a weapon, you know that. You like that. You pointed that at me. You want me to show you how to do this one too.

ALAN: . . . Shit! Do that. You do that one. Do it.

THERAPIST: You want me to do it. Ouch! That hurt your mouth.

ALAN: It got my eye.

THERAPIST: It hurt your eye, too, you're really upset about that. That bothers you.

ALAN: It really bothers me. *(Alan is softening.)*

THERAPIST: Yes, it bothers you a lot.

ALAN: What's this for?

THERAPIST: You're not sure about that.

ALAN: *(Inaudible)*

THERAPIST: You're curious about that. You're surprised.

ALAN *(in a whisper)*:   Yeah, yeah.

THERAPIST *(repeats)*:   Yeah. You like that—it pleases you. Alan, you can do almost anything you want, but one of the rules is that I'm not allowed to get wet.

Here the engagement with the therapist has become too intimate for the child and he needs to create some distance. He throws a wet ball at the therapist and hits him. Note that the therapist acknowledges the child's feelings first ("You like that—it pleases you"). Then the therapist sets the limit in a clear and accepting fashion to help the child be responsible for the limit. In the next section of dialogue the child seemingly ignores the limit; however, he does not break this rule again.

ALAN: This is a school bus.

THERAPIST: You noticed that. *(Making sounds of the bus)* You like that school bus.

ALAN: These are my targets.

THERAPIST: Those are your targets. You're taking those things out.

ALAN: I need more.

THERAPIST: You need more of those. Alan, we have five minutes to play, five more minutes.

ALAN *(repeats)*:   Four more minutes. I just want to get these targets into the gun.

THERAPIST: That's very important to you.

ALAN: Well, that's what I'm trying to do.

THERAPIST: And you want me to know that.

ALAN: And don't argue with me.

THERAPIST: You don't want me to argue with you—it's bothering you that I'm arguing with you. You don't like that when I do that.

ALAN *(very emphatic)*:   These are my guns, don't touch them.

THERAPIST: That's very important to you.

ALAN: And I can do what I want here.

THERAPIST: You know that, you like that.

ALAN: I can pour the soda by myself.

THERAPIST: You're proud of yourself.

ALAN: One more.

THERAPIST: One more, you want one more.

ALAN: It has to be a secret one.

THERAPIST: A secret one, secret. That's important.

ALAN: Okay, just one more.

THERAPIST: One more.

ALAN: I have a whole bunch to do, so don't worry about me.

THERAPIST: You want me to know that, you really want to get those things done.

ALAN *(strong)*:   By myself.

THERAPIST: By yourself, you don't want me to bother you.

ALAN: No talking at all.

THERAPIST: You don't want to talk at all.

ALAN: I don't have time to talk, I have to go home after I do this stuff.

THERAPIST: Yeah, you don't have time to talk, you're really concerned about that.

ALAN: I'm pissed off at Sandy still.

THERAPIST: You're angry with her. You sure are and you want me to know that.

ALAN: And you, don't tell anyone.

THERAPIST: You're worried about me telling someone.

ALAN *(whispering)*:   It's a secret, be quiet about it.

THERAPIST *(whispering)*:   It's a secret, be quiet about that—that worries you.

This segment exemplifies the power of the safety and security of the play therapy process. Feeling safe, the child is free to move deeper and deeper into the source of his conflicts and feelings. He begins revealing this inner conflict by asking the therapist to be quiet, that it's a "secret one." It is a secret that he is about to reveal. No one is supposed to know that his father's affair with *Sandy* caused his parent's breakup. The therapist's close acknowledgment and acceptance of this secret enables the child to bring this conflict to the surface and gain more mastery over it within himself.

Notice, too, how quickly the child moves away from the secret after revealing it. This is typical of the way children handle issues that are difficult to deal with or understand.

ALAN: How do you get this in?

THERAPIST: It's hard to get that thing in there. That isn't for you.

ALAN: Well, I'm keeping it—can I keep one of these guns?

THERAPIST: You'd like that.

ALAN: Can I keep 'em?

THERAPIST: You'd like me to answer you.

ALAN: Yeah, I want to keep these.

THERAPIST: You'd like to keep those, but one of the rules in the playroom is that all the toys in the playroom have to stay in the playroom. That's the rule.

ALAN: I can keep 'em.

THERAPIST: You'd really like to keep some—it bothers you, it's important.

ALAN: I have to have one.

THERAPIST: It's very important to you.

ALAN: Get this in.

THERAPIST: It's really frustrating for you to get that in there.

ALAN: Get it in.

THERAPIST: You want me to do it for you.

ALAN: Now, do it.

THERAPIST: You want me to do it.

ALAN: You have to rush to get these in.

THERAPIST: You want me to hurry up about this. Alan, I don't think this dart can go into this gun.

ALAN: I think so.

THERAPIST: You think so, you want me to try.

ALAN *(with lots of expression)*: Damn, shit.

THERAPIST: It makes you really mad, you're really concerned about that.

ALAN: Did you hear what I said?

THERAPIST: You want me to know that.

ALAN: . . . I'll kick you if you don't.

THERAPIST: You're really mad at me.

Again the child is struggling with issues of intimacy, mastery, and control. He has trouble differentiating from the therapist and becomes aggressive toward him. The therapist's acceptance helps create a constructive outcome, obvious as the play session progresses.

> *(Sound like a shot; both therapist and child are excited and loud and laughing hard.)*

THERAPIST: You're enjoying that—ha, ha, ha, you really like that a lot and that pleases you. *(Child is laughing)* That made you feel good.

ALAN: Now, let's do it again.

THERAPIST: You want to do that again, you liked that a lot.

ALAN: Target down.

THERAPIST: You want the target in now.

ALAN: Yeah, get the target in now—blow his head off.

THERAPIST: You want to blow his head off. *(Both therapist and child laughing loud.)*

THERAPIST: You like that idea.

ALAN: Yeah.

THERAPIST: Pushing that in there—it's hard to do. It isn't hard for you.

ALAN: I'm getting something.

THERAPIST: You're trying to get that in there.

ALAN: I can do it . . . something on the wall.

THERAPIST: You'd like that *(laughing)*, that would please you, ha, ha, ha. You'd enjoy that a lot.

ALAN: I would.

THERAPIST: Yeah, that would be fun. *(Therapist tells Alan that they have one more minute to play.)*

ALAN: *(Trying to do something—making a sound that it's very hard to do.)* Get this thing out.

THERAPIST: That bothers you.

ALAN: Get this thing out.

THERAPIST: You want me to do it for you.

ALAN: I need to get this in first.

THERAPIST: You want to get that in first. I'm thinking how to do it. *(Child making sounds again of how hard it is to do)* It's really hard, you're frustrated with this. It makes you mad.

ALAN: Well, I say damn if I want to you anytime—you don't yell at me.

THERAPIST: You're happy that I don't yell at you when you say damn and that pleases you.

Here the child acknowledges his appreciation of the therapist's acceptance and the child's good feeling about that. This is quite an intimate interaction despite its brevity.

ALAN: *(Inaudible)*

THERAPIST: You like that, and you want me to tell them. You're proud of that shot.

ALAN: Go out and tell them now.

THERAPIST: You want to go out there and tell them now.

ALAN: No, you.

THERAPIST: You want me to go out there and tell them now. Alan, our time is up. We have to leave the playroom. Time's up. Play session is over, Alan. Play session is over.

To sum up the session: As Alan became more intimate with the therapist, he became increasingly active and aggressive. His aggressive behavior peaked when the intimacy became too intense. At that point, he violated a limit, and the therapist acknowledged the limit to Alan in an accepting but clear way. This helped Alan feel more secure and trusting of the therapist. Then Alan slowly began restoring the intimate and trusting relationship with the therapist. This enabled Alan to open up and reveal this secret inner conflict. Finally, at the end of the session, Alan acknowledged his appreciation of the therapist's receptivity and acceptance.

As a result the child was able to express conflicts more openly and begin to heal some of his unhappiness. This was a powerful model for his mother and other parents, helping them to feel comfortable and confident that they, too, could conduct play sessions.

The Basic Program

As family therapy has matured, and as changes have occurred in the third-party-payment marketplace, short-term, problem-oriented treatment has emerged as an attractive and viable alternative to traditional therapies. Filial therapy meets these criteria. In addition, its consistent and clear approach can be used by many therapists with many different types of families.

The basic program consists of 10 one-and-a-half- to two-hour sessions. The time per session can be shortened, but one and a half to two hours is optimum.

Session 1

Intake

The therapist

- Introduces himself or herself.
- Begins to establish a positive and trusting relationship with clients.

- Explores the presenting problem.
- Observes entire family in a play session.
- Shares feedback with parents.
- Conducts a play session with each child as parents watch.
- Explains the play session model and the filial therapy approach.
- Distributes the *Filial Therapy Parents Manual* to the parents.

The parents

- Share feedback with the therapist.

The therapist and parents

- Discuss school and medical issues, pertinent family history, and other relevant matters.

Session 2

Modeling

The therapist

- Reviews first session.
- Elaborates on the benefits of this approach.
- Responds to parents' questions.
- Models a child-centered play session with each child.

The parents

- Raise their concerns regarding their child(ren).
- Explore the benefits of the RE approach.
- Observe each child's play session with the therapist.
- Explore each play session with the therapist.

Session 3

Modeling

The therapist

- Models the child-centered play sessions with each child for a third time as parents watch.
- Acknowledges each child's particular development and method of self-expression with parents. This helps parents improve their sensitivity toward and understanding of their children.
- Reviews play session procedures so that parents can begin to conduct play sessions at the next meeting.

The parents

- Observe the play sessions.
- Discuss their observations of the play sessions with the therapist.
- Explore child's developmental issues and self-expression with the therapist.
- Review play session procedures.

Session 4

Parent Play Sessions with a Child

The therapist

- Reviews the play session procedure before parents conduct play sessions.
- Observes the parent-child play sessions.
- Gives feedback to the parents following each play session.

The parents

- Review the play session procedures.
- Conduct a one-on-one play session with each of their children.
- Observe each other's play sessions.
- Explore feedback on each play session.

Session 5

Second Parent-Child Play Sessions

The therapist

- Reviews the play session procedure with parents before they conduct play sessions.
- Observes the parent-child play sessions.
- Gives feedback to the parents following each play session.

The parents

- Review the play session procedures.
- Conduct a one-on-one play session with each of their children.
- Observe each other's play sessions.
- Explore feedback on each play session.

Session 6

Prepare for Home Play Sessions

The therapist

- Observes parent-child play sessions.
- Discusses feedback on play sessions.
- Explores how to structure the home play sessions, making sure to address place, time, additional rules, and home play session reports. (This can be quite didactic and take up as much as half the session.)

The parents

- Conduct one-on-one play sessions with their children.
- Explore feedback with the therapist.
- Decide, in consultation with the therapist, how to structure the home play sessions.
- Discuss the specific methods of conducting play sessions in their home.

Session 7

First Home Play Sessions

The therapist

- Reviews the home play sessions with the parents.
- Makes additional suggestions to improve the structure of the home play sessions.
- Responds to parents' concerns about any problems with the home play sessions. Helps parents consider how to respond to particular child behavior and expression in the home play sessions.
- Reinforces the parents in their effort.
- Observes and provides feedback on parent-child play sessions if children are in attendance (optional).

The parents

- Report on home play sessions.
- Share their feelings on the play therapy experience.
- Describe any difficulties to the therapist for guidance.

- Plan for the next home play sessions.
- Conduct play sessions and discuss feedback if children are in attendance.

Therapist and parents

- Discuss home issues and generalization of skills to everyday life.

Session 8

Second Home Play Sessions

The therapist

- Reviews the home play sessions with parents.
- Provides additional feedback and suggestions to enhance the home play sessions.
- Suggests that office sessions with the therapist occur less frequently (e.g., every two to four weeks).
- Observes and provides feedback if children are in attendance (optional).

The parents

- Discuss the home play sessions with the therapist.
- Improve the home play session structure and enhance play therapy skills if indicated.
- Meet with the therapist less frequently.
- Continue weekly one-on-one play sessions at home.
- Conduct play sessions and discuss feedback if children are in attendance.

Therapists and parents

- Discuss home issues and generalization of skills to everyday life.

Session 9

Review of Home Play Sessions. Children are not present.

The therapist and parents

- Review the home play sessions together.
- Reconsider the presenting problem and identify any changes that have occurred.
- Decide whether further treatment is needed.

- Agree to meet in three months if there are no other concerns.
- Discuss home issues and generalization of skills to everyday life.

Session 10

Concluding Session. Children return for this session.

The therapist

- Observes parent-child play sessions.
- Provides feedback on play sessions.
- Discusses changes in the children in light of their presenting problems.

The parents

- Conduct play sessions.
- Discuss the therapist's observations and feedback.
- Review changes in the children in light of their presenting problems.

Therapist and parents

- Discuss changes in the children, family, school, and community.
- Decide on the degree to which the therapist needs to remain involved with the family.
- Agree to be in contact on a periodic basis.
- Work out any remaining concerns regarding continuation of the weekly home play sessions.
- Reinforce generalization and maintenance methods.
- Consider any other issues affecting the family and decide whether a new agreement to continue to address these issues is needed.

The 10-session program is not conducted in a rigid fashion. There are many variables when working with families, particularly those families in distress. In addition, children (the identified patients) are among the most vulnerable members in a family, and therefore their difficulties are often accompanied by stresses in other areas of family life. These other stresses may require immediate attention, which may lengthen the therapeutic process. On the other hand, a sensitive and insightful family may require fewer training sessions before being able to conduct regular and consistent home play sessions. Another variable that would affect the number of sessions or length of treatment is the difference between working with an individual family in filial therapy and conducting filial group therapy. Managing a group may require additional sessions for all group members to have sufficient training.

THE PROCESS OF FILIAL THERAPY

The following case history will help demonstrate the process of filial therapy.

> Donald is a nine-year-old boy in third grade. The oldest of three children, he has a sister Carrie, five, and brother, Ted, nine months. He has had difficulty following classroom procedures since his entry into school. In the early years, his actions were seen as stemming from immaturity. Educational programs were offered. However, in third grade, he has become more oppositional, frequently arguing with the teacher and even using foul language when confronted by teachers. His relationship with his peer group tends to be poor: He tries to bully others and get their attention, even if it is negative. At home he continually initiates conflicts with his siblings and has trouble following family rules. Typically, he expresses his dissatisfaction with the family's meal, demands something else, and makes dinner time so unpleasant that either he leaves the table or is asked to leave. Routines such as bedtime, coming home for supper after playing outside, or even getting to school are difficult for him to manage.
>
> Donald's father, George, is an executive in a multinational corporation. He works long hours and is often away from home on trips. Donald's mother, Sue, is responsible for family caregiving and family management. George tries to support Sue's efforts and reduce her stress when he is home by disciplining the children; however, the burden of responsibility for the family remains on Sue.
>
> When Donald was five and just entering kindergarten, his maternal grandmother died. This was a significant loss for Sue. Her mother had helped her manage the children, and they were very close. Sue continues to express sadness whenever she talks about this loss.

In this case, Donald can be seen as the "triangulated" child whose difficulties help to bring Sue and George together to deal with him. This could be a constructive, supportive action on behalf of the family, even though the stresses that Donald experiences may not be in his best interest.

Some of Donald's behavior seems to be characteristic of Attention Deficit Hyperactivity Disorder. The therapist made an effort to determine this through various self-report measures and a psychological evaluation; however, Donald did not show the classic signs of distractibility and inattention. Although ADHD was not ruled out altogether, parents and therapist agreed that his difficulties were mostly due to anxiety and depression. A course of psychotherapy was agreed upon.

The First Session

The initial session can be organized any number of ways. The therapist can meet with the parents alone, as was done in this case, or with the whole family. If the therapist first sees the parents alone, and then the children attend a subsequent session, both sessions are considered part of the initial session. The advantage in having everyone together is that the therapist has the opportunity to see the target child at the onset of therapy. The therapist also has a better sense of the family's concerns and can begin to intervene. Sessions with the parents alone can be scheduled to follow the initial session if that is found to be necessary. When conducting group filial therapy, it is important to have the first session without children to help foster group cohesiveness and trust.

It is important in this initial session for the therapist to convey his or her confidence in this approach. Strong beliefs in the power of the parent-child relationship as an agent of change when children have problems is essential to the outcome in filial therapy. If the child's problems occur in the home, parents need to understand the importance of their involvement in the therapy. When the presenting problem occurs outside the home (e.g., at school), parents need to be reminded that they have very little direct power. Parents also need to understand that the significance and security of the parent-child relationship can help strengthen the child's ability to cope in the outside world and ameliorate his or her difficulties. Ultimately, if the child can use his or her own resources, the potential for long-term change is assured.

The filial therapist has to skillfully relate the value of the home play sessions to the concerns that have brought the parents to therapy. One of the tenets of the child-centered play therapy approach is to provide a context in which the child's own resources are strengthened. It is this emphasis that ties the filial therapy approach to the concerns parents have about their child. The special context that the play sessions create, the improved parenting skills, and the enhancement of trust and intimacy in the parent-child and family relationships are the resources that will foster the child's competence, which in turn forms the basis for improvement in the child's behavior, affect, and relationships.

In the initial session with Donald's parents, Sue and George were seen alone. They discussed family history and their concerns about Donald's problems with the therapist. They appreciated the value of filial therapy as providing a practical, concrete approach to address these issues. They were given the *Filial Therapy Parents Manual* to review prior to the next session.

The Second Session

All three children were present with their parents for the second session. Given the father's highly variable schedule, which sometimes changed at the last minute, the therapist had to be very flexible scheduling appointments.

When the children participate in the initial session(s), the playroom or play area becomes the focus of attention. It is important to convey the special nature of the playroom and the play therapy context. It is helpful to set a rule that children can be in the "special" playroom only if an adult accompanies them. This helps set the playroom and play session apart from everyday interactions. It also helps children adjust to the different way their parents will relate to them.

After discussing the parents' concerns, the therapist invites the entire family into the playroom. The therapist stands outside the play area or observes the family play session through the two-way mirror, if that is available. Louise Guerney (VanFleet, 1994) has suggested that the therapist observe:

1. Interactions between the target child and each parent.
2. Interactions between the target child and each sibling.
3. Interactions among all children and the parents, the degree of interaction, and the absence of interaction.
4. Locus of control in the family and among the children.
5. Methods used by the target child to achieve his or her goals.
6. Methods used by the parents to control the children.
7. Verbal and nonverbal affective expressions of the target child and possible sources of the feelings.
8. General behavior and actions of the target child.

9. Neurological and other unusual signs, such as distractibility, speech difficulties, or coordination problems in the target child or siblings.
10. Problem interactions between the target child and the others.

The therapist uses these observations to detect any concerns that might need further explanation or referral (e.g., medical, audiological, visual, neurological, educational). The therapist also discusses these observations with the parents to help educate them. These observations are useful in explaining the value of the play therapy sessions and filial therapy. In this way, the RE therapist works collaboratively with the parents. For example, the therapist might note that the child turns to one parent for constant guidance and/or approval during the play session. After describing this to both parents, the therapist asks, "Does this happen at home?" Exploring these observations enriches the session, helps parents look at the family, and helps the therapist reality-test hypotheses and observations.

In this session, Donald was the center of attention. Although at times he was able to concentrate on toys and things that were of interest to him, he seemed to need constant adult attention. Once the entire family was together in the playroom, Sue immediately got on the floor while George stood directing the children's activities. Sue became engaged with Donald and tended to oversee his activities, constantly guiding and directing him. George interacted with the other two children if they turned to him or if he needed to discipline them. When Donald's infant brother crawled into his mother's lap, Donald enveloped her with hugs and kisses. Donald's sister began fantasy play and for much of the session was ignored; once Donald's mother tried to join her, and on another occasion the father tried to redirect her into another activity. At one point during the play session, Donald found the dart gun and began pointing and shooting it at his brother and sister, occasionally hitting them. At first, his parents didn't respond, but after the baby was hit both parents admonished Donald severely and took the gun away from him. In this session, George tended to act supportively toward his wife, though this was done to take care of her, which made her defensive.

Following the family play session, the therapist and parents discussed what they observed. The therapist shared his observation at how quickly Sue got down and became engaged with Donald, and that Donald seemed to depend on her involvement and guidance. The therapist also noted that George had not gotten on the floor with the children and tended to act in a more instrumental way with them. Both parents agreed that this pattern repeated itself at home. When the therapist identified Donald's seeming jealousy of his brother, Sue remarked how difficult it was for her to manage the infant when Donald was around: He would either interfere with her, begin to nurture his brother himself, or request equal nurturance.

The therapist raised his concern about Donald's sister, Carrie, who tended to be compliant and engaged in a great deal of fantasy play without much interaction with others in the family. Both parents agreed that given all the pressures within the family she tended to be ignored, yet they seemed to accept this.

Sue and George talked about how responsible and guilty they felt about Donald's difficulties. When the therapist acknowledged these feelings, Sue began to cry. It was obvious that Donald's difficulties exacted a heavy emotional toll on both his parents.

THERAPIST *(acknowledging)*:   You're really worried about him, and it's hard not to feel responsible and guilty. I'm concerned about his difficulties, too. He seems very unhappy, and all this aggressive and oppositional behavior seems to show how unhappy he really is. I'm concerned about Carrie as well. She seems depressed and tends to cope by reticence and withdrawal.

SUE: You're right. I've been very concerned about Carrie for a while, but Donald's issues seem so much more pressing that I've overlooked her. *(Sue starts to cry again. George puts his arm around her.)*

THERAPIST *(to Sue)*:   You've been worried about Carrie, too. I wonder, George, if you feel the same way about them?

GEORGE: I do, but because I'm home so much less, I depend upon Sue a lot. From what I've learned today, I think it's important we do something. When Sue first brought up coming here, I was reluctant, but now I feel good we've come."

THERAPIST: I'm pleased that you seemed to have gained from this session. I'd like to talk more about the value of the play sessions after I play with each child, so you can make an informed decision about doing this.

Individual Play Sessions with the Therapist

An important part of the initial session(s) is the one-on-one play session with the therapist while parents are watching. This is not only very instructive but also critical, in that the therapist forms a therapeutic alliance with both parents as well as the child. Filial therapy, as do other therapies using the educational model, emphasizes the importance of informing clients of its rationale, method, and the purpose of what is being offered. With this insight and understanding, clients are in the best position to choose or reject this approach. Once they are informed and choose to participate, the therapeutic alliance is strengthened.

Children, for the most part, are excited about playing in the playroom with the therapist; however, they usually feel more at ease after first using the playroom with their parents and siblings. Some younger and more anxious children insist on having a parent with them when they play with the therapist alone. Under these conditions, the parent is instructed to say little or follow the therapist's lead and model what the therapist says.

The purpose of the individual play session is to model the play therapy approach and help the therapist gain greater insight into the child's functioning. How children cope in these sessions can be an example of their coping in the larger world. Guided by the play session procedures, the therapist gains a receptive sense of the child. Following play sessions, therapists share their experience of being with each child in the playroom, relate their experiences to the presenting problem of the target child, and pay attention to the coping and functioning of the other children in the family. This is a positive and constructive interaction, because therapists relate their observations from a developmental/coping perspective rather than one of pathology and dysfunction. The therapist voices all concerns directly: "I'm concerned that the child tested the limits so often in the play session and wonder if the child's difficulties may be due to anxiety."

For the parents, the play sessions are educational opportunities. By observing play sessions in action, they gain increased insight into their children's behavior. At the same time, they can generalize the focus on the target child to the other children as well as to the entire family.

Both Sue and George observed all one-on-one play sessions with the therapist and each child. In her play session, Carrie engaged the therapist in the fantasy play in which she had previously involved the whole family. However, her affect seemed constricted and subdued.

Donald tended to be active in the playroom, moving from one object to another. At first, he had trouble finding something to focus on. Eventually, he found the dart gun and tried to shoot it directly at the therapist. When a dart hit the therapist, the therapist stated the rule about hitting. Donald put the gun down and began to play basketball. He seemed responsive to the way the therapist was playing with him, and described some of his activities at home and school. He did not seem to be satisfied with or get pleasure from his activities. He also required the therapist's constant attention, whether positive or negative.

The play session seemed to reinforce the possibility that Donald's difficulties at school and home were a result of anxiety and depression. The therapist also raised his concern that Carrie may be depressed as well. Following these observations, the therapist explained the principles and skills of filial therapy, and clarified the value of the child-centered approach to help Donald use his own resources to free himself from this depressive state and to improve his school performance and his family functioning.

The therapist explained to George and Sue that this child-sensitive response would enhance the trust and intimacy of their relationship with Donald, which certainly would improve George's involvement with the children. The therapist acknowledged how clarity, consistent structure, and limit setting during the play session would help Donald become more responsible and improve his mood. The therapist also stated his belief that as Donald's self-confidence improved, and as he felt closer to his parents and more responsible for his own behavior, his behavior with others would improve. This shift would be reinforced when others reacted to him as if he were more responsible. Both Sue and George were encouraged by this and were looking forward to learning how to conduct play sessions.

The therapists' own confidence in filial therapy is an important variable. Their confidence and optimism are usually contagious. This positive approach helps clients be more optimistic about improvement.

Preparation of the Parents

In the next session the therapist modeled play sessions with each of the children. After each play session, parents and therapist discussed the specifics of the play session methods and the application of filial therapy principles to the particular child. This session was repeated the following week to help prepare parents to conduct play sessions with each child at the next session.

Before the next session, Donald's school requested that the therapist attend a school conference with Sue and George in order to develop strategies to help improve Donald's coping and performance in school. The staff seemed reassured that the family was involved in therapy. With the parents' permission, the therapist explained that he used a filial therapy approach. Sue and George were both very positive and optimistic when talking about filial therapy.

Parent-Child Play Session

Both Sue and George were anxious about being observed conducting play therapy sessions with each child. George volunteered to go first and play with Donald. Donald was excited to play with George and concentrated on activities that showed off his prowess, particularly basketball, ring-toss, and shooting the dart gun. George had difficulty not asking questions. Even when he attempted a reflection of feeling, it sounded like a question. Nevertheless, he was making a valiant attempt to follow the play session guidelines.

After the play session, the therapist first emphasized how happy he was that George was able to follow the guidelines. George expressed his frustration at the prohibition against asking questions. The therapist acknowledged how hard that was but was pleased that George recognized it. He also acknowledged that this was a common difficulty and would dissipate.

After acknowledging George's feelings, the therapist brought up several of the interactions between George and Donald, for example, "When Donald was trying to find a dart for the gun and threw the gun down when he couldn't, what was he feeling? How would you acknowledge that to him?"

After this, the therapist modeled alternative responses for George to consider using during subsequent play sessions with his son: "You're frustrated, that's upsetting. You didn't like that." In other words, the therapist first acknowledged the positive aspects of the play session before he tried to shape the parent's play therapy behavior.

Following the discussion with George about his play session with Donald, Sue played with Carrie. She felt more at ease after watching her husband's session. When Carrie aimed the dart gun at Sue, she had difficulty setting the limit and instead just took the gun out of the girl's hand and said, "Don't do that." After the play session was over, she regretted responding in such a way that violated the play session procedures. The therapist acknowledged her being upset with herself and helped Sue practice the appropriate response ("You're enjoying that, but the rule is that the gun can't be pointed at me").

Next, George had a session with his nine-month-old son, Ted, who crawled around the room exploring everything. George found it easy to acknowledge this child and felt good at the end of the session discussing it with Sue and the therapist. Both parents were very pleased with this first play therapy opportunity with their own children. They seemed to feel proud of their accomplishments.

At the next session, Sue played with Donald and Ted and George played with Carrie. Sue had difficulty setting limits with Donald, providing an opportunity to help her improve her skills in this important area. George had a very good session with Carrie, and Sue seemed to be very pleased about that. At this point, Sue and George thought they were ready to conduct these play sessions at home. The therapist concurred. He encouraged them to complete the purchase of the special toy kit and consult with each other on the best place to conduct these sessions at home, a subject that would be discussed at the next office session.

A part of each session was devoted to how the play therapy principles are applicable to effective parenting. Typically, parents raise their concerns regarding parenting issues at home. The therapist responds by first asking how they might handle a particular concern if they were in a play session. For example, "If Donald came home late for supper, you (Sue and George) would acknowledge his feelings, reiterate the rule, and warn him of a related consequence if this happened again." This tends to enhance their understanding of the principles and how to implement them. Relating the play therapy principles and skills to everyday parenting issues helps parents improve their motivation to see the applicability of what they are learning.

At home, things were beginning to change. Donald was more cooperative and even intimately involved with his parents as well as his siblings. Carrie, whom both parents realized had been withdrawn, began to receive more attention. This shift of focus from the improving index child to another child is common in filial therapy. As the sessions progressed, Carrie became more open and spontaneous, laughed more, and improved her relationships with her peers.

Home Play Sessions

The first home play sessions went pretty well, and Sue and George were very encouraged. A few areas needed strengthening, for example, leaving the play area before time was up and use of water; however, changes were easily implemented in the following play sessions. All the children looked forward to these weekly play sessions. It was apparent that the family environment was more flexible and positive. Because George's schedule was so variable, his play sessions were scheduled a week ahead of time so that the children could anticipate them. Although home play sessions are typically held at the same time on the same day each week, a more flexible approach was required to accommodate George's schedule.

George felt very good about his increasing involvement and new role in his family. He was particularly satisfied with the skills that he was learning; previously, he had felt somewhat inadequate. As the home play sessions progressed, Donald's behavior at home and his school performance continued to improve. Typically, when home sessions begin on a consistent basis, the frequency of office sessions is scaled back. However, Donald's parents contracted to begin marital therapy: George and Sue came to therapy by themselves in the weeks between office sessions with the children. Thus, they could integrate what they had learned in the RE marital therapy with filial therapy.

Toward the end of the couple treatment period, approximately three months after home play sessions began, Sue and George reported that Donald had improved significantly in prosocial and academic behaviors, two important target areas in child therapy (Kazdin, 1995). His grades improved from Cs to Bs, and he was beginning to form friendships with his peers. He even invited a friend from school over to his house for the first time. Carrie had similarly improved. When the family was seen for follow-up a year after beginning treatment, these areas all continued to show improvement.

Supervising Parents

Parents are often anxious and insecure about going into the playroom for the first time and being observed by the therapist. They are self-conscious and concerned about being judged and making mistakes. For these reasons, supervised office play sessions need to start as soon as possible. Usually two sessions, during which the therapist models the play session procedures with each child, are sufficient; however, some parents need an extra session to feel comfortable. Some parents request that the therapist join them in the first play session. In one filial therapy program for abused and/or neglected children and families, a parent refused to go into the playroom with her child. She herself had been so abused in her childhood that she could not tolerate being in so intimate a setting with her own child. The therapist considered this therapy successful when she was willing to conduct a session along with the therapist and model his responses. However, most parents seem excited and motivated to get started in spite of their anxiousness.

Successive approximation is an important tool for the filial therapist in supervising parents. It is important to emphasize to parents that the goal of the first parent play session is to eliminate directiveness and initiation and to provide structure for the play session. Therefore, the therapist emphasizes the Nos in the *Filial Therapy Parents Manual:* no criticizing, no praise, no approval, and so on (see p. 247 in the Appendix). Parents are instructed to try to reflect the child's actions and expressions, but not to be too concerned (acknowledging their child's feeling). This is important, because it is hard enough for parents to reduce their initial directiveness; however, skill in acknowledging feelings will improve as they continue to have play sessions. In the supervision after each play session, the therapist further explores acknowledging feelings by stating, "When your child was trying to put the Tinker Toys together and then threw them down, what was the child feeling?" If the parent says, "Frustrated," the therapist responds, "Good." Then, turning to the other parent, the therapist asks, "What would another feeling response be?" That parent might respond, "Bad," "Unhappy," "That's hard," and so on. The therapist then reinforces each response (see Table 4.3).

The second time the parents play under office supervision, the therapist begins to encourage the parents to acknowledge the child's feelings. The therapist suggests to parents that if they miss a feeling or aren't sure of the feeling, they should nevertheless go on and not struggle; by the time the parent recognizes the feeling, the child has gone on to something else. Recognizing feelings more quickly comes with practice.

When supervising parent play sessions, therapists need to identify specific interactions from the session. One way to do this is to divide a sheet of paper in half. On the left side, write the child's behaviors and on the right, the parent's responses, starring those items that need to be emphasized in the supervision. Here's a helpful shorthand: "R" when a parent reflects appropriately; (R) when a parent doesn't acknowledge the child's behavior; and "F" or (F) to indicate feeling acknowledged or not.

After parents have conducted two supervised office play sessions, and each parent has had an opportunity to play with each child at least once, preparation for home sessions can begin. Spend most of a session helping prepare parents to conduct these home sessions. This attention to detail helps convey to parents the importance of carefully structuring these sessions. It also helps them learn the importance of structuring as a basic parenting skill.

Table 4.3   Steps in Supervising Parent-Child Play Sessions

1. Ask the parent how he or she felt in the play session.
2. Pick out one or more parent behaviors to which you can respond positively. (e.g., "I was pleased that you didn't do any of the Nos in the *Filial Therapy Parents Manual*"; "I liked it that you didn't initiate anything during the session"; "I'm glad you acknowledged your child's frustration with that toy").
3. Continually provide positive reinforcement throughout the supervision.
4. Pick out several points to emphasize to enhance parent skills.
5. Try to avoid negative connotations and judgments.
6. Be specific about the behavior. Ask how the behavior might be acknowledged within the guidelines of the play session (e.g., "When he handed you the toy, you tried to help him with it. How might you reflect that first before responding?" or, "When he had trouble getting the gun to work, how could you have acknowledged that?").
7. Review the rules and their application before the parent begins the play session. After the play session, emphasize limits as part of the supervision (e.g., "I liked your reaction when you were hit by the dart; you stated the limit and then acknowledged the child's concern about that." "When you were hit by the dart, you stated both the limit and its consequence. It is important to state the consequence after the second time. This allows more opportunity for trial-and-error learning.").
8. All supervision is stated in constructive, instructive, and educational terms. This enhances the parents' motivation to learn how to conduct these play sessions on their own at home.
9. Above all, the supervisor is a model for the parent. Therefore, the therapist needs to act in consonance with the principles and methods of filial therapy. *Acceptance* and *nonjudgment* are the cornerstones of all therapist behaviors.

THE TOY KIT

After the initial session, parents are encouraged to begin assembling a creative toy kit. The toys should stimulate activity, fantasy, and mastery, and be relatively unstructured so that the children impose their own direction on their use. A deck of cards, ring-toss, a bowling set, and checkers may be included, particularly for older children between the ages of 9 and 12. Toys that the children already own but haven't used for a while can also be included, but parents must first ask the child's permission (since these toys will be off-limits except during play sessions). Children can be involved in the toy selection process. This enhances their motivation for home play sessions. All toys are to be kept in a large box for easy storage.

STRUCTURING THE HOME PLAY SESSION

Before discussing the structuring of home sessions, parents have to consider the best place to conduct them. Next they must explore any additional limits that need to be set and whether privacy can be maintained. Sometimes asking parents to draw the area and review each element within its boundaries is helpful. It's important to take a lot of time with the parents, going over where the weekly play sessions will be conducted. The RE therapist inquires if there will be enough room, if water can be used, if the setting is private enough, what additional limits might need to be set, and so forth. It is important to inquire about the furniture, if it can be moved, if there is any concern about damage. Next the RE therapist talks with the parents about when the home play sessions will be held. The therapist helps the parents negotiate a practical time for both parent and child to reduce the chances that play sessions will be missed. It's important to guide parents in choosing a time that won't disrupt the child's routine or is not competing with some other issue (e.g., when the child normally plays with other children).

Once the place and time are agreed upon between parents and children home play sessions can begin. Parents are instructed to organize the room for the play session and set up the toys before getting the child. Then the parents get the child, saying, "It's time for our play session." The child is allowed one bathroom break during the play session, but it counts as part of the play session time. At the end of the home play session, the parent takes the child out of the play area, returning later to clear the toys and return the room to its initial status.

Once home play sessions have begun, responsibility shifts from the therapist to the parents. Parents are encouraged to maintain these scheduled weekly play sessions for at least six months, preferably until the child begins to lose interest. Periodically, the time for the play session may need to be changed to accommodate summer schedules and/or activities of various family members. (See Table 4.4 for additional instructions to parents for conducting home play sessions.)

Generalization and Maintenance

As discussed earlier in this chapter, generalization and maintenance begin during the first session. This process is established by suggesting home assignments between sessions. In the very first session, parents are given the handout *Filial Therapy Parents Manual*. They are asked to

Table 4.4   Things to Consider in Structuring Home Play Sessions

---

Find a suitable area in your home.

- Pick a room that best accommodates the play session, in which furniture that has to be removed can be removed easily, and which contains the fewest limits. Remove anything that stands in the way of setting a clear limit (e.g., important papers, small objects you don't want touched).
- Sit in the room before setting up play sessions and figure out all necessary limits, such as what can be removed and what would be dangerous. Decide how to state the limit.
- Consider the size of the area. It needs to be large enough for your child to be free to hit the bop bag without worrying that you'll get hit. An area that is too large, however, may not provide the intimacy that is important for this type of play session.

Pick the times for play sessions.

- Play sessions are best conducted on the same day of the week and at the same time.

Ask yourself: When will I be most physically and psychologically available? When is the best time for the child?

Keep in mind.

- Don't answer the telephone or go to the door during a play session.
- If both parents are available, conduct the play sessions consecutively on the same day so the parent not conducting the play session can watch the other children, answer the phone, and so on. It's important that these play sessions not be interrupted.
- If the other parent is not available or you are a single parent, decide how the other children will be managed. Do you need to add to or eliminate any rules from the basic rules?
- If the play session must be canceled, establish an alternative time for a session the same week.
- Occasionally a play session must be canceled and can't be rescheduled during the same week due to unavoidable circumstances. Don't try to make it up. Continue with the scheduled play sessions.
- However, if a child is upset about missing the play session arrange a "special make-up time."
- Use the toy kit only during play sessions.
- Toys can be replaced and new toys purchased to complement the kit.

---

read it thoroughly and discuss it with the therapist at the next session. Home assignments for subsequent sessions may include reading a chapter of *Parenting: A Skills Training Manual* (L. Guerney, 1995) and discussing it with each other at a specific time. At the third session, they are asked to set up a toy kit and begin to prepare for home sessions. Regularly, throughout the course of office meetings, parents are encouraged to apply the play session procedures to their everyday parenting efforts.

Special Times

When children begin to lose interest in the formal, structured play session, parents can suggest that "special times" replace them. Special times, like the regular play sessions, are scheduled upon agreement by parent and child. A designated amount of time also is agreed on. However, special times can take place anywhere at home, in the community, or at a place of the child's choosing. During special times, parents try to apply the principles and skills that they have learned. Special times can also be useful with an older child for whom play sessions may not be appropriate.

SUPERVISING HOME PLAY SESSIONS

When parents are conducting home play sessions, the role of the therapist becomes more consultative. At each subsequent meeting, parents and therapists review the home play sessions. This reinforces the continuity of the home play sessions at each of the office sessions. Even when meetings with the therapist focus on other concerns—for example, parenting skills, marital issues, other family issues—home play sessions need to be reviewed to maintain continuity. Guidelines for home session reports (Table 4.5) help parents structure these discussions with the therapist.

Table 4.5   Guidelines for Home Play Session Notes

1. Describe in general terms the process of the play session.
   - How did you feel?
   - How did the child feel?
   - How did each session begin and end?
   - What was happening before the play session began?
   - What happened afterward?
   - What changes have you noticed in your child? in you?
2. State at least one interaction with your child that you liked. Try to be specific (e.g., "She tried hard to draw the picture she wanted. I acknowledged, 'You're frustrated,' and she tried again. Finally, she got it and I acknowledged, 'You're proud of that.' Then she gave me a hug and I said, 'It makes you feel good.'").
3. State at least one interaction that you found difficult or weren't sure how to respond to. Again, try to be specific (e.g., "He kicked the rubber ball and I was afraid it would hit me so I set a rule that it couldn't be kicked. I wasn't sure about this"; or, "She kept putting her dolls in the water, and I wasn't sure how to respond.").
4. Identify any other questions or concerns.
5. Keep a play session notebook so you can review the play sessions over time. Don't take notes during play sessions.

DIFFERENT FORMATS FOR FILIAL THERAPY

Filial therapy can be used in many formats:

- Single-family group.
- Multiple-family group.
- Single-parent group.
- Extended family group (e.g., parents and grandparents and/or others providing child care).
- In-home therapy.
- Integration with other interventions.
- Intensive and extended therapy.
- Preventive therapy.

In all these variations of the filial approach, the basic elements remain: Parents are the agents of change, and the child-centered play session is the method of change.

Single-Family Group

When applying filial therapy to one family, all or as many family members as possible need to be included. If a parent has a busy schedule, the therapist makes every effort to accommodate that parent's schedule so that both parents can attend each session. If one parent can't do this, the therapist asks that this parent at least attend with some regularity (biweekly, monthly). Because it is important that both parents learn to conduct home play sessions, it may be necessary to schedule office sessions only when this parent is available. This may lengthen treatment and make the learning process less efficient. Nevertheless, it is important to involve both parents in this process as much as possible.

A parent who cannot attend all sessions should be encouraged to come to those sessions during which the therapist models the play session and when home play sessions are being planned. At other times, this parent should consult with his or her partner if any questions or difficulties arise in conducting home play sessions. Above all, the therapist tries to convey the importance of the home play sessions to achieve the objectives of both parents.

Involving all the children in the family in these home play sessions is important. With an older child, "special times" can be substituted for the structured play sessions. Involving all the children in this process is an act of prevention, since different children experience difficulties at different times in the family's development. Though the target child is often the primary concern, other children may be having difficulties of equal or greater importance. Often during filial therapy, a therapist or parent raises concerns about another child. Thus, involving all the children takes the pressure off the "target child" by generalizing concern for all the children. Also, singling out the target child for special attention (i.e., therapy) often reinforces the child's negative behaviors. Involving all the children tends to preclude this possibility. In addition, playing with all the children helps parents become more skillful, as they often learn more readily from a child with whom they feel more comfortable. Often the siblings of the target child feel left out and/or resentful because so much attention is being given to the "problem" child. Having everyone participate in these special play sessions or special times fosters greater family cohesiveness and cooperation.

Multiple-Family Group

Filial group therapy is an efficient therapeutic method, for several families can benefit from the expertise of one therapist. Parents in a group can support each other. In addition, they become more realistic about their own concerns as they relate to the concerns of other parents. Finally, once home play sessions have begun, the group can continue meeting at each other's homes without the therapist, drawing upon their trust and cohesiveness to address other concerns.

Balancing dynamic and didactic issues is particularly important in a multiple-family group (Andronico, 1983; Andronico, Fidler, Guerney, & Guerney, 1967). Exploring dynamic issues can help group cohesiveness, but focusing too much on these issues diverts attention from the children's issues and the children's relationship with parents. Turning to didactic issues helps refocus the group and maintain continuity. To do this, therapists need to (a) acknowledge the feelings that underlie these dynamic issues; (b) identify how the play session will help address them; and (c) focus on the specifics of the play session. An example follows.

> A parent complains that she and her partner can't agree on most parenting issues. The other parent jumps in on the defensive. The therapist acknowledges how *frustrating* that is, and tells them that learning to conduct the play sessions will help them achieve more of a consensus on these issues. Then the therapist begins to talk about the importance of acceptance in the play session.

Multiple-family groups proceed similarly to single-family groups. However, each family needs attention. To facilitate this, schedule families to bring their children to play sessions at specified times. When an individual family's issues tend to take over the group, schedule a single session with that family alone, to address these issues in a more in-depth manner without interfering with the group progress. Consider having cotherapists in multiple-family filial groups.

Andronico (1983) emphasizes that it is highly desirable to have both parents take part in filial therapy. But when both parents are not willing or available, he suggests that the willing or able parent be included in a mixed group of couples and single parents who are separated, divorced, or widowed. He believes that a mixed group offers many advantages. Among them, there is carryover of learning from one family to another:

> The couples can observe the difficulties that single parents have and learn to appreciate even the limited help they get from their spouses. The group members can learn from the mistakes of other parents in the group, and learn more positive ways from couples who get along well together, especially when the group progresses into the group therapy phases of filial therapy. (p. 6)

If a parent is not going to participate in the group, it is useful to encourage that parent to participate in the training phase when the therapist models the play therapy approach. When this is not possible, it is helpful to schedule a single session with one family or a group of all the parents who are not participating. This acknowledges that parent's permission for the home play sessions and helps to reduce negative attitudes toward this intervention. In the case of separated or divorced parents, it is useful to encourage both parents to attend a group either together or separately.

It is important that therapy groups, as in other forms of filial therapy, are time designated. This helps to support the task orientation consistent with the educational model. At the end of the time-designated period, a new agreement can be formulated. Progress can be assessed at this time and new objectives can be included or substituted. Sometimes the group continues to meet without the therapist, or meets with the therapist but on a less frequent basis. This is part of the shift to client responsibility for the intervention.

Ginsberg, Stutman, and Hummel (1978) reported on group filial therapy that evolved from a play therapy group into a training program for parents. The group was conducted in a school in a low socioeconomic, multiethnic community. Parents who came to observe were encouraged to participate. Therapists modeled the skills and parents were encouraged to follow the therapists' lead. Eventually, this group began to meet in each other's homes, frequently without the therapists.

Single-Parent Group

Single-parent families, by virtue of the fact that they don't have a coparent, are more likely to depend on the therapist. Helping single parents improve their resource network is an important part of the intervention; a single-parent filial therapy group can fulfill this function. It also helps single parents become more realistic as they encounter other parents in the same situation. Methods for conducting single-parent filial therapy groups are similar to those for couples groups (see the previous section). A single-parent filial therapy group may become a support group for the parents after they have begun home play sessions.

Extended Family Group

In many families, particularly single-parent families, other family members, friends, and other caregivers become very involved with the children and their parents. It is useful to include all these people in filial therapy. This involvement can range from a single informative session to participating fully in the therapy.

Single parents living with their parents often have a great deal of trouble being independent and resisting the pull to be treated as a child alongside their own child. Involving a grandparent who provides a major caregiving function can be useful in helping parent and grandparent differentiate their roles while helping them find more mutuality and consistency in providing care for the children. Having the entire living system participate, at least in a single session, may help children receive more consistent parenting from all the adults with whom they are living.

In-Home Format

In 1990, social workers in a county children and youth social service agency in Bucks County, Pennsylvania, were trained in filial therapy. The social workers in this agency typically would see families in their home as part of their responsibility. An in-home filial therapy program was established. As part of their regular visits, the social workers introduced home play sessions to these families. Special toy kits were assembled to be used for home play sessions, and parents were given kits free upon agreeing to continue play sessions at home. Outcomes (from anecdotal reports) were very positive (Ginsberg, 1990). Some important considerations for the therapist include: structuring the home environment for play sessions; managing the other children while an individual play session is being conducted; generalizing principles and skills to general parenting methods; and arranging time for play sessions. In some cases the therapist may continue to visit the home (though less and less frequently) during the course of home play sessions.

Integration with Other Interventions

Relationship Enhancement therapies, by virtue of their educational basis, can be quite compatible with other interventions, and children will benefit from ecologically integrated services. All aspects of the child's environment (home, school, and community) need to be considered. Many children, especially those with handicaps or physical impairments, benefit from medical services. In-school and community services are important components of any intervention program. Associated family variables (e.g., marital difficulties, an adolescent in treatment) can be integrated with filial therapy. The therapeutic work of a child or other family member being seen by other therapists or self-help groups can also be integrated with this approach. In fact, integration with other interventions enhances outcomes.

Intensive and Extensive Formats

Filial therapy is flexible and can be modified to meet the needs of the family. Time constraints are common variables that have to be considered. The family may live far away from the therapist, which may limit how often they are able to come to therapy. It may be hard for one parent to attend consistently. Everyday constraints of living add to the difficulty some families have maintaining regular contact with a therapist. The intensive format helps to address these issues. Families are seen for an intensive period of time ranging from three hours to two days. The purpose of the session is to help parents learn the play therapy skills well enough to conduct home play sessions. Subsequent sessions, which may take place after a period of months, are used to provide supervision and support for the home play sessions. Other concerns and issues can be attended to at these times as well.

Some families continue to need therapist involvement throughout the course of therapy in order to maintain sufficient family stability. This extensive format should be adapted to the particular needs of the family. The therapist encourages less frequent meetings, but weekly meetings may extend over a considerable period of time (more than six months). This often becomes a comprehensive treatment plan integrating marital, sibling, family, family-of-origin, community, and school issues. Obviously, in today's healthcare marketplace, short-term treatment is emphasized. If asked to justify an extensive format, therapists can emphasize that many family members are being treated concurrently. It is also likely that the cost of treatment is reduced when all relevant members are seen together rather than individually.

Prevention

The filial program is an effective preventive intervention that improves child competence in the parent-child relationship, parenting skills, and overall family functioning. Preventive filial programs differ little from therapeutic programs except that they emphasize enhancement rather than problems. Filial programs can be advertised to the larger community and offered as an educative program. Coufal and Brock (1983) have developed a 10-week parent education program based on this model. VanFleet (1994) has discussed some of the hallmarks of prevention programs, which include having fun together and having parents improve their understanding of child development and family functioning.

TREATING DEVELOPMENTAL DYSFUNCTION AND IMPROVING ADAPTATION

Kazdin and Kagan (1994) have written about enlarging our perspective on childhood dysfunction to include attention to clusters of influences and outcomes and their dynamic relations. They argue that we all need to expand our assumptions regarding these factors that contribute to psychopathology. The development of psychopathology, they claim, is

> inherently a study of transitions and change. It remains important
> to understand isolated variables, simple effects, and isomorphic

relations to the extent demonstrable. At the same time, effort
needed as well to understand the complexity. Rather than defi
complexity out of our models, or research, we need to embrac
and to adjust our models suitably to handle the relations. It is in-
portant to understand the complexity of those phenomena that define the appearance and maintenance of dysfunction. (p. 49)

By involving the primary and significant people in the life of the
child, and by engaging them with each other in a structured, systematic,
and time-designated fashion, filial therapy helps us better understand this
complexity and intervene more effectively.

CHAPTER 5

The Adolescent in Relationship Enhancement Therapy

Including adolescents and young adults—with their increasing competencies and independence—in Relationship Enhancement therapy adds a new, or different, dimension to RE. Working with more than two family members in the same room at the same time challenges the balance of power. This makes therapist leadership more difficult, as the many triangulations that are normative (and/or dysfunctional) can interrupt any two-person interaction. As all the family members try to meet their needs in relation to each other, they create a complex interactional system that operates beyond the therapist's and their own awareness or understanding.

Families function in consistent and habitual ways. Spontaneous interruptions of the therapeutic process, which often occur when these recursive habits are challenged or blocked, are inevitable. Therapists need to master new skills so that they can work directly with the complexity of this larger relationship system. They must also strive to grasp the complexity of an interactional system that often operates outside of the awareness of its participants. Therefore, the RE therapist turns to RE's four pillars—empathy, language and relationship, emotional expression, and acceptance (nonjudgment and equivalence)—discussed in Chapter 1. Rather than trying to directly restructure the family's interactional system, the RE therapist emphasizes skill learning and practice.

The RE therapist can use perspectives and methods of working with families that have been developed by other approaches to family therapy. For example, it is helpful to recognize that triangulation is a natural interactional response, particularly in close relationship systems that elicit the recursive processes so characteristic of these relationships. By attending to elements of these cycles, the RE therapist can focus the family on skill learning and on the values inherent in the four pillars of RE. In addition, the importance of respecting the boundaries that mark the distinctions between members and between subsystems corresponds to RE's emphasis on acceptance and equivalence. This respect for boundaries elicits stable leadership in the family while allowing each member to respect each other's equivalence and autonomy. From this a secure and cohesive family unit emerges that fosters intimacy and trust.

Adolescence is a stage in itself, not just a transitional period between childhood and adulthood (Kazdin, 1993). According to Garcia-Preto and Travis (1985), "Adolescence involves such significant shifts in the experience, identity and structure of the family that the family itself is transformed" (p. 21). In many families, children become adolescents at the same time their parents reach midlife with its own dramatic changes.

According to Feldman and Elliott (1990), the adolescent period begins at age 10 and extends through the mid-20s. Early adolescence ranges from ages 10 to 14, the middle period from ages 15 to 17, and late adolescence–early adulthood extends from age 18 through the mid-20s (Goldberg, 1993). This is a long period of evolution for all family members. The launching of children is not as clear-cut as it may have been earlier in this century and through the post–World War II period. Puberty begins at younger ages and young adults frequently remain at their parents' home or return to it well through their twenties. In addition, the high incidence of teenage pregnancy can make adolescents and young adults more dependent on their parents.

According to B. Carter and McGoldrick (1988), the shifts and changes that occur during adolescence mark a new definition of children and of the parents' roles. Qualitatively different boundaries from those of families with younger children must be established during adolescence. B. Carter and McGoldrick believe that this transition is made more difficult in our times by the lack of built-in rituals to facilitate it. They suggest that the important second-order changes (changes in the system itself) include: "a. shifting of parent/child relationships [to] permit the adolescent [to] move in and out of [the] system; b. refocusing on mid-life marital and career issues; c. beginning to shift toward joint caring for the older generation" (p. 15).

It is important for these families to develop permeable boundaries that will help adolescents separate without cutting off their families of origin. Indeed, independence, autonomy, and differentiation are the objectives during these stages of development. Adolescents are affected strongly by their increasing intellectual skills, new self-awareness, and broader awareness of the world. The family must be strong and flexible so that a balance of power is created, which allows family members to experiment while at the same time feel protected. According to Garcia-Preto and Travis (1985), "Parents can respond to the adolescent's dependency needs by setting clear limits and expectations, and at the same time respect[ing] the adolescent's struggle for independence by being flexible and willing to change rules in the family" (p. 27). Garcia-Preto and Travis believe that some generational conflict is necessary for developmental growth to take place, and that the family's ability to be flexible is essential to provide a safe environment in which to resolve this struggle.

Cooper, Grotevant, and Condon (1983) suggest several types of communication patterns that lead to individuality and connectedness for adolescents and their families. When family members are free to express their views, positive or negative, individuality is enhanced. When the family is open, responsive to, and respectful of the views of others, connectedness is fostered. In these families, the individuation of the adolescent occurs within a context of connectedness. Adolescents from these families have a point of view, are open to accepting the views of others, and can make distinctions between their own views and those of others.

Adolescence is a rich, full, dynamic, and creative developmental period. It is a stage during which differentiation and independence are accentuated. Profound changes occur not only in the adolescent, but in the parents as well. The hierarchy in the family is continually challenged during this time. As a result, greater collaboration between adolescent and adult is required to work on these difficulties.

"Autonomous-relatedness," a term coined by John Bowlby (cited in Murphy, Silber, Coelko, Hamburg, & Greenberg, 1963), is considered an optimal outcome for the adolescent-parent relationship (Allen, Hauser, Bell, & O'Connor, 1994). According to Allen et al. (1994), adolescents' self-reports of autonomy and relatedness vis-à-vis parents have been linked to a range of positive outcomes, including better adjustment to separation, increased assertiveness and dating competence, more resistance to peer pressure, enhanced self-esteem, and less loneliness after leaving home to attend college. They defined those behaviors exhibiting autonomy as "differentiating a person from others, reflecting independence of thought and self-determination in social interaction," while those behaviors exhibiting relatedness were defined as "reflecting interest, involvement and validation of another person's thoughts and feelings"

(p. 181). After studying the links between processes of establishing autonomy and relatedness in adolescent-family interactions and adolescent psychosocial functioning, they suggest that there is a relationship between expression of autonomous-relatedness and concurrent ego development as well as self-esteem. They found that fathers' displays of autonomy and relatedness were predictive of adolescents' development of self-esteem and ego development over time. They also suggest that an overall positive, engaging interaction characterized by autonomous-relatedness may stimulate the adolescent to develop more complex views of self and others, as well as more firmly grounded positive views of self in relation to others. RE, with its emphasis on equivalence, acceptance, and acknowledgment, facilitates this kind of interaction between adolescents and their parents.

THE PARENT-ADOLESCENT DEVELOPMENT PROGRAM (PARD)

The outcomes of studies of the Parent-Adolescent Relationship Development (PARD) program, an RE approach to therapy with adolescents and parents developed by Ginsberg (1977), point to improvement in self-concept of both adolescent and parent. In addition, the quality of the relationship improved, particularly in areas of trust, empathy, genuineness, intimacy, openness, and relationship satisfaction (Ginsberg, 1977; Grando & Ginsberg, 1976; B. G. Guerney, Coufal, & Vogelsong, 1981, B. G. Guerney, Vogelsong & Coufal, 1982).

Engaging adolescents and their parents in a structured communication process undermines the defensive posture that both parties so easily generate in conversation with each other. Much of the time this defensive posture arises from a sense of not being acknowledged. Adolescents are desperate to be acknowledged as grown up and to have their point of view respected. Because they are more egocentric during this period, they are less likely to consider or acknowledge the perspective of others. This is often the source of conflict with their parents, who are threatened by the seeming change of power in the relationship. Parents' need for acknowledgment of their continued importance to their children can be threatened by this very self-centeredness on the part of their offspring.

One of the most important components of the RE approach is its vigorous emphasis on acknowledging the other person before conveying one's own perspective. This is accomplished primarily by emphasizing receptive listening, one of the core skills of RE. Acknowledgment also occurs in the engagement skill when the new speaker conveys how it feels to know the other person's thoughts and feelings. Furthermore, RE's emphasis on understanding the positive underlying message enhances the meaning of conversation between parents and their adolescent children.

It is important to help parents recognize that the egotism of adolescence is a normative developmental phase. This helps parents allow some latitude in accepting the self-centered expressions of their adolescent children. In other words, parents need to remain in a listening position for long periods of time. This enables adolescents to feel freer to express themselves with a greater confidence that their parents will not only listen to them but acknowledge both their importance and the importance of what they are expressing.

At the same time, RE therapy with adolescents stresses the importance of equivalent conversation between parents and teenagers. Many parents subject their adolescents to long lectures rather than carefully considering their teens' explanation. Mastering the RE listening skill goes a long way to rebalance parent-adolescent expression.

This is not to say that the parent must acquiesce to the adolescent's expectation. In fact, if we accept the concept of autonomous-relatedness, it is essential for parents to genuinely challenge the adolescent's perspective while remaining supportive of him or her. RE's emphasis on allowing greater opportunity for adolescent expression helps to create a supportive relationship context. However, it is important for parents to convey their own honest response and perspective. Establishing this supportive context allows parents and teens to genuinely encounter each other; this, in turn, sets the stage for the setting and negotiating of limits that fosters the changes seen in RE. When parents learn to stand their ground without becoming defensive, they create a supportive context for their teenage children. By being flexible and openly receptive to their child's perspectives, parents can achieve more collaborative outcomes. At the same time, adolescents who experience this receptivity from their parents are more inclined to acknowledge their parents' perspectives when asked to be listeners to them in an RE conversation. Engaging adolescents and their parents in this way helps to open up the relationship, build more trust, and foster a more collaborative relationship.

THREE RE APPROACHES WITH ADOLESCENTS AND THEIR FAMILIES

Three formats are available in RE therapy to accommodate adolescents and their families: multiple-family groups, single-family groups, and process-oriented groups. The original RE program for adolescents and their families was called the Parent-Adolescent Relationship Development (PARD) program. Initially it was designed for fathers and their adolescent sons (B. G. Ginsberg, 1977; Grando & Ginsberg, 1976). Later it focused on mothers and daughters (B. G. Guerney et al., 1981; B. G. Guerney et al., 1982). PARD is a structured, multiple-family group therapy. It is time designated (usually 10 two-hour sessions) and includes three to four adolescent-parent dyads. Same-sex dyads were included in the original research program, but the format can accommodate cross-sex dyads and/or any adolescent-parent dyad. Developing such multiple-family therapy groups requires a great deal of planning, marketing, and organizing.

In clinical practice, referrals tend to be crisis-oriented and problem-focused and demand a quick response that usually includes all or most family members. The RE therapist should welcome the opportunity to explore the presenting problem with and learn about each family member and the family process in order to ascertain each family's readiness for therapy. Some families quickly recognize the value of engaging in a structured communication approach in which skill learning is emphasized. They are responsive to a task-oriented and time-designated (negotiated) methodology.

Other families—often those under greater stress—respond better to a process-oriented family therapy approach. In this situation, a problem focus works well. Therapy proceeds much like typical family therapy in which RE is incorporated. This approach stays within the principles of RE, but allows the therapist greater flexibility responding to the crisis and/or heightened anxiety in these families. In some cases, after a few initial sessions (considered extended intake), the family is ready for a more structured and systematic approach. Even if the therapy does not evolve into a more structured RE therapy, it continues to incorporate the skill-learning, task-oriented, and time-designated emphasis typical of RE therapies.

Structured Multiple-Family Group RE Therapy

The PARD program was drawn from earlier RE work with couples in group therapy. It is a structured program of 10 two-hour sessions. The format of these sessions is modeled after the 10-session model explained in Chapter 3. Table 5.1 presents a brief overview of the ten sessions.

RE's structured skill-training and practice approach may elicit some defensiveness and resistance from adolescents, for it may remind them of school. Many adolescents are naturally reticent and reluctant to express

Table 5.1   10-Session Outline of the PARD Program

Session 1. *Intake and Introduction: Developing Trust and Rapport*

• Group members and therapist(s) introduce themselves.
• Members share their reasons for joining the group.
• Therapists: describe the PARD program and the skills; model speaking and listening skills with a volunteer group member; assign a home activity (e.g., "Bring in a list of six or more important issues to talk about next session. Try to include two positive issues.").

Session 2. *Beginning Skill Practice*

• The group discusses the previous session, the home activity, and the development of group rapport.
• Therapists supervise conversation between a member who agrees to talk about something positive and one who agrees to listen.
• Each participant practices speaking and listening roles with unrelated partners under therapist supervision.
• Home activity: "Decide on a time (one hour) to spend with each other each week" (eventually this will be used for home practice).

Session 3. *Continued Skill Practice with Related Partners*

• Members review previous session and home activity.
• Role-play begins between volunteer parent-adolescent dyad.
• Therapists introduce and model conversive skill.
• Participants practice three core skills: expressive, receptive, and conversive. They begin with positive issues.
• Each adolescent-parent pair practices role-playing.
• Therapists supervise skill practice.
• Home activity: "Don't talk about anything serious during the weekly time you've set aside to spend together and/or play a game."

Session 4. *Continued Skill Practice with Related Partners*

• Same as Session 3.

Session 5. *Continued Skill Practice with Related Partners*

• Same as Session 3.

Session 6. *Generalization and Maintenance: Begin Home Practice*

• Members review previous session and home activity.
• Therapists distribute home practice handout (see Table 2.6); prepare adolescent-parent dyads for home practice; discuss audiotaping of home practice and use in therapy sessions.
• Members continue role-play practice.
• Home activity: "Practice three core skills during agreed upon time and audiotape them."

Table 5.1   *(Continued)*

Sessions 7–9. *Generalization and Maintenance Supervision of Home Practice*

• Members review previous session and home activity; listen to audiotapes and supervision of home practice.
• Home activity: "Continue home practice and audiotaping."

Session 10. *Concluding Session*

• Members plan for continued home practice; review home practice; discuss PARD program evaluation and suggestions; plan for a follow-up session in three months.

---

themselves. Over-involved, intrusive parents may inadvertently trigger an adolescent's defensiveness, resistance, and even rebellion. Typically, adolescents don't request therapy. Many of those who do are usually encouraged by a parent. Most often, adolescents come to therapy to please, placate, and/or satisfy the parent's concern. Many feel forced to participate.

Pitta (1995), referring to adolescent-centered family treatment (Guerin & Gordon, 1983), sees the adolescent as the scapegoat and absorber of the family's anxiety. She believes implicit statements such as "Fix my adolescent; don't trouble my marriage; don't expose other children to therapy; let's keep therapy a secret; and it is something to be ashamed of" (Pitta, 1995, p. 100) often underlie therapy when an adolescent is the identified patient. Quite frequently, adolescents referred for therapy are struggling with their own emerging developmental need for independence and autonomy while trying to maintain allegiance to the family system. This task is made harder when the parent or family system is rigid and not responsive to this developmental need. Such a scenario leaves the adolescent few options other than withdrawal, acting out, or a change in school performance, which is often most effective. Paradoxically, these actions tie the adolescent even closer to the family, which then delays his or her emerging independence. The situation is exacerbated when the adolescent struggling to be independent acts out to such an extent that the larger society becomes involved, in the form of juvenile authorities, youth services, school officials, or other community agencies.

Working with adolescents and their families requires great patience. It is important for RE therapists to maintain a commitment to the principles and methods of this systematic and structured skill-learning approach. Their belief in the value of learning communication and relationship skills and its effectiveness in fostering change is essential.

Doubling

When the PARD program was being developed with sons and fathers, many therapists were concerned about two issues: adolescents' natural reticence, and the degree to which fathers and sons have difficulty expressing their feelings. A technique called doubling, drawn from psychodrama (I. A. Greenberg, 1974; Moreno, 1959), was employed to ease the pressure on any one participant or adolescent-parent dyad to be expressive and acknowledge feelings. Using doubling, a second pair of participants restates the expressions of the primary pair. For example, the Smith teenager expresses himself to his father; the Jones teenager reiterates the expression of the Smith teenager; Mr. Smith responds; and Mr. Jones restates the expression of Mr. Smith. Each member of the pair doubling the primary pair maintains the same mode (speaker or listener) as the participant he is doubling. An example of a dialogue taken from an actual session illustrates this doubling technique.

MR. SMITH: I have a feeling that as a father I could be a lot more help to Jerry if he felt he could talk about his problems to me. And seek more counseling and discussion *(pause)* in many areas. In other words, I see him down in the dumps one day and he's up the next day and I don't know why and . . . and . . . and this bothers me. In other words, if he'd talk more about problems, even boy, even girl-boy relationships, I think there are some things I could help you with, if you'd feel free to express them.

LEADER M: I like what you're telling me. Tell Jerry that you're concerned about this. *(Redirecting.)*

MR. SMITH: I would feel a lot better if you would come to me and talk about it.

LEADER M *(modeling):*   It bothers me, Jerry, that you won't come to me when it's obvious to me that you have a problem and as your father maybe I can help you with it.

JERRY: In other words, maybe we do talk about a lot of things, but maybe some issues we're just not . . . I don't tell you about things as much and, uh, it kind of bothers you not to know why some days I'm really happy and really going and other days I'm really down. You'd really like to know about these feelings when I have them.

LEADER M: Good! *(Reinforcement.)*

JERRY: And if you did know I was down you'd like to help me with it.

(The therapist encourages Mike, another boy in the group, to double.)

MIKE *(doubling):*   Like maybe when I have a problem that's really disturbing me, like maybe I should come see you instead of keeping it all inside.
(Short pause.)

MR. SMITH: Yeah, I . . . it really bothers me that, uh, 'cause I know that you, uh, do have some problems and it just leaves me to intuit what they are and I'd feel a lot better if you'd come right out and tell me what they are.

MR. JONES *(doubling):* I'm the kind of guy that if I know there's a problem and I can't understand what the problem is then it's upsetting to me.

JERRY: It bothers you that the times when I take . . . when I take the responsibility and figure out these problems for myself, you think some of these . . . maybe I do a little bit too much for myself and you'd like to help once in a while; maybe make things a little easier.

MIKE: Yes. *(Some laughter.)*

LEADER M: Do you want to add to this? *(Someone says "No.")* All right then, why don't we switch?

Earlier the therapist had encouraged a switch, but Jerry remained in the listener role and his father continued talking; this time Jerry accepts the switch. It has taken Mr. Smith a long time to feel acknowledged. The dialogue continues in this way for a lengthy period of time.

JERRY: I think your point was very well taken. *(Some laughter)* I can really understand that, but I think maybe to make it a little clearer to you . . . I suppose the reason I do make a lot of the decisions myself, on things that I do is that I . . . I'm really doing something myself. This is really me, when I make a decision I did it without any help so really I feel proud. Maybe whenever I do something and stand behind it and it comes out okay. I can see your concern, that maybe someday I might get let down by my own decisions for being wrong.

MIKE *(doubling):* Like, I make my own decisions because, like maybe, maybe some kind of problem would concern you, but like there's some things I have to make, I just have to make my own decision, but then like if there's anytime like I make the wrong decision you'll like be there to help. *(A long quiet pause.)*

MR. SMITH: In other words, you have an inner feeling that you'd like to accomplish something on your own. In other words, you're trying to find your own identity. You feel that this is important and one of the ways you can do this is take things on yourself, and make decisions.

LEADER M: Good. *(To Mr. Jones)* Did you want to add something?

MR. JONES *(doubling):* It gives you a, uh, uh, that your, uh, feeling of maturity to make these decisions without my help.

LEADER M: Good. *(To Jerry)* Shall we switch back to your dad or do you have something more to say about that? Do you want to keep the speaker's role?

JERRY: We can switch.

MR. SMITH: Yeah, well what I wanted to say . . . I feel and understand the fact that it's important to you and makes you feel good that you can make decisions and, uh, and I also have a strong feeling that whenever I have influence into your decisions I won't be making decisions for you, that makes me feel good.

JERRY: That makes you feel good. So you're saying that maybe you wouldn't actually be making decisions for me, but you'd like to hear what my decisions are before I . . . before I get into trouble with them or before they come out real well.

MR. SMITH: Yeah, switch. *(Feeling acknowledged and less anxious, he is able to switch on his own.)*

JERRY: I'm glad to know you'll respect my decisions and I'll try to let you in on them more often.

MR. SMITH: You feel good I'll respect your decisions and you'll try to clue me in more.

JERRY: Yes.

MR. SMITH: That makes me feel good.

LEADER M: Good.

This is a positive interaction on a very difficult subject common to most adolescent-parent relationships. Obviously, Mr. Smith and his son enjoyed a trusting and respectful relationship before they began therapy. Nevertheless, it is poignant to see father and son grapple with this sensitive issue and the profound change in their relationship. They are struggling to maintain the respect, trust, and importance of their relationship while coping with the insecurities arising from the dynamic changes that are occurring. At the end of this dialogue, they have achieved a measure of mutual understanding and reiterate their closeness. However, they will need to repeat this dialogue to keep their underlying positive feelings in full view while struggling with their ongoing differentiation.

Mr. Smith's and Jerry's depth of expression and openness with each other was facilitated by doubling. The doubling was also good practice for Mr. Jones and his son. When Mr. Jones doubled, for example, he tended to speak less as the conversation between the Smiths became more intimate. Later, when it was the Joneses' turn, their conversation was less defensive and more accepting.

Doubling can also be used when one of the adolescents isn't willing to role-play. In this case, another teenager is encouraged to volunteer to take that adolescent's place. The therapist asks the second teenager to check with the first to ascertain whether the role-playing is accurate. Often, after a short period, the first adolescent will engage with the parent on his or her own.

Another example of doubling is to have parents role-play the adolescent of other parents and adolescents role-play parents other than their own. This use of doubling often enhances empathy between adolescents and parents.

Doubling is only one of the methods that RE therapists use in the early, structured sessions to avoid defensiveness on the part of adolescents. Therapists also rely on positive reinforcement, avoid criticism, and elicit resistance. They do this by taking the time to acknowledge the stilted nature of the therapeutic process and by accepting clients' feelings of frustration and discomfort. Taken together, these efforts help clients feel more comfortable and trusting. Only then can therapists talk about the value of learning and using RE skills.

Structured Single-Family RE Therapy

This format is used with single-family groups and can include all family members. It is useful to meet with the entire family at first to ascertain their readiness for structured therapy. When families enter therapy, they are typically not prepared for all they will encounter. In fact, the more structured and systematic the therapy, the less prepared they may be. Some families, however, are relieved at the prospect of therapy with a clear structure, defined methods, and a more directive style of therapeutic leadership. Obviously, these families are more likely to be amenable to a structured RE approach earlier in the therapy.

Therapists working with adolescents and their families in RE therapy need to address a number of sensitive and complex issues that may not be as pertinent in dyadic and multiple-family forms of RE. Wakshul (1973) has identified five major issues that therapists should consider when working with adolescents and their families:

1. Size of the family group.
2. History of their relationship with each other.
3. Complexity of the family group.
4. Different motivations of each family member.
5. Power differential between different family members (particularly between parents and children).

Size of the Family Group

As RE therapy evolved from working with groups of dyads to family groups with three or more members, a question emerged: Who should be seen: the target child/adolescent and parents, or the entire family? A number of factors favored seeing the entire family together. First, it has long been accepted in family therapy circles that one person's problems and symptoms represent the same in other family members and in the family as a whole. Therefore, including all family members has the greatest potential for effecting improvement and change in family patterns and dynamics. Second, the skill-training approach or RE would be most effective if all family members were more skilled in interpersonal communication. Third, involving all the members of the family in skill training would generalize the problem and its solution to the entire family. This would bring more resources to bear and improve family flexibility. Finally, designating one person as responsible for the problem leads to a more rigid family system and less opportunity for change. RE therapists were also concerned that involving only the target adolescent might reward that person and maintain or exacerbate the existing difficulties. It could also create resentment on the part of other adolescents and children in the family.

There are, however, some reasons for including only the target adolescent, foremost of which is the adolescent's own request for privacy. Sometimes, adolescents will insist on meeting alone with therapists and parents, and although this is not preferable, it often encourages the adolescent to cooperate and open up. Another obvious reason for not including all family members is the developmental level and ages of the other children. Younger, less mature children might distract and undermine the process of the therapy. On the other hand, younger children—even preschoolers—can be motivated and are able (with the help of the therapist) to learn these skills. It is always helpful to elicit the collaboration of parents and other family members in making this decision.

History of the Family

Inquiring about family history is a useful technique. Most families respond positively to genuine interest in their history. History-taking helps develop rapport with and trust in the therapist, particularly if done during the early phases of beginning skill practice. Since all members have some interest in the family's development, this activity also helps to keep them engaged. Also, because each family member has a somewhat different view of the same event, airing these divergent views allows other members to gain perspective on the events. Reviewing family history also helps therapists in two ways: They understand better how the target person came to be a concern for the parents or family, and they can generalize the concerns and issues aired during history-taking to other family members and to the family itself.

Complexity of the Family Group

Having more than two related persons in RE therapy creates some management problems that do not arise during RE therapy with dyads. The most important fact of family life is that each family member has a vested interest in all other members and in the family itself. Thus, when any two members are communicating feelings and issues, they stimulate feelings and issues in other family members and elicit the natural coalitions and triangulations that all families develop. The RE therapist needs to find ways to set boundaries that limit the intrusion these triangulations can create. A very effective way to establish these limits is to develop additional rules for practicing family RE therapy, (see Table 5.2, Guidelines for Family RE Therapy) for example, to maintain that a family member cannot talk about another family member unless the latter is acting as a listener. This can help to counteract some of the rigid coalitions that are formed in families.

Another problem is the complex scheme of relationships that exist in families. For the therapist to give each relationship sufficient importance and attention is difficult, if not ultimately impossible. However, balancing all the relationships so none is ignored is an important therapist structuring skill. One way to accomplish this is to make sure that each person has an opportunity to have a conversation with each family member, and that all potential dyads have an opportunity to practice. It is also helpful to

Table 5.2   Guidelines for Family RE Therapy

- Agree to meet once a week at the same time.
- Make sure that everyone will be available on the day and time picked.
- Each week, a new person acts as designated facilitator, so that everyone has a chance to be the facilitator (see "Guidelines for Facilitative Skill").
- If the designated facilitator does not want the responsibility, a parent assumes the facilitator's role.
- Each week a different family member takes a turn at being the first speaker.
- The speaker chooses whom to talk to first: That person becomes the listener.
- If someone else wishes to participate, that person first must receive permission from both parties already talking.
- The person requesting to speak must first acknowledge (reflect) the other person's expression before beginning. This is a switch.
- The facilitator tries to give everyone a chance to talk. If someone does not get a chance to talk about his or her issue, that person is the first speaker the next week.
- It's important for all members to stay at the meeting for its duration.
- If someone wants to leave early, that person asks if anyone has anything to discuss with him or her.
- If someone has something more to discuss, then the person who wants to leave must first have an RE conversation. If that person insists on leaving without having the conversation, the person who wished to raise an issue with the departing person becomes first speaker next week. Everyone agrees that the person speaking may not talk about another person present unless that person is the listener.

begin each session by focusing on the person who had the least opportunity to practice in the earlier sessions. This tends to reduce the dominance of one or two members.

Another concern is how to organize home practice when there are so many dyadic relationships to contend with. One solution is to alternate dyads for weekly practice sessions. The therapist can also suggest that the family evolve from having individual dyad practice sessions to having weekly family meetings for all members. An intermediate step would have three members practice alternating roles of speaker, listener, and facilitator. Of course, additional structure and rules will probably be needed to establish a practice time for all members, which limits the opportunities for interruption and triangulation.

Different Motivations of Family Members

Motivational factors are intimately connected to the issue of the power differential in the family, but deserve special acknowledgment. Although adolescents occasionally request therapy and are open to being seen with their parents and other family members, it is far more typical for parents to initiate therapy and insist that their children attend. In some ways, adolescents are relieved by their parents' initiative: They see that their concerns are being taken seriously. At the same time, however, they distrust their parents' action, fearing that they will feel controlled or unacknowledged. This lack of trust and fear that they won't be treated with equivalence combined with their desire to feel acknowledged and understood creates tremendous ambivalence and elicits greater initial defensiveness upon entering therapy.

The issue of motivation, then, is an important consideration when involving adolescents in family therapy. Since children and adolescents aren't usually the initiators, they are often reluctant participants. Children and adolescents share the concern that they will be forced to be honest and open, leaving them even more vulnerable to parental power. The resulting anxiety and defensiveness further exacerbate the motivational differential that already exists between children and parents.

It's crucial that therapists understand and accept this differential in motivation; otherwise, their expectations will almost certainly turn the teenager away.

Power Differential

Related to the issue of differential motivation is the power differential between adolescents and their parents. Parent power is certainly a strong factor in bringing adolescents to therapy. Therapists who are forced to deal with this power differential are working at a considerable disadvantage: They have to maintain a delicate balance between respecting parental power (hierarchy) and creating a context of equivalence. For this to be successful, the therapist has to work at protecting the adolescent's vulnerability while helping him or her be more open and engaging him or her in a more direct and equivalent way. This task is made even harder when adolescents express themselves in an accusative and judgmental way, which in turn makes it more difficult for parents to remain receptive to what the adolescent is trying to say. This quickly leads to defensiveness and loss of control.

Liddle (1995) suggests yet another factor that often confounds family therapy with adolescents: Parents of troubled and troubling teenagers don't want to participate in therapy. He believes that these parents feel (a) helpless because they've tried everything and nothing has worked, (b) hopeless about change, (c) estranged (emotionally and physically) from their child, and (d) reluctant to view the adolescent's problems as theirs to solve. Usually, a combination of these factors contributes to the parent's reticence to begin therapy. Often, parents hope or fantasize that the therapist can fix the problem by seeing the adolescent alone, and use their power to insist that this transpire.

Both parents and adolescents have expectations when they begin therapy. Because the therapist is an adult, parents often assume that the therapist will side with the adults—and so does the adolescent. When the therapist tries to balance the interaction by acknowledging the relevance of the adolescent's perspective, parents often become defensive and feel threatened about losing power. This vulnerability is comparable to the vulnerability of the adolescent discussed earlier. The success of the therapy depends on how well the therapist can maintain a therapeutic alliance that feels safe and productive enough for both adolescent and parents to continue to be engaged in therapy.

Engaging Adolescents and Parents in RE Family Therapy

A paramount concern whenever adolescents and their families are involved in treatment is how to engage teenagers in the process for the duration of the therapy.

Liddle's multidimensional family therapy (1995) includes an excellent and useful summary of the philosophy and principles of engagement for therapy with adolescents and families. These 12 points are paraphrased to include RE:

1. The therapist doesn't assume that family members are motivated to continue therapy. The therapist must inform (motivate) clients about the value of therapy.

2. Even though RE emphasizes the learning of skills through practice, RE therapists must acknowledge that the presenting problem is the reason clients have entered therapy. The RE therapist must directly address the presenting issues by connecting change in the presenting problem to learning skills.

3. The therapist communicates to both parents and adolescents that he or she will work directly with the adolescent and those resources pertaining to the adolescent's life, such as community agencies, schools, and the peer group when appropriate.

4. The RE therapist needs to inform clients of the value of RE and its direct connection to the presenting problem.

5. Paying attention to the history of the family, the presenting problem, and the family's interaction with its larger relationship context (e.g., family of origin, work, school) can help the therapist more effectively engage family members.

6. The RE therapist needs to be sensitive to the everyday struggles that family members are experiencing, particularly those struggles pertaining to the implications of being in therapy. RE acknowledges that life is larger than therapy.

7. The context of people's lives, which includes their stresses and living conditions, needs to be respected. Some of these factors can be changed, but many cannot. Receptivity and acceptance (core RE skills) are essential attributes of the therapist.

8. According to most family therapy perspectives, the therapist needs to be skilled in addressing the multidimensional aspect of family therapy. Liddle (1995) emphasizes a realistic but upbeat attitude on the part of the therapist to engender hopefulness; RE emphasizes the underlying positive message, which helps to elicit and maintain optimism.

9. The RE therapist never assumes that the therapy process is secure once the family becomes engaged. Many factors can interrupt or challenge the initial trust. The RE therapist regularly directs attention to these mediating issues to keep them alive in the therapy when they surface. This helps to maintain continuity and motivation.

10. Many factors may arise and threaten not only the initial therapeutic agreement but also the progress of therapy. Rather than ignore these challenges, the RE therapist uses the time-designated nature of RE to address them when they arise. In other words, the initial therapeutic agreement calls for clients to practice RE skills for a specified number of sessions before evaluating the benefit of the therapy. With this contract in hand, there is less likelihood that challenges to the therapy will arise, and those that do are more easily managed. These issues are addressed in each session. Often an appropriate home assignment can help clients feel less need to challenge the therapy.

11. The RE therapist is aware that defensiveness and regression often accompany change. Remembering this can help therapists remain optimistic and work through difficulties with the family.

12. Many families requesting treatment are overwhelmed by forces not amenable to therapeutic intervention. RE therapists need to recognize the limits of their abilities and resources to adequately meet the family's need. Referring the family to others and/or integrating treatment with other interventions is essential to the success of RE therapy. As mentioned earlier, RE therapy works well when clients are concurrently engaged with other therapies and interventions.

These 12 factors are particularly relevant when an RE therapist is conducting a more traditional family therapy approach (process-oriented RE family therapy). However, they also apply whenever working with adolescents and their families. One way these factors can be used in the more structured RE approaches is through the concept of extended intake.

Extended Intake

It takes time to engage a family in therapy. Patience is critical when working with adolescents. With this in mind, B. G. Guerney (1977) developed the concept of "extended intake or early stage of therapy" (p. 171), which essentially encourages therapists to take more time to allow family participants to express themselves and for the therapist to obtain a better understanding of the family, its members, and their issues. B. G. Guerney identifies the three benefits of extending the early phase of therapy: Helping participants:

1. Fully air their feelings and be open to structured RE training.
2. Feel that they have been able to fully present their perspectives, including the depth and scope of their problems.
3. Be able to listen to each other without emotional breakdown or interruptions.

Extended intake is a crisis method that relieves the family of its initial stress; this allows them to feel more secure and be open to the thrust of the therapy itself. All families have the need to be sure that the therapist understands them and has insight into their presenting issues. It is also important for the therapist to have a grasp of the family's concerns, issues, and objectives so that the intervention strategy addresses these. If the therapist is receptive and skillfully acknowledges their feelings, there is a moment during the intake or early stage of the therapy when it becomes clear that clients are ready to hear the therapist's ideas for intervention. In RE, it is very important that clients understand the value of the skill training and of each skill. This understanding is the basis of the collaborative relationship between clients and therapists upon which successful RE therapies depend.

Once therapists inform clients about RE rationale and methodology, they engage several members in a model RE interaction to show clients how RE works. Often they play the part of a family member. After this, an agreement is reached to continue therapy over a specified time. Typically, the therapist suggests meeting weekly for four sessions before evaluating the progress of the therapy. This short-term, concrete contract is often very attractive to families. Four sessions allows the therapist to focus on skill training without paying a great deal of attention to the ongoing dynamics of the family. It also reduces the possibility of resistance, which can undermine the therapy process. It is helpful, however, to suggest that clients perform certain tasks between sessions. This helps bridge the sessions and gives clients and therapist specific, concrete topics to discuss at each session. In addition, it helps prepare clients for home practice. Another significant benefit to contracting for only four sessions is that adolescents are likely to cooperate with a short-term agreement. After four sessions, therapists can suggest that the adolescent attend sessions less frequently (e.g., every other week). When appropriate, adolescents can be referred to a concurrent adolescent group. Meeting with parents without the adolescent present helps strengthen the parenting skills of the parent dyad and single parents (particularly if they also meet in a group with other single parents). Another advantage of alternate-week attendance by the adolescent is that it allows sufficient time to audiotape a home practice between sessions. *Parenting: A Skills Training Approach* (L. Guerney, 1995) contains a supplement about adolescents that is useful for home practice activities for the parents-only sessions.

Doubling (by the Therapist) for the Adolescent in the Extended Intake

Doubling for the adolescent by the therapist can be very useful during the extended intake or early phase. It helps to bring to the surface issues that the adolescent might be reluctant to share and provides an opportunity for parents to become more receptive.

The following dialogue illustrates how an RE therapist engages an adolescent through doubling. It occurs at a point during intake when the family is ready to be introduced to the model through role-playing.

THERAPIST: I wonder, Joe, if there are some issues that concern you?

JOE: No.

THERAPIST: I know that it's hard as a teenager to talk about things with your parents.

JOE: *(Nods his head yes.)*

THERAPIST: I've heard a number of things that teenagers talk about here which seems to affect most people. *(Pause)*

JOE: *(Seems interested.)*

THERAPIST: One of the most frequent issues is that parents don't listen when you're trying to tell them something.

JOE: *(Nods his head yes.)*

THERAPIST: That's frustrating.

JOE: *(Acknowledges this nonverbally.)*

THERAPIST: I wonder, Joe, if you could talk to your folks about that. I'll help.

JOE: *(Quiet)*

THERAPIST: Okay, suppose I pretend to be you, is that okay?

JOE: *(Shrugs)*

THERAPIST: It's important to me that if I'm not right, that you let me know, okay?

JOE: *(Nods his head yes.)*

THERAPIST: Whom do you think I should talk about this with first?

JOE: *(Shrugs)*

THERAPIST: How about if I talk with Dad first? Okay with you, Dad?

   (Both the father and son acknowledge affirmatively.)

   Okay, Bill (father), you'll be the listener first. Remember, no questions or judgments and you can't state your point of view. Your job is to reflect back what I say and feel as Joe. Okay? I'll begin.

THERAPIST *(as Joe):* You know, when I try to tell you my side when we get into an argument, you don't listen to me. That makes me mad.

BILL: You get mad at me when I don't listen to you.

THERAPIST *(as Joe):* Yes. As soon as I try, you tell me what I should do. That really makes me mad.

BILL: It really makes you mad when I don't listen to you and instead tell you what you should do.

THERAPIST *(as Joe):* Yes. *(As therapist)* Switch. Is that okay Joe?

JOE: Okay.

THERAPIST *(to Bill):* Now you're the speaker and you can state your side, but first you have to say how it makes you feel to know that Joe is mad about that.

BILL: Well, it makes me feel bad that you're angry with me about that 'cause I recognize that there is some truth to that.

THERAPIST *(as Joe):* That makes you feel bad 'cause there is some truth to it.

BILL: Yes.

THERAPIST *(to Joe):* How about if you take over for me?

JOE: Okay. *(He's tentative.)*

THERAPIST: Say to your dad, "That makes you feel bad."

JOE: That makes you feel bad.

BILL: Yes, and I want to try not to do it.

JOE: You'll try not to do it.

BILL: Yes, but it would make me feel good if you could help me by letting me know when I'm doing that.

JOE: *(Quiet)*

THERAPIST: It would make your dad feel better if you could let him know when he's doing that. Could you tell him that, Joe?

JOE: You'd feel better if I told you when you do that.

THERAPIST: Bill, I think this would be a good time to switch.

BILL: Okay, switch.

THERAPIST: Joe, how does it make you feel that your dad would feel better if you'd do that?

JOE: Well *(long pause),* it kinda makes me feel good, but I'm afraid too that he'll get mad at me.

THERAPIST: Good. How about if you tell him.

JOE: I'm glad you'd like my help, but I'm afraid you'll yell at me if I try to do that.

BILL: You're glad, but you're afraid I'll get mad.

JOE: Yes.

THERAPIST: Okay to switch, Joe? *(The therapist switches quickly here to enhance engagement and short-circuit Joe's defensiveness.)*

JOE: *(Nods his head.)*

THERAPIST: Bill, how does that make you feel?

BILL: I feel bad. It's important, you know, that I'll try not to do that and really listen to you.

JOE: You'll listen to me, you want me to know that.

BILL: Yep, switch. *(Bill switches spontaneously to give Joe more of a chance to talk.)*

JOE: Well, I'll try to help.

BILL: You want me to know that.

THERAPIST *(to Joe and Bill):*   Good. That was a great conversation. *(To mother)* Jane, how about you pick someone to talk with in this way?

Though the preceding dialogue was extrapolated from a tape of a real conversation, it is rare for an adolescent to open up so quickly. Often, the therapist must double as the adolescent for a good deal longer before such openness takes place. Nevertheless, even adolescents find it difficult to remain reticent when the issues the therapist role-plays and models create so much emotion in them. Once they get drawn into the conversation, it's easier to engage them in direct practice.

At the end of this conversation, the therapist positively reinforces father and son and then turns to the mother to continue the skill practice. Because RE is task oriented, it's important for the therapist to keep the clients engaged in skill practice. Once Jane picks a family member to talk with in this way, the therapist inquires if they have any questions before beginning the conversation. Sometimes they will comment on the previous interaction. Most of the time they ask questions regarding rules and procedures.

Next, Jane as speaker picks someone to speak to (the listener), and the process continues. (She can choose to talk with Joe, but she must follow the conversive skill and relate how she felt about the conversation between Joe and his father. Then she can continue on her own theme.) To reduce the pressure on Joe, the therapist encourages Jane to continue practicing with another family member. This overt suggestion maintains the collaborative nature of the therapy.

Jane decides to talk with Joe first, before picking her older daughter, Allison.

JANE *(to Joe):*   I just want you to know that I think you did a good job talking with Dad.

THERAPIST: That's a little judgmental—"good job." Instead, tell Joe how that conversation makes you feel.

JANE: It makes me feel good.

THERAPIST: Tell Joe.

JANE: It makes me feel good that you talked to Dad.

THERAPIST: Joe, you're the listener.

JOE: You feel good.

JANE: Yes, switch.

THERAPIST: How does that make you feel, Joe?

JOE: *(Silence)*

THERAPIST *(to Joe):*   You like it that Mom feels good.

JOE: Yeah.

THERAPIST: Tell her.

JOE: I like it.

JANE: You like it that I feel good about how you talked to Dad.

JOE: Uh huh. Switch.

JANE: I'm glad to know that.

THERAPIST: This could be the end of the conversation, Jane. Do you want to say more to Joe or talk to Allison now?

JANE: I'll talk to Allison now.

THERAPIST: Okay, Joe?

JOE: *(Nods his head yes.)*

Note the therapist's supervision and structuring to keep the focus on feelings and engagement. Note also that the therapist accepts Joe's level of communication even though Joe needs the therapist's structuring. Thanks to these efforts, Joe was able to continue to engage in conversation with his mother.

The rest of the session was devoted to the conversation between Allison and Jane. At the end of the conversation, the therapist acknowledged to Allison that she would be first speaker next session, thus ensuring that all members of the family will converse with each other.

The Knight Family

For some families, the extended intake requires a number of sessions. Others, like the Knight family, are ready to engage in a more structured process right away. In their case, the therapist was introduced by an agency social worker who continued to consult with the family as an expert in family communication. The Knight family was referred for therapy after tremendous family conflicts brought them to the attention of several community agencies. The family consists of Tina, age 16, Betty, age 42, and Ralph, age 38. Betty is Tina's birth mother, and Ralph is her stepfather. They have been together as a family for more than 10 years. Betty has two older children not living at home.

BETTY: We have a lack of communication. Tina and I talk a lot. Ralph doesn't like to talk, so that interferes with his relationship with me and his relationship with

Tina. It interferes because with the three of us, well, me and her start fighting because he says certain things, then she says certain things and they'll be two different things and then I'm upset with both of them.

It's hard to leave home in this family. Betty's two older children left home under conflictual conditions, and only now are they beginning to talk to her, a fact acknowledged at the beginning of the therapy. Tina, too, is struggling with the issue of leaving home. She is the youngest and is having the most difficulty. Most likely, her mother's overinvolvement and their resultant enmeshment makes it hard for Tina to differentiate. She has coped with this by becoming depressed and oppositional. Her condition became so serious that she was hospitalized for three weeks due to suicidal ideation. During the time that included this session, she was in an adolescent partial-hospitalization program, where she received schooling.

It is also likely that the mother-daughter enmeshment led to serious marital conflicts as well.

TINA: Like Mom said, it's like me and Ralph and her and Ralph and I hate it when they fight, I hate it, I get drastically wild. They haven't fought, like, a lot, but they used to fight a lot. It used to drive me crazy, I just hated it. It made me anxious. Like he would ground me for something without confronting her first and that would get her upset, and then I'd ask why I should be grounded for that because I didn't mean to do it. I'd say, "I'm sorry" and everything like that and they would get into a big fight and they would start screaming. Or like something would happen and I would see it one way and he would see it another. Then I would go tell her and then he would go tell her after I told her, and then they'd get into another fight. It's just no good. Everybody's always fighting.

THERAPIST: Now if you have a fight, does it get resolved?

TINA: No, we just drop it.

The therapist poses the question, "Does it get resolved?" to assess the functionality of the conflict. In RE, conflict is seen as potentially constructive when it keeps relationships flexible and better able to evolve. Helping families to more constructively engage around conflict is the thrust of RE.

TINA: I understand everybody has to yell at one point in time, but Mom'll yell at me and she'll say, "Why didn't you do this, and why didn't you that?" But then she'll come back later after she calms down and say, "Well, I'm sorry, why didn't you do this? I didn't mean to yell at you, but why didn't you do it?" Ralph just yelled at me and I get into this major rage, and I either go outside and smoke a cigarette or run upstairs and slam the doors.

THERAPIST: You get pretty frustrated and upset.

TINA: Yeah.

THERAPIST *(to Ralph):*   I guess you get pretty frustrated and upset, too. *(Here the therapist begins to engage both of them.)*

RALPH: You're damned right. She never listens to me.

THERAPIST: That makes you mad and it keeps happening over and over again.

RALPH: Yeah.

BETTY: Well, this is just an example of how bad our communication is.

THERAPIST: This concerns you, too.

BETTY: Yeah.

> *(At this point, the therapist introduces RE and a lively discussion ensues, which indicates the interest and motivation of the family. Tina decides to talk with Ralph.)*

TINA: I disliked it very much when you hit Inky [the dog]. It scared me and I want you to know that.

THERAPIST *(to Ralph):*   Do you want me to model it for you? You have to start with "You." You can't talk about your feeling. You can't tell her you're sorry.

RALPH: I was going to tell her I was sorry she got upset.

THERAPIST: Right, but you're talking about your feelings. Say to her, "You were scared . . ."

RALPH: You were scared when I yelled and you want me to know that.

THERAPIST *(to Tina):*   Why does that scare you? *(The therapist asks Tina to express her feelings in more depth.)*

TINA: I don't know. I don't know why I thought it but it just scared me at the time and he might hit Mom. *(She goes a little deeper.)*

THERAPIST *(modeling):*   So, the way that you hit Inky, you were afraid that he might do that to Mom.

TINA *(repeating):*   The way that you hit Inky scared me that you might do that to Mom or me.

THERAPIST *(modeling to Ralph):*   That really scared you when I hit Inky because you're afraid it might happen to you or Mom.

RALPH: That really scared you when I hit Inky because you were afraid that it might happen to you or Mom.

THERAPIST: All right. You can continue or say switch.

TINA: Switch.

THERAPIST *(to Tina):*   Good. Now you are the listener. *(To Ralph)* Now it's important to say how it makes you feel to know that she was scared about that.

RALPH: I was scared a little bit. I didn't know I had that effect.

THERAPIST *(to Tina):*   Now, you say that back. Do you want some help?

TINA: Uh huh.

THERAPIST: Say, "You feel bad that I was scared."

TINA: You feel bad that I was scared.

THERAPIST *(to Ralph):*   Now, you can go on or you can ask for my help. It's up to you.

RALPH: Yeah, I need some help 'cause I want to say something—*(Ralph is struggling with his feelings, and the therapist is structuring to allow him to feel safe.)* It's something she said about hitting her and her mom, and that's something that I've never done and something that has never crossed my mind, and I was wondering why they . . .

THERAPIST: Well, it upsets you because it made you feel bad. Now before you tell her that, it would be helpful to go on and talk about why you got scared—understand why you got scared.

RALPH: Sometimes when I'm angry I just act out. Like I just made lunch and I was getting ready to eat my lunch and, well, Inky decided to eat it for me, and it pissed me off. He was there and I whaled him.

THERAPIST *(to Ralph):*   I would say to her, "I got scared because I reacted so quickly and it really upset me." *(Restating the underlying feeling.)*

(Everybody is laughing. They are anxious.)

RALPH: It scared me when I reacted towards Inky for eating my lunch, but what's got me upset now is what you said about me. You were afraid I would hit you or your mom, and it's important for me that you know that.

THERAPIST *(to Tina):*   He wants you to know that he, too, got scared. *(Structuring to keep her in the listening role.)*

TINA: You want me to know that you wouldn't hit me or my mom. It makes you scared because you would never do that to us and you want me to know that.

THERAPIST: Good. Ralph can continue.

RALPH: I would just like to apologize to you. I was scared for the way I acted and I want you to know that.

TINA: You want to apologize to me because you want me to know that you were scared and you want me to know that.

RALPH: Switch.

THERAPIST *(to Tina):*   Now you're the speaker. How does it make you feel to know Ralph's feeling?

TINA: It makes me feel safer now, because you are communicating to me and I know now . . . I knew before, but I know now much better . . . that you would never hit me and that makes me feel good.

RALPH: It makes you feel safer now that I've told you that, and that makes you feel good.

TINA: I accept your apology and thank you for apologizing and it makes me feel good, and I want you to know that.

THERAPIST: Good.

RALPH: You feel better that I've apologized, and you want me to know that.

TINA: Switch.

THERAPIST: How does it make you feel to know that?

RALPH: That makes me feel better, because I didn't know I had that effect on you.

TINA: It makes you feel better 'cause you didn't know that you had that effect on me, and you want me to know that.

Tina has raised a sensitive subject and it surprises Ralph. He is somewhat taken aback and struggles with his feelings. The therapist's structuring helps Ralph own his feelings. Tina feels better after hearing Ralph's feelings. Though Ralph says he feels better, he becomes upset that Tina would think he would hit her or her mother. In the midst of a general discussion of the conversation, Ralph returns to this concern. With the therapist's structuring, Ralph is able to express his feelings constructively.

This was a very difficult conversation. Ralph was so upset that it was hard for him to accept Tina's underlying positive feelings. The therapist not only structured and modeled, but also acted as a troubleshooter by engaging Ralph directly at a very tense moment. Thanks to the therapist's interventions, Ralph and Tina's dialogue elicited the underlying positive feelings they have for each other, and they became more constructively engaged.

While this tense conversation was going on, Betty had difficulty restraining herself from interrupting and trying to mediate the stress by explaining Tina's feelings to Ralph. That she didn't is a good example of how the structure of RE undermines the very triangulations that maintain family conflict. However, it was important to engage Betty in the process before the end of the session; otherwise, her unprocessed feelings had the potential to create conflict during the week.

THERAPIST: Is there anything you guys want to say about this at all from your perspective? Betty, you were watching; maybe you want to say something.

BETTY: No, it was really good to watch them two and to sort out their feelings about how each other is reacting.

THERAPIST: That makes you feel good.

BETTY: I thought it was very good.

Betty turns to talk with her husband. Because she appreciates the effort he made in the conversation with Tina, her feelings for Ralph are enhanced. In turn, Betty's positive feelings make Ralph feel good and closer to her as well. This closeness echoes a finding of the informal follow-up of the PARD program (Grando & Ginsberg, 1976), which indicated that the marital relationship improved after the father and son participated in the program.

Next the therapist engages Betty and Ralph in a short RE conversation. This is a positive interaction.

BETTY *(to Ralph):* I feel really good that you listened to Tina and were trying so hard to communicate with each other. It makes me feel good that you tried so hard.

This was the first positive conversation this family had had for some time. Obviously, there is a lot to deal with, and one session can't possibly resolve long-standing, intergenerational difficulties. In fact, the next session with the family was very difficult. Conflict emerged immediately and both Tina and Ralph withdrew from the session. However, the increment of change that occurred in the first session influenced subsequent interactions. In fact, as sessions continued with the Knight family, they were increasingly able to tolerate and trust their underlying caring and positive feelings. Tina was encouraged to come to biweekly sessions as she was also involved in an adolescent therapy group and receiving therapy at her partial-hospitalization program. In her absence, the therapist worked on the marital relationship. As a result, there were many fewer conflicts in the family. Betty and Ralph worked more closely together in formulating limits for Tina. As their weekly sessions with the therapist became less frequent, they were able to hold biweekly family meetings during which they used RE to address any difficulties. Ralph found that Tina was coming to him more often. One interesting outcome was that Tina's irritability and defensiveness ("My guard is always up") seemed to dissipate during these sessions, and her relationship with her peer group improved. Of course, one hopes that she will achieve greater independence and be better able to face the kind of conflict experienced by her siblings.

Home Practice in Family RE

When more than two family members participate in family RE therapy, the home practice format begins with family members practicing in alternating dyads. Sessions are taped and reviewed in the sessions with the therapist. The therapist also helps the family practice RE by supervising their home practice sessions in the office. In a subsequent office session, the therapist can suggest they schedule and audiotape a family meeting during which they will use RE skills. The tape is reviewed at the next office session and the family is encouraged to have another practice session at home for review in the therapist's office. As families practice more at home, they meet less frequently for office sessions.

In order to reduce interruptions and provide opportunity for each family member to bring up issues during home RE family meetings, some additional rules apply. Clients are given "Guidelines for Family RE Therapy" (Table 5.2), and "Client Guidelines for Facilitative Skill" (Table 2.11). The role of facilitator alternates weekly allowing all family members a chance to assume this role.

Typically, home practice begins with family members forming dyads. Each dyad practices and tapes its conversation. The tapes are brought for shared supervision to the office sessions. Once all family members have practiced at least once with each other, family meetings can begin. In the interim, the family is asked to agree on a mutually acceptable time each week or every other week to have family meetings. Once a time has been designated, the family is asked to try out the time, but not to practice RE skills during this time. Instead, they are asked to raise positive issues until they have completed the dyadic practice. Family meetings are taped and brought in for supervision with the therapist; who makes suggestions to strengthen these meetings. Thereafter, the therapist meets with the family less often, which helps the family generalize the skills they've learned. Therapists working with adolescents and their families may continue to meet weekly with the parents to enhance their leadership role and/or work with them on marital issues. Many parents also benefit from participating in a parenting group when one is available.

Process-Oriented RE Family Therapy

This type of RE family therapy most closely approximates typical approaches to family therapy. In some ways, it resembles an extended intake that doesn't lead to formal, structured skill training. This approach remains primarily problem focused, and ends when a solution is reached or change occurs. It can also evolve into more structured skill-training sessions to enhance the gains made in earlier sessions. The direction that the therapy takes very much depends upon the client's and family's needs, readiness, and motivation. After the initial crisis is relieved, some families are open and ready to focus on improving their communication and relationships with each other. Other families are satisfied (or dissatisfied) with the changes arising from therapy and choose to end therapy before embarking on more formal skill learning. Still other families, because of their sensitivity or fragility, are too threatened by the vulnerability RE elicits and would not be good candidates (at least at this time) for more formal skill practice. Whatever form it takes, the process-oriented RE approach consistently adheres to RE's principles and methods, and RE therapists remain true to the four pillars: empathy, language and relationship, emotion, and acceptance/equivalence. In addition, RE therapists always keep in mind the principles of nonjudgment, acceptance, and acknowledgment and the core skills of receptivity, owning, and engagement.

Rules, Limits, and Consequences in Therapy with Adolescents

All those who work with adolescents—parents and therapists—must learn how to handle rules, limits, and consequences. For adolescents, this area becomes the interface through which they struggle for independence and autonomy. At the same time, parents struggle with the threat that their children's independence and autonomy pose, as illustrated in Joe's dialogue, quoted earlier. Typically, adolescents continually question and challenge the rules parents generate. According to Paikoff and Brooks-Gunn (1991), parents and adolescents agree that they most frequently disagree over rules and regulations.

As they get older, adolescents are more likely to view a situation in terms of personal choice, while parents perceive the same situation to be regulated by social conventions (Smetana, 1989). Paikoff and Brooks-Gunn (1991) conclude, "The developmental task for the young adolescent involves acceptance of higher levels of reasoning about social conventions that result in enhanced perspective-taking and understanding of the necessities and limitations of social expectations," whereas "The parent's developmental task may involve acceptance of more personal jurisdiction by the adolescent over her or his behavior, or separating social conventional expectations from the adolescent's more personal expectations" (p. 57).

Feldman and Gehring (1988) emphasize that this increasing disagreement is a reworking of power relations. In this light, the conflict revolves around generational boundaries (Minuchin, 1974); that is, weak boundaries lead to conflict. Those parenting skills that stress principles and methods of limit setting and consequences help to maintain strong boundaries and greater flexibility in the face of evolving family change. Therefore, those conflicts that arise in the parent-child relationship and bring families into therapy are necessary and constructive even though the patterns (habits) that underlie them may be dysfunctional at the time.

Educating families—not just parents—in the principles and methods of limit setting and consequences is instrumental in the success of family therapy with adolescents. This emphasis echoes the educative basis of RE and is easily incorporated into PARD. In fact, working on limits and consequences early in the therapy can help a family focus on communication skills: Because the family is already motivated around these issues of discipline, it is easy to engage them on the subject of rules and consequences. In these cases, RE therapists follow the systematic course of RE therapy: They elicit the problem; discuss and identify the principles and methods they will suggest to address the problem; model principles and methods; supervise in-session practice sessions and home practice via audiotape; and explain generalization and maintenance of skills in all areas of life.

The principles and methods of establishing rules, limits, and consequences can be found in Louise Guerney's book, *Parenting: A Skills Training Manual,* and its adolescent supplement (1980). Rules and consequences are best negotiated collaboratively between teenagers and their parents. At best, rules (limits) are effective when parents and children agree to them before they are tested; the same applies to consequences. Rule setting is easiest when both adolescents and parents agree on the *consequence* of an action before the rule is violated, instead of the parents deciding on the *punishment* after the fact. Even when the consequence has not been agreed on beforehand, it is best to try to negotiate a collaborative agreement. When conflicts of this nature arise during therapy, the RE therapist has the perfect opportunity to introduce RE as a means to facilitate collaboration by saying, "It's hard to come to an agreement if both talk at one time. How about one of you talk first, and when you're done, we can switch and the other person can talk? It's also helpful to let the other person know that you understand what that person said before you talk. Is it okay if we try to do that?" Note that the therapist is *modeling* a collaborative approach ("Is it okay if we try to do that?") so central to RE methodology.

The therapist negotiates directly with all parties to help them come to an agreement. They are asked to try to stick to this agreement between sessions and report the outcome at the next session. If there have been problems with the agreement, the therapist helps them renegotiate the agreement and suggests that they again try to stick to it between sessions. Once the outcome is successful, the therapist can ask them to negotiate another rule and consequence on their own, reporting the outcome at the next session. This can go on concurrently with in-office sessions focused on RE communication training.

The Kramer Family

A summary of a beginning family therapy session may help to illustrate the process-oriented PARD approach. The county children and youth agency has asked a local family therapist to consult on a case with their social worker. The Kramer family consists of a father, Bob, and three daughters, Caroline, age 16, Annabelle, age 12, and Tanya, age 10. The mother died more than three years earlier. The circumstances of her death were not clear. The family has come to the attention of the county children and youth agency because of frequent calls to 911 (police emergency). These calls were a result of conflicts between Caroline and her father.

It seemed apparent to the agency and the family therapist that these conflicts were related to the loss of the girls' mother and the overinvolvement between the father and the oldest daughter. As happens in many single-parent families, one of the children, Caroline, had taken on the role of parental child. Bob's wish not to involve the two younger girls in the conflict exacerbated the situation, because he had frequent private talks with Caroline. Although there was no hint of sexual involvement between father and adolescent daughter, sexual tension could have been a factor. Taken together, the anxiety in the Kramer home was affecting Caroline's school performance. Her frequent conflicts with her teachers could have been a way to externalize her grief over the loss of her mother by projecting it onto all female teachers.

The therapist and youth social worker met with all four family members at home one afternoon. Bob's sister was waiting in the next room to take the two younger children with her because he didn't want to involve them in the conflicts. The therapist, however, wanted the girls to remain. Their absence would only exacerbate the conflict between Bob and Caroline and maintain their overinvolvement. Keeping the two younger girls in therapy would also enhance the family's ability to test the reality of this conflict. The two younger children certainly are aware of the conflicts and are affected by everything that goes on in the family.

Having her siblings present would also help Caroline, giving her the benefit of the natural coalitions with her siblings. This balances the distribution of power, which should reduce the frequency of and the underlying factors contributing to the conflicts. A sensitive and skillful therapist allows the opportunity for the redistribution of power while supporting the parent's authority and responsibility to maintain a safe, secure, and constructive environment for the children. Adolescents appreciate the security that good limits provide even as they need to feel respected for their growing independence.

In this session, there were a number of times when Bob wanted the younger girls to leave, but the therapist was able to keep them involved. One key issue—worry over the father's drinking—would not have surfaced without the presence of all three daughters. His drinking ultimately became a metaphor through which to negotiate the family's relationships and balance of power therein. This was a very sensitive issue because the father's drinking posed a genuine threat to his ability to care for his children. Such issues often arise in single-parent families, where the security of the family is dependent on one parent. In these situations, power is easily undermined and/or overemphasized. The negotiation of how to handle the children's anxiety when their father drinks helps to rebalance power constructively and foster a more secure environment for all parties.

The therapist engaged Bob and all three daughters in a discussion focusing on the girls' anxiety over their father's drinking. During this conversation, there were references to their mother's alcoholism and its relation to her death. Bob acknowledged their fears about his drinking and their underlying fear of his death. Using RE, the therapist helped all four work out the following agreement: When the father chooses to drink, the girls can stay with friends who meet his approval. This led to a lively discussion regarding limits and the need to work on developing clear and realistic rules. They all were assigned the task to separately develop a list of the rules that each thought would be important and bring it to the next session. Helping adolescents and their parents develop realistic and clear limits and consequences is essential. This enables them to negotiate differentiation more constructively. RE can be useful in these discussions, helping the participants be clear about what they are saying, understand each other better, and come to constructive agreements that can last.

The therapist, concerned that the conflict between Caroline and her father would escalate before the next session, needed to return to the presenting problem. He engaged Caroline and Bob in an RE conversation. As a result, at the end of the session, Bob agreed to have a meeting with Caroline and her teachers to try to address the school problems. Caroline stated that she would try not to be so aggressive with her father. Bob agreed to try not to provoke her by accusing her.

Following this session, Caroline agreed to drug and alcohol counseling. The whole family continued in RE family therapy with the social worker. In subsequent sessions the agreement about the father's drinking was honored. There were no further crisis calls to 911. It seemed obvious that as this family learned how to communicate more constructively, intergenerational boundaries grew clearer and the family was more stable and secure. Focusing on the impact of the mother's death did not play a significant part in the changes, but the children were better able to express their feelings about this loss.

There is no doubt that any type of therapeutic work with adolescents and families with adolescents is unpredictable. Adolescence is such a quickly changing time and feelings become so acute that engaging and keeping these families engaged is very difficult. Often, the conflicts are so pronounced by the time these families enter therapy that youth agencies and/or juvenile probation officers may already be involved. This further complicates the therapy, as it extends the possible triangulations. Keeping families engaged in more structured and consistent therapy sessions is even harder. RE therapists have to be flexible during sessions, waiting for the right moments during which to engage family members in RE communication and skill practice. The RE therapist is always ready to pursue a more structured, systematic direction, but can use RE for facilitation of family process at any time without the therapy becoming more structured. Typically, once the crisis is past, families may be more ready to engage in a structured RE process—that is, if they remain in therapy. But often, even those families who leave return three months, six months, or a year later and are more open to a structured approach.

In some ways, Caroline and her family followed this pattern. For a period of some months, there was crisis after crisis. The involvement of the social worker over time began to triangulate with the family to ease the anxiety and elicit more stability. At that point, the family was ready for more structured RE therapy. This was not smooth; there were a number of crises that interrupted the process. But as the social worker continued to work with the family, maintaining support and focusing on skill practice, the family became increasingly stable.

Adolescence today is less clearly defined than in the past, but in many ways it is more interesting and exciting. Our children are exposed to many influences of the world at earlier and earlier periods of development. Perhaps the fast pace and increasing complexity of our society have contributed to this. Perhaps the degree to which the media today intrude on our lives is responsible. Perhaps the prevalence of single-parent families, latchkey children, and families in which both parents work causes problems. In any case, it is imperative that individuals and families become more skillful in coping with these influences. Time for connection with each other, intimacy, and the security that accompanies our engagement with each other are becoming scarce. Adolescents benefit from being more independent and autonomous yet connected to those who have helped them form who they are. Relationship Enhancement therapy can be a resource to help this happen.

CHAPTER 6

The Young Adult in Relationship Enhancement Therapy

In our society, adolescence often extends well into the twenties, sometimes the thirties. Then begins young adulthood, a period very much like adolescence. Children take longer to move out of their parents' homes. Those who leave often return, sometimes several times, because of financial difficulties, to return to school, and for many other reasons. Even married children may return to a parent's home either with their spouse and children or, if separated or divorced, alone or with children in tow. Special problems arise when adult children live with their parents: Are they adults or children? Obviously, they are both, and their ambiguous role and the unclear boundaries between adult child and parent engender stress and conflict.

In some cases, adult children who live at home are not ready to separate. Sometimes a trauma or other life event (e.g., death of parent, economic instability) causes adult children to delay moving out. This overinvolvement or enmeshment can be exacerbated when the adult child feels inadequate and insecure. Littwin (1986) believes that children today take a decade longer to grow up than their parents did. She identified four factors contributing to this change. Young people today feel trapped because of their own expectations, which derive from their sense of entitlement. They are psychologically unprepared, believing that they are special and deserve special treatment. This is not the fault of parents, but part of our culture. Second, the harshest reality that this generation faces is the fact that choice is limited. This is a time of lowered expectation and diminished opportunity. The third factor has to do with the change in men's and women's roles and its effect on the family and society. The options created by these role changes influence life's timetable. In other words, "If you don't have to marry, settle down and raise a family, then what is the big rush about growing up?" (p. 248). Our changing values and the confusion they create is the fourth factor affecting young adults and their growing up. Once it counted to help others or work for ideals. Today the bottom line seems to be all that matters. This makes it harder for the young adult to know what path to pursue or what ideals to value. The internal ambivalence with which the young adult views becoming a full adult can create excruciating difficulties in the family. Sometimes, young adults are so triangulated that the rigid roles they play in the family are severely threatened by their need to be independent. This can lead to recurring cycles during which periods of closeness alternate with periods of terrible conflict.

The primary goal of single young adults is to accept emotional and financial responsibility for themselves and to "become a (self) before joining with another to form a new family subsystem" (Carter & McGoldrick, 1988, p. 13). This life-cycle transition requires a shift to a less hierarchical form of relating that leads to greater differentiation of self in relation to the family. It is also a shift to a greater sense of equivalence during which we form more adult-to-adult relationships. This is integrated with the development of intimate peer relationships and the establishment of self in relation to work and financial independence. According to Carter and McGoldrick (1988),

> The shift toward adult-to-adult status requires a mutually respectful and personal form of relating, in which young adults can appreciate parents as they are, needing neither to make them into what they are not nor to blame them for what they could not be. Neither do young adults need to comply with parental expectations at their own expense. Therapy at this phase most often involves coaching young adults to reengage with their parents in a new way that accomplishes the shifting of their status in the system. When the parents are the ones seeking help, therapy usually involves helping them to recognize the new status of their adult children and to relate to them as such. (p. 14)

In RE family therapy, young adults and parents are brought together to help them make changes in the family and reach these objectives. The goal of therapy is not simply to help the family to become aware of the importance of seeing and relating to each other in more differentiated ways: Often, young adults and their family members entering therapy already know this. However, nonconscious, emotionally motivated behaviors and habits make the process of change difficult and emotionally wrenching.

The following transcriptions of therapy sessions with a young adult in the throes of this difficulty poignantly identify the ambivalence and mixed feelings with which young people struggle. Louise, 21 years old, has just quit college in midsemester to return home to live with her parents. She had difficulty adjusting to her first two years of college and called or came home frequently. During this period, she experienced a parallel ambivalence in a relationship with Bill, a young man she had known from early adolescence. She expressed confusion and dissatisfaction with "where she was going." Expressing a need to take some time to "find herself," Louise moved back home. She has been in family therapy since her teens. Her family was seen originally because of her parents' serious marital difficulties.

Louise's sister, Sharon, 24, was also affected by her family's difficulties, but she tended to internalize her experience. Often, she would complain how hard it was for her to access her feelings. She, too, had gone through some tough times in college; alcohol often played a part in these difficulties.

Louise's parents both came from abusive family backgrounds in which drugs and alcohol were also abused. A sibling of the mother committed suicide several years before Louise's family entered therapy. Louise's mother, Betsy, became suicidal herself at one point during their therapy. Betsy was a closet alcoholic. Louise and Sharon often knew when their mother had been drinking, but Betsy would always deny it.

As the marital relationship improved, the focus of the therapy turned to the two daughters and their involvement in the process. Soon, a pattern emerged: The family's interactions and coping skills would improve, they would withdraw from treatment for a year or two, and then return again for three to six months. During one hiatus from therapy after Louise left for college, Betsy finally admitted her alcoholism and entered a 28-day residential program for alcohol abuse; subsequently, Tom, her husband, was treated for depression.

At the time recorded by the first transcript, Sharon had just moved in with her fiancé. It is likely that this move destabilized the fragile family's ability to cope, and that Louise's return brought the family system into tentative balance again. Helping Louise differentiate more and fulfill the goals outlined by Carter and McGoldrick (1988) were important objectives of the therapy. However, such changes would inevitably cause unresolved stress in the marital relationship to surface, necessitating therapeutic work with both parents.

Although both Sharon and Louise had difficulties, these transcripts will focus on Louise's turmoil and will document her developmental process. The first transcript is drawn from one of four sessions during which Louise and Sharon saw the therapist together. Louise had requested an individual session with the therapist during the summer between her sophomore and junior years as she had done in the past. (Away at school, far from home, she sought individual therapy with a college counselor.) Usually, these sessions included her parents and, on occasion, her sister. During one individual session, the therapist suggested that Sharon be invited to subsequent sessions so that Louise could use RE in the context of this important relationship to help her sort out her feelings. Louise liked the suggestion and invited her sister to attend. This was a familiar context, as they had met without their parents in the past to help strengthen their relationship and improve their ability to cope with the difficulties in their family. The session was very productive. As a result, Louise requested her sister's participation thereafter. Sharon also found the sessions meaningful and gladly participated.

The sibling relationship and its potential to create constructive change within the family are often overlooked in family therapy. This is particularly true when siblings reach adulthood and build more independent lives for themselves. Though many siblings are competitive and their relationships conflictual (particularly at younger ages), they often begin to look to each other for support as they mature. Forming increasingly stronger coalitions with each other, siblings can strengthen their differentiation vis-à-vis their parents. Sharing the same family background, they are able to understand and be a resource to each other. Sharon, for example, became a resource for Louise during these sibling RE sessions, at the same time understanding herself better. The sessions also marked a transition for them: They were evolving from an older-younger sibling system to one with greater equivalence and mutuality. Perhaps this change was enhanced by Sharon's decision to live with her fiancé, and her upcoming marriage.

In the following excerpt, which is representative of that summer's sibling sessions, Louise talks about the importance of being able to confide in her sister because she feels trapped in her relationship with their parents. Louise herself requested that they use the RE format for these sessions. They had been introduced to RE as young teenagers in family therapy, and RE had become a resource for them in other areas of their lives as well. Note that the therapist intervenes only to point out that a "judgment" is being made or because one of them turns to him directly for help clarifying her experience. Louise emphasizes the importance of being acknowledged and understood. Sharon validates her experience through listening and acknowledging that she recognizes what Louise is struggling with, having grown up in the same family.

LOUISE: It makes me feel good that we came to the therapist together and that you didn't make me come by myself. It made me feel good that we kept the commitment to come, even though there are other things going on in our lives and we're busy doing other things. It makes me feel good I guess because you understood that this was something important.

SHARON: It makes you feel good that you think that this is important. You're glad I came.

LOUISE: It also makes me feel good that we have been getting along better this summer.

SHARON: I don't know what the hell happened.

LOUISE: But I don't know, like, I can call you, and talk to you and I don't know—it's no pressures and it just makes me feel good that I can talk easier now.

SHARON: It makes you feel good that you feel more comfortable talking to me.

LOUISE: And we're able to share and relate.

SHARON: You feel good we can share more and relate.

LOUISE: Switch.

SHARON: That makes me feel good to know you feel good about that.

LOUISE: It makes you feel good to know that I feel good about that because I'm glad that we've been talking.

SHARON: I didn't think about it until we talked about it. That makes me feel good that we're doing more sisterly bonding.

LOUISE: It makes you feel good that we're doing some more sisterly bonding.

SHARON: It was important to me that we came tonight. I just wanted you to know that because I was worried that you were afraid that I wouldn't come.

LOUISE: You want me to know that coming here was important to you because you were afraid that I was thinking differently.

SHARON: It makes me feel good that you talked to me last night when you were feeling upset and worried.

LOUISE: It makes you feel good that I could talk to you last night.

SHARON: Because it felt good to be like a friend.

LOUISE: It felt good to be a friend to me.

They are acknowledging the changes in their relationship and are becoming more equivalent to each other more.

Louise still struggles with her dependence on her parents. She wants to confide in them and have them take care of her as they did in her childhood. But when she comes face to face with their overinvolvement and control, she regrets it and grows angry with herself.

SHARON: You get angry with yourself when you tell Mom and Dad things.

LOUISE: Yeah. I think it makes me feel better now that I know I can come to you with things instead of going to them with it.

SHARON: It makes you feel better when you can come to me.

LOUISE: I'm frustrated right now because I'm stuck everywhere. It's nothing but shit, Mom and Dad's shit, and it doesn't stop. No matter what, they're always bitching about something. I always feel bad about myself. They put me down for everyday things, like I don't do the dishes right—and they have to interfere with that. I guess I just want you to know how helpless I feel right now.

THERAPIST: It's really hard and you feel bad.

(She is feeling scared, so she looks at the therapist for support. He acknowledges her and with his support continues to talk to her sister.)

LOUISE: I'm very, very scared right now that I'm not going to make it through this. Sometimes I just don't know, I'm sick of trying to choke through all these things that have come up, and it makes me feel like shit, makes me feel bad. I'm scared that I don't know if I will make it and it makes me feel bad because I'm so tired of doing it and I'm afraid I'll never get better, and I want to ask you for your help, but I'm afraid it's going to be a burden on you and that would make me feel bad.

SHARON: You would feel bad that it would put a burden on me, and you want to ask for help.

LOUISE: I don't want to scare you. I'm afraid I will.

SHARON: You're afraid you will scare me and it worries you.

LOUISE: I want you to know that I feel a lot less crazy when I'm talking to you now.

(She acknowledges the power of this RE interaction.)

SHARON: You want me to know that you feel a lot less crazy when you talk to me now, and it makes you feel normal.

LOUISE: It makes me feel normal because you can sit here and act like everybody does, but with Mommy, it's like, "Oh my god, oh my god, something's going to happen, you can't be sad, oh my god, you can't be angry. You can only be happy and content and just happy-go-lucky in life." I feel good that I can say this, but it makes me feel bad when Mommy does that to me. It makes me feel crazy.

SHARON: It makes you feel bad or crazy when Mom gets all uptight when you're upset, and it makes you feel good to talk about this now.

LOUISE: Switch.

SHARON: It makes me feel good that you feel comfortable talking with me and that you're feeling better by talking.

LOUISE: It makes you feel good that I feel better by talking and I feel better.

SHARON: It makes me feel bad that you're going through such a hard time and you're so frustrated with yourself.

LOUISE: It makes you feel bad that I'm feeling so frustrated with myself.

SHARON: I feel good about talking. I like when you tell me things because I feel included in your life.

LOUISE: It makes you feel good when I tell you things because then you feel included in my life.

SHARON: I like to share things because it makes me feel good.

LOUISE: You like to share things and it makes you feel good.

SHARON: I feel good because it helps us get along better when we share different things about ourselves and we understand each better. It helps, and it's important because you're important to me.

LOUISE: You want me to know that it's important that we get along better because I'm important to you.

SHARON: I feel good and it makes me feel good that you've been talking to me.

LOUISE: It's important that I know that I feel good that I've been talking to you and you feel good that I talk with you.

SHARON: Switch.

LOUISE: That makes me feel good. It gives me a little bit of hope that I'm going to be able to chug along through this thing.

SHARON: That makes you feel good.

LOUISE: It makes me feel good that I have someone to depend on. I was feeling hopeless, because I was thinking that I don't have my family to depend on; I don't have you because you have your life, with Jay [fiancé] and the wedding, and I don't want to be a burden, and I worried that I was going to be a burden.

SHARON: You were worried that you were going to be a burden.

LOUISE: It's important that you know that and I don't want you to feel bad for not taking time out, and I'm worried that you're going to feel bad because you're not going to take time out for me.

SHARON: You're worried that I'm going to feel bad because I'm not taking time out for you.

LOUISE: Well, yeah, but we sat there on the phone one day when I was at work and talked for an hour. That was really cool, because I needed to talk to you.

SHARON: You needed to talk to me.

LOUISE: I think this is what I needed. I needed to know that there is someone there for me.

SHARON: It's very important to you to know that someone is there.

LOUISE: Yes, because it saddens me that Mom can't be there for me.

SHARON: You're hurt by that.

(Sharon has added a facilitative statement by changing the feeling word to one that is close in meaning.)

LOUISE: But I also feel good because I realized that she can't, she just can't, I don't think that she can be there. She has too much stuff of her own, and it makes me feel good to realize that.

(She is beginning to differentiate.)

SHARON: It makes you feel good to realize that Mom can't be there the way you want her to be.

LOUISE: Yes, but it angers me because she can't let go of me. Like I said, she wants to keep taking care of me until I find someone who can take care of me. But I don't want her to. I want to be able to take care of myself before I go out and find someone else. It makes me very angry.

(Struggling to be independent.)

SHARON: It makes you angry that Mom wants to take care of you.

LOUISE: And, I'm supposed to like her. It's very hard. It's very hard to have a relationship with her and it makes me feel bad because it has to be on her terms. I have to take all of her shit and then we'll have a relationship. I don't want to do it that way anymore and that makes me feel angry with her.

(Torn, Louise is struggling in her relationship with her mother. The strong allegiance she feels toward her mother and the family conflicts with her need to be independent. Sharon succinctly acknowledges this and then helps Louise go deeper.)

SHARON: You're angry with her.

LOUISE *(turning to the therapist)*:   What is wrong with me? I haven't felt this good in so long.

THERAPIST: That makes you feel terrific.

LOUISE: Yes, but why?

THERAPIST: You're surprised, it makes you feel good.

LOUISE: But why? Why do I feel so good?

THERAPIST: You want me to answer that question. I'm supposed to know why you feel so good because it surprises you so. I'll be glad to answer that, but first I would like your sister to talk. *(To Sharon)* How does it make you feel to know that she is feeling like that?

(He keeps them engaged.)

SHARON: It makes me feel good to know that you feel so good right now.

LOUISE: It makes you feel good that I feel so good.

SHARON: I'm glad that you feel very good.

THERAPIST: Anything you have to say about what she's struggling with, because you know Mom? How can you relate to it? How does it affect you? What is your reaction to what she is going through? Can you understand it?

(He tries to elicit Sharon's own awareness that she has similar struggles with her mother, which would validate Louise's feelings. It's often the case that children know the unacknowledged family secret.)

SHARON: I remember not too many months ago I was ready to pull my hair out because I had to be out of that house. I don't know for sure, but I'm assuming you feel this way now, and I'm telling you this because I want you to understand how I feel.

(She acknowledges sharing similar feelings and struggling with their mother over independence. This leads to more intimate sharing of even deeper feelings. It also relieves Louise.)

LOUISE: You want me to know that you understand how I'm feeling and it's important to you.

(Pause)

SHARON: I'm glad that you can come and talk to me. You're welcome any time and I want you to believe that.

LOUISE: You're glad that I can come and talk to you and I'm welcome anytime and you want me to know that.

This session poignantly exemplifies the struggle that young adults experience as they mature into adulthood. The transition from dependence to independence is rarely smooth. Family loyalty and the degree to which childhood roles become entrenched make the process of leaving home and becoming independent gradual and conflictual.

In this family, Sharon moved back home after finishing college. Though the move was primarily economic, it seems clear from the family's dynamics that she and her parents needed more time to differentiate and become more independent. At one point, Sharon's fiancé moved in with her family—another incremental step in the transition to independence and differentiation. During the summer in which this session took place, Sharon and her fiancé had moved into their own apartment and had set a wedding date for the spring. This increased the pressure on Louise, causing her more stress and eliciting more conflicts with her parents. The transcribed session was valuable because it allowed the sisters to reiterate the importance of their relationship, to note their emergence into more equivalence with each other, and to enhance their sibling coalition, which in turn strengthened their differentiation and independence.

Interestingly, the same summer that Sharon moved out and Louise moved back home, Betsy began to drink again and the parent's marital relationship deteriorated, becoming increasingly distant. This family is representative of many families who have difficulty "launching" their children into adulthood. Often these families tend to be rigid and have histories of stress and trauma, as Louise's family did. Certainly the history of alcoholism is significant. Nevertheless, following each conflictual period throughout their adolescence and adulthood, Louise and Sharon seemed to grow more independent. Their decision to return to therapy at stressful junctures helped them engage in a constructive process of change.

When Louise returned home, she began a full-time job and resumed a relationship with her long-time boyfriend, Bill. Soon thereafter, Bill moved in with the family, just as Sharon's boyfriend had. After several months, Louise requested a session with the therapist. At that time, she expressed satisfaction with her decision to leave college, return home, and work full time. She was enjoying her job and was pleased that her relationship with Bill had resumed. She was excited about her sister's upcoming wedding and was looking forward to participating in it. However, she found it difficult to live at home with her parents. She experienced her mother as controlling and was very angry with her father, Tom, who had withdrawn into a depressive state. She did not return to therapy after that session; however, two months later, she asked her mother to accompany her to therapy. They met for several sessions and focused on their relationship, struggling with how much they meant to each other and their need to be more independent. At Louise's request, they used the RE structure. Interestingly, Betsy and Tom's relationship improved during this time.

In the following transcript, from Betsy and Louise's last session, the therapist relied mostly on his receptive listening skills, allowing the interaction between Louise and Betsy to unfold on its own. He only entered the conversation to keep it safe, to keep the parties engaged, to help the speaker clarify her feelings and own them, and to defuse defensiveness (troubleshooting). In the latter case, the therapist tried to help the speaker return to a receptive position (through modeling and structuring). If this didn't work, he engaged directly with her (doubling), helping to ease her stress, which was threatening to derail the constructive process. The excerpt begins with Betsy exploring her anger toward her daughter.

THERAPIST: So, is there anything you want to bring up or say to me or should I just get you into talking with each other?

BETSY: I'm furious.

LOUISE: You can talk first then.

BETSY: I don't want to talk with you yet.

LOUISE: Okay then.

THERAPIST: You can talk to me then *(troubleshooting)*.

BETSY: I'm just, I was so angry this morning—very, very angry, and then I started to cry, and I was so emotional, like I thought I was losing it. I'm just so angry at her.

THERAPIST: At Louise?

BETSY: Yeah. You know Louise was away at school and in November she started to have problems and anxiety, and she wanted to come home, and I said okay. I mean she was talking about suicide at times, and I was dying inside. I did nothing but cry every day and night. She said, "I want to come home where I'm loved," and she did. It killed me. This went on for about a month. She comes home to the safe environment. We gave her love and support. Then she decides to get a full-time job, now she has decided to move out of the house with Bill. You know all those things are natural, I mean leaving college happened, whatever was going on with her happened and it's like *(she snaps her fingers)* in two months, she leaves school, comes home, gets a full-time job. I don't know where school is right now; I guess it's put on the back burner, and she's moving out with Bill? To a month-to-month lease, which tells me that neither one of them is ready to commit. And I think it's good that she's going to move out, but why does she have to move in with him? Why can't it be with another girl or on her own? I mean everything is in two months, all this has happened, and as a mother and 45-year-old woman, I'm sitting back watching this happen, knowing, feeling inside that this is not a healthy situation.

THERAPIST: It's very worrisome to you.

BETSY: And her sister is getting married in two months. When Sharon moved out, you know I helped them with buying certain things and going with her for certain things to help set up house. I don't have that time to do that right now. I think it's very unfair for Louise to do this at this time when her sister is getting married in two months. She should be concentrating on her sister's shower because she is the maid of honor, and that's her responsibility, and she's not.

THERAPIST: That's very upsetting to you too.

BETSY: I am so frustrated. And luckily Tom and I are together on this. Tom and I were so far apart it wasn't even funny over the last three months.

THERAPIST: Is that right?

BETSY: I was leaving, that was it. And one week Louise was gone, house-sitting for a friend. I don't know, Tom started to talk and we started to talk, nothing serious, just not sarcastically, 'cause that's how he always gets. And he wasn't going to bed every night—before that he always came home and went right into the bedroom.

THERAPIST: Well, I'm glad to hear that.

BETSY: And as it went on we started to talk to each other, because it was just us, and we focused on each other instead of all the other shit going on. It got really good. So, where it's at now, we're into talking, and trying to work things through.

(The parents are struggling with their own independence from their children. It's interesting that their relationship seemed to improve after Louise's absence. This suggests that some differentiation is already occurring.)

THERAPIST: Well, that's encouraging.

BETSY: Yes, it is. I'm worried sick about this whole situation, and I said to her, "Why don't you two get engaged, and then move out?"

THERAPIST: Why would that be, I don't understand.

BETSY: Then they would be committing to each other.

THERAPIST: I see. The fact that they are not committed makes you so worried.

BETSY: Right, because of his past history. There's never a commitment. It's "See ya."

THERAPIST: I understand. You're afraid of the devastating effect on her after Bill abandons her another time. That's what you're scared about.

BETSY: Yes.

THERAPIST: I think that what you're talking about really is a struggle between you and her that you have to work on. The only way to do it is to talk about it with her because it's a lot deeper than what you described. You really need to face this with each other; it's a very important issue. And, of course, you can't do it until you're ready to talk to her.

BETSY: I can talk to her, she's just . . .

THERAPIST: Why don't you just continue. Talk to Louise and we'll do it in the structure, so maybe we can help you get somewhere.

This is a good example of how a therapist troubleshoots for the client and begins to engage clients with each other. Because Betsy's feelings were too strong to be able to talk with her daughter, the therapist himself engaged her by using the receptive skill. After Betsy clarifies her feelings, she will be ready to talk with Louise. Louise, trusting her previous RE experience, responds by being the listener.

BETSY: I'm very angry with you.

LOUISE: You're very angry with me.

BETSY: I'm very worried about you.

LOUISE: And you're very worried about me.

Betsy continues to talk about her anger and hurt that Louise is moving out just before her sister's wedding. Louise reflects her feelings.

LOUISE: It makes you angry that I want to move out right now and Sharon's wedding is only two months away.

BETSY *(sighs)*:   I would like to share in the same thing that I did with Sharon. Going shopping for things, buy you things. I can't afford to do that right now with the wedding, Louise. I feel cheated that I'm not going to go and help you with it. *(It's hard for her to let go.)*

LOUISE: You feel cheated that you're not going to be there to help me with this because of Sharon's wedding.

BETSY: Can I say this? I think it's very selfish of her.

THERAPIST: That's a judgment. Why is it selfish? What makes it selfish?

BETSY: Because of the time.

THERAPIST: Why does that make it selfish?

BETSY: Because it's taking away from Sharon's shower and her wedding.

THERAPIST: How does it do that?

BETSY: Because to me, first of all this is very hard for me. It's very hard to let go of the last one. You know, in a way her leaving for school was hard and now it's a permanent thing. It's very hard.

THERAPIST: Good, that's the way you say it to her.

> *(Again, the therapist helps Betsy clarify her feelings. She is now able to express her struggle with letting her daughter go and be independent.)*

BETSY: It's very hard to let you go, although I want you to because Dad and I need our time now. But that's hard for me to let go, so that's a pain that I'm dealing with. Then for you to choose to do it now when I can't focus on you and shop with you and make it a happy experience leaving, it makes me so angry because I would like to share in that with you, and I'm sure you would like me to do that too. It's very important to me.

LOUISE: It's very important to you that you take the time with me to shop with me when I move out. You want it to be a happy time when I move out. It's very hard for you to let go of the last one. It's going to be very difficult and it makes it even harder that I'm not allowing you the time to take with me so that we can go. It's very painful for you.

BETSY: Switch.

Louise continues to struggle with her feelings. She feels guilty and trapped and expresses this to her mother. Trying to ease her guilt by explaining her motivations for moving out, she becomes a little defensive.

LOUISE: I feel trapped between Sharon's wedding and moving out, as if I'm not allowed because of Sharon's wedding and if I do, you're going to feel bad about it and you're going to feel guilty and I don't want any of that. I don't want any of those feelings. It would make me feel bad if we had those feelings between us. I understand that you want to do things for me. It's hard letting go of the last one, and it's hard for you to think about me moving out. It's hard, and you said . . . well it's a 30-day lease and you're worried about that with Bill, but most of it is for me. If I don't like that particular place, then I don't want to be there and I'm going to change and it's not because of Bill's and my relationship. I don't know how to make you feel better about that. It makes me angry that I'm sitting here trying, 'cause nothing I ever say or do ever makes you feel better and it makes me feel bad that I have to justify all of this.

BETSY: It makes you feel bad that you have to justify all this.

THERAPIST *(to Louise)*:   What you want to convey to her, I think, is that you really are prepared to face the responsibility of this decision yourself, and you'd like her to trust that.

> *(Here the therapist emphasizes how important it is to Louise to have her mother's trust.)*

LOUISE: I would like you to trust *(crying)* any decision I make.

BETSY: You would like me to trust any decision you would make, and that's very important to you.

(Pause)

LOUISE: Yes, lately I have taken some pretty big steps, some pretty outrageous steps off the beaten path, but I think that I'm going to be okay, and I think that everything is going to work out. I believe that I have a good head on my shoulders and I know what I want and where I want to go and someday I will achieve it, but right at this moment is not the time. And yes, I do want to go back to school and you know that and I have discussed that, and if I'm going to do it, I'm going to do it. If I put my head to it, I'll do it. You say all you ever want for me is to be is happy, and I want to do that, and I want you to trust that.

(Helped by her mother's acknowledgment and acceptance, Louise is strongly asserting confidence in herself.)

BETSY: You want me to trust that if you put your head to it you'll do it.

LOUISE: That's how important you are to me.

BETSY: That's how important I am to you.

(Here the underlying positive message emerges spontaneously.)

LOUISE: Switch.

BETSY: It makes me feel good to know that I'm very important to you, but I'm worried because two months ago there was this little girl who was crumbled in a ball and couldn't think, couldn't do anything. I held you and watched you cry. You didn't even know where you were, what you were doing *(crying),* and now you know everything and you're fine and that's very hard for me.

LOUISE: It's very hard for you to believe that everything is just fine right now when just a few months ago you were holding me and I didn't know what I was doing or anything. Now I know everything and that's why you're so worried. *(Louise is not ready to switch even though she said so. She continues crying.)* When I came home from school, I was looking for somewhere safe. I needed that because being in a hick town where I had tons of worries other than school—meaning bills to be paid—was one of my worries. I didn't want to keep asking you for money; I wanted to do my own thing. I enjoyed my classes, but I didn't feel like I had anything. I needed somewhere safe to be, so I came home 'cause that was safe, and I don't feel that way anymore. I have another source of safety I guess, me or Bill, or us together, and I mean I think I have found more with me. I have to look at me to find happiness and me to find safety, not you, because you're not always going to be there and it's not always going to be the same. That makes me feel better that I told you that.

BETSY: It makes you feel good that you have to find safety with yourself now and you can't be running somewhere else to find it and you feel good that you feel that way.

(Louise is able to recognize and acknowledge her need to find security in herself instead of depending on her mother.)

LOUISE: And I want you to know that.

BETSY: And you want me to know that.

LOUISE: It's important to me that you understand that your acceptance of me is so important.

BETSY: It's important to you that I understand . . .

LOUISE: Wait, wait . . .

BETSY: Well, I don't want to miss anything.

LOUISE: No, you won't. That your acceptance of me is so important that it influences my own choices which causes the anger.

(She has more insight into herself.)

I feel bad that I don't choose your decisions and that's where the guilt comes in.

BETSY: You feel bad that you don't choose my decisions and that's where the guilt comes in.

LOUISE: Yes. It would make me feel good if we could resolve this and that I can understand the way that you accept me and I would feel better.

BETSY: It would make you feel better if we could resolve this and understand how I accept you.

LOUISE: Switch.

BETSY: It makes me feel good to know that.

LOUISE: It makes you feel good to know that.

(Pause)

BETSY: I don't know what to say.

THERAPIST: Let me offer you another possibility. Can I? Say, "I'd like to try to work on that with you 'cause that would make me feel good for you to understand how much I really do accept you."

BETSY: Yeah, I'd like to work on that with you. It would make you feel good so that we could have a relationship.

LOUISE: It would make you feel good if we could work on that and we could have a relationship.

BETSY: Yeah, but I feel very leery about that because every time we walk out of this office and go home we don't really talk much, and then it's the same old thing. It worries me that it happens.

THERAPIST: Good.

LOUISE: It worries you that when we leave here the same old thing happens.

BETSY: Yes, but I would really like us to try to do that. That would make me happy.

LOUISE: It would make you happy if we would try to do this.

BETSY: Louise, you are just exactly like your mother.

LOUISE: You are damn right, and it's freaking scary. You and me are a mirror, do you realize that? I'm looking in a mirror.

BETSY: That is why I worry about you.

LOUISE: I am following in your footsteps.

BETSY: No, I don't want that to happen. That's what I'm worried about. *(Laughing, they are both feeling relieved and better.)*

LOUISE: I know. Tell me about it. I can't change it.

BETSY: Do you want to end up 27 years later like this?

LOUISE: Yes, yes.

BETSY: I'm not going to stop worrying.

LOUISE: Mom, all your worrying, at least for me, isn't that necessary. Because you worry so, I think I need to do this, that, and the other thing to make you not worry.

BETSY: That's your problem. I can't not ever stop worrying.

LOUISE: Well, how do we deal with this, is what I need.

BETSY: I know. I will not express my worry to you, okay? I will share it with someone else.

LOUISE: And I won't tell you every single detail about my life, my fights, my arguments, my bad days.

(They are beginning to problem-solve, and act more equivalently.)

THERAPIST: I have to see you in two weeks, just to see how this pans out. *(Laughing)* But I like it. At least you're working on this. Understand, if this agreement doesn't work, as long as you keep working on this kind of thing with each other things can improve. That was terrific tonight what you guys did together. I liked it very much.

The session ends on a very positive note. The therapist acknowledges the good feeling and the shift to a more constructive interaction. He also reinforces their agreement.

Betsy and Louise canceled their appointment scheduled to take place two weeks after this session. When the therapist placed a follow-up call a month later, he found that this positive change in their relationship had continued. Louise moved out on the appointed date and Betsy accepted it.

The therapy is now in the consultative phase. Family members contact the therapist periodically for booster sessions. In the interim, they apply the skills they learned and benefit from the changes elicited from these RE interactions.

Young adulthood is a time of profound transition. Young adults resemble adolescents, although they are able to act more independently. As this transcript indicates, they are not free from family influences. In fact, they are strongly affected by their families. They want to leave home, but they still need their parents to accept them as independent, equivalent, and autonomous. Parents, on their part, find it hard to let go of their need to protect their children. They struggle with the realization that they no longer play as pivotal a role in their children's lives as they had when their children were younger. This transcript makes it very clear that this struggle doesn't end in young adulthood, but continues throughout life. Relationship Enhancement therapy with young adults helps multigeneration families cope with the significant influence of family-of-origin issues across the life span.

CHAPTER 7

Adulthood, Marriage, Coupling, and Close Relationships

In March 1995, the Council on Families in America published a report, *Marriage in America: A Report to the Nation,* which stated: "Relationships between men and women are not getting better; by many measures, they are getting worse. They are becoming more difficult, fragile, and unhappy" (p. 3). According to the American Psychological Association (Azar, 1995), relationships between men and women are evolving faster than many marriages can withstand. Most marriage researchers agree that the shifts in women's roles in society, among other factors (e.g., economic changes, increased mobility, the influence of the media, the growing complexity of our society, increasing longevity) have created changes in marriage and contributed to the rise in divorce rates (Azar, 1995). In particular, the advances in women's work status have forced more egalitarian marriages. Furthermore, with the increasing acceptance of same gender relationships, communication and negotiation, particularly of conflict, have become essential to all couple relationships. Attesting to the difficulties inherent in modern relationships are the following statistics: The number of unmarried adults nearly doubled between 1970 and 1993, and more than half this group has never married; those who do marry are waiting longer to do so; and many more couples are living together unmarried (Azar, 1995).

Yet the importance of having a primary and significant partnering relationship, whether with a member of the same or opposite gender, is something most of us want and need. People identify marriage as one of the most important sources of happiness, and 90 percent of adults marry at least once by the time they reach age 50 (Azar, 1995). The mental health and functioning of each of us is greatly influenced by the strength, intimacy, and security of our couple relationship. Many clients come to therapy because of dissatisfaction with their partners. Many others come in with emotional and/or physical complaints that are strongly influenced by the quality of such a relationship.

THE NATURE OF THE COUPLE RELATIONSHIP

The couple relationship is probably the most difficult relationship to sustain; much of the difficulty is inherent in the very nature of this primary and significant relationship. For one thing, the couple relationship is devoid of the hierarchical protection that other primary and significant relationships afford (e.g., parent-child and family of origin). As in any peer relationship, the boundary distinctions are less clear. Because of this, both partners are vulnerable and negotiating intimacy and differentiation can be very difficult. In addition, couples, particularly married couples, find themselves the focal point of all family development with both family-of-origin and family-of-procreation needs continually impinging on them. Now that people live longer, the concept of the "sandwich generation" has emerged and taken root in our culture, as adults struggle to meet the needs of both their parents and children while trying to maintain the strength and security of their couplehood. Yet the extent to which people strive to have such relationships attests to its importance.

Each of us develops out of the context of our primary and significant (family) relationship. We bring habits, values, and goals drawn from this context to our couple relationship just as our partners do. Amid the stress and struggle emerging from our particular perspectives, we forge a new context (relationship system) to carry on the mandates of this developmental process for the future. This is an ongoing process that is never free of intergenerational influences or present-day pressures. It is in the negotiation of these stresses that the strength or weakness of the relationship resides. Communication is the vehicle through which this negotiation is accomplished.

Intimacy in Couple Relationships

Jacobson (1989) noted that although he and his colleagues were successful in teaching couples to communicate more effectively, couples continued to evidence intense and destructive conflicts. These conflicts were almost invariably about how much closeness or distance existed in the relationship. He concluded that the core conflict in intimate heterosexual adult relationships is over intimacy: "What I contend is that, in a substantial portion of the intensely conflictual issues that couples bring into therapy, the battle over how much closeness there will be in the relationship is the underlying theme" (p. 31).

Weingarten (1991) proposes a shift away from a global assessment of an individual's capacity for intimacy or the quality of a relationship to how each intimate (and nonintimate) interaction is produced. Intimacy is a reality that people construct with each other, and these unique constructions affect and are affected by prevailing discourse. Weingarten defines intimate interactions as occurring "when people share meaning or co-create meaning and are able to coordinate their actions to reflect their mutual meaning-making" (p. 287). The experience of intimacy occurs out of repeated intimate interactions.

Maggie Scarf (1986) defines intimacy as "a person's ability to talk about who he really is, and say what he wants and needs and to be heard by an intimate partner" (p. 49). Wynne and Wynne (1986) believe that it is not useful to define intimacy with such terms as "closeness," "warmth," "love," or "sexuality." Rather, they define intimacy as

> a subjective relational experience in which the core components are *trusting self-disclosure* to which the response is *communicated empathy.* . . . a key component is the willingness to share verbally or non-verbally, personal feelings, fantasies and emotionally meaningful experiences and actions, positive or negative, with the expectation and trust that the other person will emotionally comprehend, accept what has been revealed and will not betray or exploit this trust. (p. 384)

They emphasize that an intimate experience has not occurred until empathic feedback (acceptance and acknowledgment) is communicated.

Relationship Enhancement emphasizes the learning of skills that help couples construct intimate interactions with each other. The use of these skills over time elicits intimacy. The skills RE emphasizes are trusting self-disclosure (expressive skill-owning) and empathic responding (receptivity). However, in RE intimacy is established primarily through the conversive (interactive/engagement) skill, whereby couples acknowledge what the relationship means to them. Trust and acceptance are key ingredients of this intimate experience through which mutuality emerges. As Wynne, Ryckoff, Day, and Hirsch (1958) indicate, mutuality incorporates both distancing, or disengagement, and constructive reengagement. Perhaps the ultimate objective of RE therapy is to help couples learn to continue to reengage and maintain the continuity of their mutuality.

The Importance of Communication

Communication in the couple relationship has been identified as important by practitioners from a wide variety of theoretical backgrounds (Ackerman, 1966; Bloch & Simon, 1982; Gottman, Notarius, Gonso, & Markman, 1976; L. S. Greenberg & Johnson, 1986b; Jacobson & Holtzworth-Monroe, 1986; Lederer & Jackson, 1968; Satir, 1967; Wile, 1981). Gottman (1979) suggested that distressed couples are characterized by specific deficits in communication skills, particularly those having to do with conflict. He emphasized the role of affect in controlling both functional and dysfunctional marital processes. In a longitudinal study of premarital relationships, Markman (1981) found that "unrewarding" patterns of communication were predictive of marital distress five years later and that deficits in communication preceded the development of marital distress. In addition, defensiveness, stubbornness, and withdrawal from interaction were associated with long-term deterioration in marital satisfaction (Gottman & Krokoff, 1989).

Gottman (1993) has proposed a theory of marriage based on the relative balance of positive and negative speaker and listener behaviors. He identifies three types of stable couples: validators, volatiles, and avoiders, which coincide with Fitzpatrick's (1988) typology of traditional, independent, and separate couples. Validators carefully choose when to disagree and confront conflict while conveying some measure of support. Volatiles thrive on conflict and easily express disagreement, but are also characterized by laughter, positivity, and passion. Avoiders, who minimize the importance of disagreement, are characterized by separateness and emotional distance. Gottman (1993) posited that all three stable marital types shared a ratio of five positive to one negative expression during conflict resolution. He also acknowledged that as this ratio goes down, all three "stable" marriages change in ways that become increasingly apparent.

A recent study of short- and long-term effects of marital therapy (Snyder, Mangrum, & Wills, 1993) found that long-term outcomes were better predicted by couple communication, particularly emotional expressiveness and conflict resolution, than by other factors. This research indicates that communication training can be beneficial to any form of marital therapy. Relationship Enhancement therapy focuses in a structured and systematic way on emotional expressiveness, receptivity, and engagement by teaching three core skills: speaking, listening, and conversive. What makes RE effective as a couples therapy is that it trains couples in those communication skills that pertain so directly to long-term outcomes of marital therapy. Clearly, deficits in these skills are responsible for some of the difficulties couples experience that propel them to enter marital therapy. Of course, many other variables contribute to a couple's stress (economic pressures, traumatic events, developmental changes, family-of-origin issues, children, etc.), but what helps them cope with these pressures and will most likely keep them together is the degree of mutuality they can sustain by using these communication/relationship skills.

Surprisingly, the degree to which a couple attempts to problem-solve may not be a good measure of long-term outcomes. Snyder et al., (1993) state:

> Subjects engaging in proportionately higher rates of problem solving and information exchange at termination, also showed poorer outcome four years later; this latter finding was unexpected and may reflect couples who prematurely propose unacceptable problem solutions without sufficient disclosure and affirmation of each partner's *feelings* regarding the conflict. (p. 67)

This clearly supports RE's emphasis on teaching the three core skills that improve a couple's ability to disclose and acknowledge feelings *before* problem solving is taught. Often, as couples in RE sessions disclose and acknowledge their feelings regarding problems, the meaning of the problem dissipates and new underlying understandings emerge, making problem solution no longer pertinent or less so. Much of the time, after couples understand the problem by expressing and acknowledging their feelings, problem solution emerges naturally and spontaneously. This is particularly true when couples use the third core skill, conversive (interactive/engagement), to acknowledge the value to their relationship of understanding each other's feelings. This fosters *constructive engagement,* which includes constructive conflict engagement, an important part of conflict resolution (Gottman & Krokoff, 1989). It is this constructive engagement, fostered by the improvement of the three core skills, that makes the effects of RE couple therapy in the short- and long-term so powerful.

Support for the value of training couples in these essential communication skills comes from the work of Leslie Greenberg and colleagues.

Their approach, emotionally focused therapy, has many similarities to RE: It combines the interactional emphasis of systemic therapy with an emphasis on the importance of acknowledging and expressing disowned feelings and needs (L. S. Greenberg, Ford, Alden, & Johnson, 1993). Jacobson and Addis (1993) suggest that most of the process of change research in couples therapy has been done by examining couples in emotionally focused therapy. In one study (Johnson & Greenberg, 1988), successful couples showed higher levels of experiencing (greater emotional involvement and self-affirmation in the sessions) and more autonomous and affiliative actions (more acceptance and less hostility and coercion) than couples who were not successful in couples therapy. Another study (L. S. Greenberg, James, & Conroy, 1988) that strongly supports the importance of the core skills of RE found five significant change processes: the speaker's emotional expression leading to a change of perception in the listener; learning to express needs; acquiring understanding; taking responsibility for one's own experiences; and receiving validation from the partner. Relationship Enhancement emphasizes that these elements are most effective in a context of nonjudgment and acceptance in which one takes responsibility for one's own experience and does not project one's needs onto others. This is called "assertive expression." When speakers own their feelings without judgment, listeners' perceptions are enhanced. The listener then validates the speaker by acknowledging the speaker's feelings without judgment and with acceptance.

This process sets up a recursive cycle similar to that suggested by emotionally focused therapy (L. S. Greenberg, Ford et al., 1993). The increase in emotional expressiveness leads to new levels of self-disclosure, assertion, and self-awareness, which elicits a changed perception of the self by the other. This changed perception by the other leads to more receptivity (affiliative behavior) on the part of one's partner. When both parties acknowledge their feelings about this new awareness of the other (conversive skills), a greater mutuality (affiliation) emerges in which they are more accessible to each other, more responsive and more trusting. This process engenders more positive interactional cycles. They are more able to inhabit the relationship (Wile, 1981).

Change

Change in RE therapy is similar to Johnson and Greenberg's definition of change (1988). Essentially, a "softening" occurs, which makes the interaction more open, receptive, and intimate. Johnson and Greenberg define "softening" as a time "when a blaming spouse accesses vulnerability and asks for closeness or comfort from a previously distant partner. This event . . . constitutes a redefinition of relationship structure" (p. 176).

Change in RE marital therapy is also similar to change in emotionally focused marital therapy, "in which the emotional responses underlying interactional positions are experienced and reprocessed so as to create a change in such positions in the direction of increased accessibility and responsiveness" (Johnson & Greenberg, 1988, p. 176). The emphasis in RE on "owning" one's emotional expression promotes one's ability to access and acknowledge a new awareness of self, which in turn elicits new responses from one's partner. According to Johnson and Greenberg, "the process variables associated with change in Emotionally Focused Therapy are, then, deeper levels of experiencing and corresponding affiliative and accepting interpersonal responses" (p. 176). In RE, these process variables emerge when couples learn and practice *expressive* (speaker) and *receptive* (listener) skills. At the same time, learning and practicing the *conversive* skill increases engagement, mutuality, and intimacy and fosters couple satisfaction.

L. S. Greenberg and Johnson (1986b) summarize the process of change as a deepening of experience and an increasing awareness of the new aspects of self. This emerges when interactional behaviors are reframed positively in terms of underlying emotional states. Both partners then experience a redefinition of self in their relationship, which leads to a change in interactional sequences. As L. S. Greenberg and Johnson (1986b) state: "the partners' views of each other are framed in new terms, and so their responses to their partners are different, and they are more able to accept certain behaviors in their spouses that were previously unacceptable" (p. 261). L. S. Greenberg and Johnson (1986b) suggest five processes of change that occur in emotionally focused couples therapy that approximate change processes in RE therapy, outlined in Table 7.1

Deeper Levels of Experiencing and "Softening" in RE Therapy

An example of a couple interaction will exemplify how RE fosters deeper levels of experiencing leading to a "softening" very much like that described by Johnson and Greenberg (1988). Jerry and Sonia have just come through a very difficult period. Their relationship suffered significantly for seven years following a miscarriage of their third child. Jerry coped with this loss by absorbing himself in his business while Sonia turned all her attention to their two children (Alex, age 8, and Diane, age 10). At one point, Jerry included a female partner in his business about whom Sonia

Table 7.1 Specific Processes of Change in RE Therapy

- Partner A (speaker) is able to "own" responsibility for his or her intent by not projecting it onto another (not judging, accusing, or questioning). This leads the speaker to greater insight into self and motivations (feelings) and conveys an openness and vulnerability. (Expressive Skill)
- Partner B (listener) recognizing the speaker's openness and vulnerability, responds more receptively and empathically by acknowledging and accepting the speaker's feelings. This helps the listener perceive the speaker differently. (Receptive Skill)
- Partner B (as new speaker) lets Partner A (new listener) know how he or she feels to understand Partner A's feelings. This gives meaning to the relationship, fostering engagement and intimacy. (Conversive Skill)
- Partner A (listener) acknowledges Partner B's feelings, further deepening engagement and intimacy. (Receptive Skill)
- Finally, Partner A expresses how it makes him or her feel to understand Partner B's feelings, thereby engaging the couple in an even deeper level of experiencing. (Conversive Skill)

became particularly distressed. She grew depressed and withdrew from Jerry. When she did talk with him, she attacked him. Jerry became increasingly anxious. He insisted she seek psychological help. She refused. Desperate and helpless, he moved out. He then began an affair with the other woman, but ended it when she became more serious. Soon after he returned home, and out of guilt and remorse, he revealed the affair to Sonia. This session follows the revelation of the affair.

SONIA: I have a really hard time understanding how it got to where it got, as far as your friendship with her and that whole thing. I mean, you know, you have a way of . . . You keep blaming me—I pushed you out the door, I did this—and that makes me frustrated because, I mean, he felt pushed out, I felt pushed out. I felt pushed away. I feel frustrated because I can't seem to get that through.

JERRY: It makes you feel frustrated you can't get through to me, that I say you pushed me out and you yourself felt pushed out and that frustrates you.

SONIA: Yeah, and when you tell me I pushed you out, that's when this whole thing with her started, well, that's not true, that's not being honest with me. First, she came around, then she was calling and then I said something one day, and he said, "Well, you're out of it [the business]." You went like this right in my face, "You know you have nothing to do with this," and that hurt.

JERRY: It hurt you when I told you that you weren't going to be involved with any kind of the business.

SONIA: Just she was and that hurt. This girl is just working her way in. Here I am, Alex is back in school now and I'm trying to get my act together. You talk about being bummed out; my head was so clogged, it wasn't funny. I couldn't even think straight. I don't know how I functioned, like get those kids off, do homework, do all the responsibilities I had; I don't know how I did it. That's how much it upset me. I don't think I'll ever be the same person again and I just feel different inside all the time. Sometimes I feel lost, sad, by myself.

JERRY: You feel sad and alone because our relationship has changed.

SONIA: No, that's not what I said. I feel sad and alone sometimes because of what has happened. *(He didn't adequately recognize her meaning and she corrected him.)* I can't change it, I can't erase it. I feel I could have prevented it, but I'm not ever going to forget it and have to live with it. I'll never be the same.

JERRY: It makes you feel upset that things will never be the same; you feel they will never be the same. You're sad about that.

(He got it right this time.)

SONIA: Switch.

JERRY: That makes me feel sad that you feel that way.

SONIA: It makes you feel sad that I feel this way.

JERRY: It makes me feel like shit that I did that, but I feel two ways about that. It makes me feel shitty even talking about it because I'm embarrassed that I did that, but it makes me feel uncomfortable that you feel that way—that I was looking for that relationship and when I found this relationship, when I felt cornered or when I felt it was a relationship I had to get the f——out and quit and as quick as I jumped in I jumped the f——out . . .

(Jerry initially engages with Sonia through conversive skill and is open and vulnerable to her. But then he becomes defensive and explanatory. This makes it difficult for Sonia to be receptive to him. The therapist needs to step in to keep the conversation safe and maintain the boundaries.)

THERAPIST *(coaching Sonia to stay in role and not to become defensive)*:   Now listen to what he is telling you. *(To Jerry)* The last part was defensive on your part. The reason it is a problem is that she is going to get defensive. She won't be able to hear what you have to say. Now, what's the message he gave you?

SONIA: He's telling me as soon as he saw that she was getting too involved emotionally, he jumped out.

(She is still defensive.)

THERAPIST: It's important that you recognize the most important part. He feels bad and embarrassed about what he has done, and furthermore he feels bad, and is concerned that you won't believe that she didn't mean anything to him. If you didn't hear that, I'll have him tell you again.

(The therapist intervenes in two ways: using the expressive skill to reiterate Jerry's feelings, and structuring to maintain the boundary that Jerry is still the speaker.)

SONIA: I heard it. You feel embarrassed and upset that you did that and you feel bad that I would think she meant a lot and she didn't and it's important that I know that.

JERRY: It's important that you realize I just felt beat up too. As angry as you were with yourself, you were directing it all to me and I couldn't take any more. It's important that you understand that.

SONIA: It's important that I understand that you were just as upset as I was because of how I was acting, and it's important that I understand that.

JERRY: And then, I guess, when I realized I couldn't help you, I f——ing dug myself in—and I absorbed myself in that f——ing shit, lost sight of reality even though I didn't lose control, and I feel ridiculous about the whole thing, absolutely ridiculous, because I'm not that kind of person and I want you to know that.

SONIA: You want me to know that you're not that kind of person and that's why you feel so bad.

(Jerry is more able to own his feelings, and Sonia remains receptive.)

JERRY: Switch.

SONIA: I feel sad too because I feel like we just beat each other up. I guess it had to come to a head—it was ridiculous the way it went down, but I guess it had to come to a head. I feel sad, but I feel good and relieved that all that's over and a lot of stuff has come out. I feel like we've been renewed.

JERRY: It makes you feel good that all that stuff is over and you feel relieved now. It makes you feel good that we renewed our relationship.

SONIA: I feel like a big load has been lifted off my shoulders. I just look at things different now. It makes me feel good. I needed to make these changes. I couldn't go on the way I was going; I wouldn't be here today. I feel good about that.

JERRY: You feel good about that. You needed to make the changes and you feel good about that.

SONIA: Switch.

JERRY: I'm glad you feel that way because I think I've changed too.

SONIA: It's important I know that.

A softening has occurred in these last few exchanges as they express and acknowledge deeper levels of experiencing. They have become intimate and engaged in a more constructive way. Now that they understand themselves better, their interaction has *changed.*

PHASES OF RE COUPLE THERAPY

Relationship Enhancement therapy progresses in a systematic way through four distinct phases:

1. Initial/Introduction.
2. Skill learning/Supervision.

3. Home practice.
4. Consultation.

Initial Stage

The initial stage is extremely important, for the success of the therapy hinges on the degree of engagement and trust between clients and therapist. The empathy, acceptance, and receptivity of the therapist is critical to the development of trust and security within the therapeutic context. At the same time, the therapist also models these skills for clients.

After an introductory period during which clients and therapist get to know each other, share preliminary information, and become more comfortable with each other, the therapist asks about the presenting problem. The inquiry process proceeds in a consistent way (similar to the nine-step approach delineated by L. S. Greenberg & Johnson, 1986b). The RE therapist:

1. Helps the couple elicit the presenting issues/problems and the ways they have been dealing with them.
2. Acknowledges and accepts the underlying feelings that often are not expressed or even recognized by the couple.
3. Associates each person's perceptions and behaviors to the other's responses/cues as soon as this step seems appropriate.
4. Identifies the negative interaction cycles.
5. Reframes the negative interaction cycles in terms of underlying feelings.
6. Explains the principles and skills of RE and supervises the couple in a short, structured RE intervention to let them experience the process.
7. Describes how learning RE skills changes the negative cycles to positive ones, and agrees upon a designated number of sessions with the clients.

As noted by L. S. Greenberg and Johnson (1986b), this is a circular, not linear, process; deepening occurs as underlying feelings are acknowledged and accepted. Many clients experience sufficient "deepening" in the initial phase to change their perceptions of themselves, each other, and their relationship. As a result of this change, they become more motivated to work on their relationship and learn RE skills.

The following dialogue is taken from an initial session. As the clients describe the presenting problem, the therapist begins to guide the conversation to include elements of RE.

JOAN: He's always reading my mind. It makes me feel like I'm not responsible for my own thoughts.

THERAPIST: You don't like that.

JOAN: No. Sometimes he does that before I get a chance to think about what I want to say.

THERAPIST: It's hard for you when he knows what you are thinking before you've had a chance even to think about it. That's frustrating. *(To Ted)* I wonder if you understand that.

(The therapist begins to engage the couple with each other.)

TED: Well, she never lets me know what's on her mind. She never lets me know anything unless I question her and then she'll just say anything to get me off her back.

THERAPIST: You're upset about that.

TED: You're damned right. If she would only share things with me more I wouldn't be so upset.

THERAPIST: You feel bad about it.

(The therapist models acknowledging feeling.)

TED: I do!

THERAPIST *(to Joan)*:   Do you understand his feelings? *(The therapist attempts to introduce the receptive skill.)*

JOAN: Well, he's always disparaging me!

THERAPIST: That makes you feel bad.

JOAN: Real bad.

THERAPIST: It hurts.

JOAN: *(Cries)*

THERAPIST: You feel very bad when he does that.

JOAN: Yes.

THERAPIST: But I was wondering how you felt knowing that he's frustrated and feels bad when you don't share things with him? *(Conversive skill.)*

JOAN: Well, I feel bad about it too. I wish I could be different, but it's so hard when he interprets me before I get a chance to say anything.

THERAPIST *(to Ted)*:   How does it make you feel that she feels bad that you're so upset, but that's hard for her when you interpret her and she gets hurt? *(Receptive and conversive skills.)*

TED: I don't know . . . I guess I feel bad that she's hurt. It's just so frustrating. *(He has softened and become more receptive.)*

THERAPIST: You both feel real bad about this. I think this is a good example of the merry-go-round you two are on. Ted, you're frustrated and feel bad because Joan doesn't seem open to you. And Joan, you're hurt and angry when Ted interrupts and interprets you. This causes you both to be more defensive and repeat yourselves over and over again. You both feel bad about the effect on the other person, but are too defensive to change this negative cycle. If you could learn to be more open and understanding of each other, I think this would change.

(Both Ted and Joan nod their heads affirmatively.)

Working on your communication is important and I think could help change this merry-go-round.

They concur and the therapist introduces the structure, rationale, and method of RE. Joan and Ted indicate that they are willing to try it.

In the initial session(s), couples are probably not ready to engage in a structured skill-learning approach. They may resist too much engagement or intimacy, behaving so defensively with each other that they reject any closeness whatsoever. Mostly, they are eager for the therapist to understand how unhappy they are. Though they really want to communicate these feelings to their partners, they express themselves more fluently and feel safer talking to the therapist. This is therefore a critical time for the therapist to troubleshoot: both to engage with the clients using RE skills, which enhance trust and openness, and to model these skills. The RE therapist first integrates dynamic and didactic methods to help couples recognize the circular communication processes that keep them defensive toward and distant from each other. Then the therapist can help them understand the value of learning RE skills to undermine these negative circular habits.

When couples are in "crisis," anxious about the stresses in their lives, what they most want is to feel less anxious and hurt. At this stage, they aren't ready to engage in RE skill practice. However, the structured nature of RE can help ensure safety and reduce conflict. Once the stress is reduced, the therapist can identify the value of using the RE structure to develop the skills to improve their understanding of their own feelings and their feelings about each other, which can lead to greater intimacy and closeness.

Skill Learning/Supervision

This is the basic training phase of RE. During these sessions, the therapist directly provides structure, models skills, and facilitates skill learning. In subsequent sessions, the therapist gradually disengages as clients become increasingly able to use the RE skills on their own.

At the beginning of each session, the therapist asks if the couple has any comments or questions regarding the previous session, if any change has occurred in the interim, and if either partner has any concerns about the present session. Then the therapist suggests starting an RE conversation. One partner begins as speaker (partners take turns speaking first). For the balance of the session, clients continue in RE practice under therapist supervision.

The following vignette provides an example of the supervised skill-learning phase. Chris and her husband, Bob, a recovering alcoholic only six months out of a 28-day rehab program, began to see Dr. Jones out of concern for their oldest child, Samuel, who had been diagnosed with ADHD and was having school and peer-related problems. Samuel and his two siblings were seen in filial therapy, during which the parents requested an appointment for themselves. Concurrent with this, Chris had a recurrence of an anxiety attack. The initial session focused on her anxiety. In time, cognitive behavioral treatment combined with medication was integrated into the couples therapy. Bob also continued attending AA meetings.

The following excerpts are drawn from a subsequent couples session. Chris and Bob have been looking to move to a new house within the same school district. Last summer, before Bob entered his rehabilitation program and at the height of Chris's anxiety disorder, they chose Annie, a friend of Chris, as their real estate agent. During this conversation, Bob is expressing his anger over this choice: He doesn't trust Annie. Chris has been acknowledging his feelings as we pick up the conversation.

CHRIS: You talked about you not being able to communicate with her [Annie] on the phone. You felt you didn't get a choice of a realtor, and that makes me feel upset because I feel in August you made it very clear that you wanted a choice of realtor and I feel that you backed off and I gave you time and options; that's why we stopped. I feel upset that now he didn't have a choice. That upsets me.

BOB: You feel upset that you felt that I had a choice in August to pick a realtor. You're upset that I didn't know that.

CHRIS: And I also understand that my anxiety came into play a little bit and we decided not to go on with buying or selling the house anyway and it makes me feel good, because I didn't have to think about buying and selling a house (*anxious and defensive, she turns to the therapist*)—so he doesn't have to feel it's all his responsibility. The reasons I feel that Bob is thinking right now is that he had his chance to find a different realtor, but then we stopped the whole process anyway.

THERAPIST: How does it make you feel now to recognize that it did make you feel good to stop the process when you were feeling so anxious, but somehow or another that may be related to some of Bob's difficulties? I think that is what you are suggesting. (*The therapist helps her to acknowledge the underlying feeling in order to bypass her defensiveness, help her assert herself, and return the conversation back to Bob.*)

CHRIS: Well, I'm saying to Bob that we stopped the other agreement for a number of reasons. One, they turned us down and we didn't pursue it in August because Bob felt very strongly about having the house listed with somebody else. He wanted his choice. That was one of the reasons why we stopped. And then we stopped the whole process because of my anxiety, and I'm telling you that now because I want you to know how I feel; I care, and I'm concerned. *(Note the relevance of this topic to Chris's anxiety disorder and to Bob's rehabilitation. Very likely, this discussion elicits many unresolved feelings that pertain to the difficult period of time in their recent past.)*

THERAPIST *(models Chris's underlying positive feeling)*:   I would say that I feel bad that you're so angry and upset about this now because during the summer I tried to respect your wanting to find your own realtor and then of course I recognize that we stopped the process because I was feeling anxious, so I feel really bad that you're so angry about this now.

CHRIS: I feel bad that you feel bad about this.

BOB: You feel bad that I'm angry about this.

CHRIS: I feel bad that you feel angry about all this, and it upsets me and it makes me feel upset.

BOB: You feel bad and upset about how I'm feeling.

CHRIS: Please, that makes me feel very upset because now *(crying)* we're sitting here and I'm feeling—you just should have said "No" a long time ago.

BOB: And you're angry about that.

CHRIS: Switch.

BOB *(softening)*:   It concerns me that you're so upset about this because I care.

CHRIS: You're upset because it concerns you how I feel because you care and it's important for me to know that.

The therapist structures the conversation to keep Chris and Bob engaged, reduce defensiveness, and help them remain within the boundaries of RE therapy. Maintaining these boundaries helps to elicit the underlying positive feeling that they have for each other.

The following excerpt from the same session demonstrates how much therapist structuring may be required when the conversation gets "hot." Chris and Bob are both defensive.

CHRIS: I don't know if he got it all. I want to repeat it just one more time. I feel I protect you in a certain way to Annie, because I know how you feel, but when Annie did provide information about the house—I said, "Oh great, I'll talk to Bob, and I'll twist the little finger and do it." I could have prevented this whole thing, by you just saying "No" then. That's why I feel so bad now and I want you to understand that.

BOB: You feel upset about the fact that you didn't go to Annie and you didn't say, "Well, I'll twist his little finger and tell him about the house and get him to sign an agreement." You said, "I will mention it to Bob and see what happens." You want me to know that because that's why you're upset about it.

THERAPIST *(to Bob)*: Why is she so upset about that? Because she cares about your feelings. She feels bad to know you're so upset now, and she feels worse especially since she could have stopped it before and now it's really hard. That's why she wants you to know why she is so upset now, do you understand that? How does it make you feel to know that—that she feels that way? *(The therapist is structuring by emphasizing the underlying feelings. He then initiates the switch so that the couple will engage more with each other.)*

BOB: It makes me feel good, but upset to know that you feel that way. I do need to clarify that I was very interested in the house. Whether I had to deal with her or not, I was willing to deal with Annie to get that house and that's important for me that you know that because it's important for me that you know that I was not putting the way I feel about Annie in front of the way I feel about the house and about your relationship with her.

THERAPIST: Why do you want her to know that now? *(The therapist is trying to get Bob to own the underlying feeling.)*

BOB: I want you to know because you're upset about that and that makes me feel pissed, angry, that you're upset about something that if I had followed my instincts long ago, I would not have done . . .

THERAPIST: You shifted. You want her to know that you are willing to go through with this with Annie because you wanted the house. Why do you want her to know that? *(Trying to elicit the feelings underlying his defensiveness.)*

BOB: Because I care about her [Chris].

THERAPIST: That's why you're telling her that, but she hasn't gotten that message yet. You were going off into your frustration. Instead, try to tell her how much you care about her. *(Reinforcing the underlying positive feeling.)*

BOB: I want you to know that I care about you and that I was putting my feelings about Annie aside because I knew that you loved that house so much and I loved that house as well, and I thought it would be a neat place for us. Now I feel bad that you're so upset and that's why I want you to know that.

CHRIS: You feel bad. *(To therapist)* Yes, I understand what he said.

BOB: Can I speak? I don't think it's irresponsible to call Annie and get out of this deal. I think if you did that it is something that you are choosing to do.

THERAPIST *(to Bob)*: You're being aggressive—you're not owning it enough. What do you want to do here? Instead of telling her what you want, say, "It would please me if . . ." *(Trying to elicit a more assertive, feeling-based expression.)*

BOB: It would please me if I could sit down with Annie and discuss the way I am feeling about the way she has represented us and also about my feeling about the house with the problems that are occurring. *(He takes ownership.)*

CHRIS: It would please you to tell Annie how you are feeling about her as a realtor and your feelings on the house. That would make you feel good. That makes me feel good to know that. *(Natural switch.)*

BOB: That makes you feel good that I'm willing to call Annie and tell her how I feel about this. *(They are beginning to resolve this.)*

CHRIS: It would please me.

BOB: That would please you.

CHRIS: Switch.

BOB: It makes me feel good to know that.

CHRIS: It makes you feel good to know that.

THERAPIST: Great. It was a good conversation—a tough conversation.

Chris and Bob managed to stay close to the RE structure, but their dialogue was very emotional and they needed the therapist at times to provide boundaries and structure to keep them engaged. Nevertheless, they found a way to resolve this difficult matter. What kept them engaged was the fact that they both acknowledged, with the therapist's help, their underlying positive feelings. They also spontaneously switched speaker and listener roles as couples learn to do following the formal practice period.

Chris and Bob continued to work on their relationship for several sessions. They then began home practice, and after several sessions with the therapist, continued home practice on their own. At the same time that they were working on their relationship, they continued to have weekly home play sessions with their children. Chris was able to gain control of her anxiety attacks using a combination of the relaxation, imagery, and cognitive techniques that she had learned in the therapy sessions. She became markedly less dependent on her medication, which she began to take on a "when needed" basis. Bob continued to attend AA meetings and did not relapse. Six months after they had discontinued scheduled therapy sessions, Chris wrote a note to the therapist saying that they all were getting along much better. They were still conducting home play sessions, she wrote, and frequently used skills they had learned in therapy.

Home Practice

During this critical component of RE therapy, the therapist guides couples to practice RE skills at home in a structured and formal manner. Couples are encouraged to set aside a specific time on a specific day each week to practice RE skills; these home sessions run parallel to the sessions with the therapist. During home practice, couples maintain the formal structure of RE, having one speaker at a time who is responsible for the switch (see Table 2.6, Relationship Enhancement Instructions for Home Practice). They audiotape these home practice sessions and bring the most recent tape to the sessions with the therapist along with any other tapes during which difficulties emerged or questions arose.

Betty and Ken have been meeting monthly with their therapist for the past four months. This followed an intensive period of 12 weekly

RE therapy sessions. Supported by the monthly therapy session, they have become skilled in conducting home practice conversations. At the monthly meetings, they listen to the home tape for about half the session, practice problem solving, and then discuss issues and concerns that have emerged over the past month. The therapist identifies RE principles and skills that can best address these difficulties. It's important that the therapist emphasize the couple's improvement and positively reinforce their effort when listening to the home practice tapes with the clients during the session. Though home practice has become sporadic due to the pressures of daily life, the therapist urges them to maintain the sessions.

The following excerpt from one of Betty and Ken's home practice tapes exemplifies a skillful interaction. Ken is initially defensive, but quickly enters into a more revealing conversation with Betty that elicits his underlying issue. Note that Betty begins the conversation by expressing concern for the relationship—a concern many women share. Typical of many men, Ken appears to struggle with achievement and competency, which causes him to withdraw into himself and away from the relationship. This is especially acute in Ken's case, as he has just completed an extensive period of study in order to change careers. He is older than his wife and is beginning to experience some serious physical problems that interfere with his career objectives. Anxious and depressed, he further withdraws from the relationship. Betty, sensitive to her husband, has probably sensed his retreat into depression. Her concern about the relationship, though important, may mask her concern for his emotional state. Until this issue can be acknowledged, they may not find a more constructive way to deal with it. By the end of the conversation, however, this underlying issue has emerged—much to their mutual relief.

It is important to emphasize that their mere engagement in this dialogue fosters openness, intimacy, and understanding. This engagement is the primary therapeutic variable; solving their issues is secondary. In fact, it is only through this engagement that the relevant underlying problems *can* be resolved. This type of engaged conversation elicits trust and caring, so that many problems naturally resolve.

BETTY: I feel concerned how we converse with each other some times, and I feel unsatisfied with it a lot of the times.

KEN: You're concerned and unsatisfied about it.

BETTY: Yes, and it worries me because I feel like we have a pretty good relationship right now, and I feel like you're understanding me, but it concerns me because . . . we had been coming to a counselor on a regular basis, and I'm concerned that when we're not able to come that our level of communication will not be as good. That really concerns me.

KEN: You're worried about that.

BETTY: Yes, and it's really important to me to have a good relationship with you and I want to be able to look forward to having good communication in my relationships. Now as I get older, that's very important to me. And it frustrates me when I think that that might not happen and I want you to know that.

KEN: It's important to you that we have a good relationship and good communication, and it frustrates you when you think that we might not.

BETTY: Yes. Switch.

KEN: It worries me when you say that you are worried about our communication.

BETTY: You feel worried when I say that.

KEN: Yes. And I suppose it worries me that I need to be concerned about that . . . I would rather just . . . it's sort of like when you're short of breath, you're thinking all the time about breathing, and I would rather not have to think about that. It would make me feel better if I didn't have to worry that our communication might not be good at some point and what might happen.

(Ken is acting defensive.)

BETTY: You want me to know that you would feel better if you didn't have to worry about the quality of our conversation, and the fact that I might not be happy with it.

KEN: Yes. Switch.

BETTY: I feel bad that it puts a strain on you to worry about that. *(The positive underlying feeling naturally emerges.)* But I want you to know that it's important to me to keep our relationship good.

KEN: That's important to you.

BETTY: Yes, it is important to me and I believe that working on this will help us keep a good relationship, so that's why it's important to me.

KEN: It's important that we work on our relationship and you feel it's important that we have good communication.

BETTY: Switch.

KEN: It makes me worried when you tell me how important it is to you because I worry that I won't be able to live up to it. It's sort of like a threat, because if I can't do this sort of thing good enough, then you're not going to stick around.

BETTY: You want me to know that it scares you and you want me to know that you feel threatened by it.

KEN: It really makes me . . . it doesn't come across to me as simply a statement of fact; it comes across as a threat.

BETTY: You want me to understand that.

KEN: Yes. It's possible that it reminds me of some of the things that my parents did. Instead of coming right out and saying something, they would say it indirectly, and maybe that's why it scares me so much.

BETTY: You want me to understand that it seems indirect to you and that's particularly scary for you. It's like an indirect threat.

KEN: It also makes me mad because I don't like that sort of indirection. *(He is accusing and attacking her.)*

BETTY: You want me to know that you feel mad about it.

(Notice how Betty's succinct acknowledgment helps her acknowledge Ken's anger without becoming defensive.)

KEN: Switch.

BETTY: It makes me angry because it makes me feel like . . . it pisses me off that it's immediately threatening to you. It upsets me because I feel like I have to be distracted by your worry about the relationship and I'm afraid that it's already hard enough to work on our communication. I'm worried that it will keep us from being motivated to work on things. *(By expressing her anger and worry, she is encountering his defensiveness and his subtle accusation of her.)*

KEN: You're worried that my reaction will make it more difficult for us.

BETTY: Yes. Switch.

KEN: It makes me feel bad that I react that way, but I almost can't help it . . . *(Softening. Ken becomes more open as a result of Betty's encountering him.)*

BETTY: You want me to understand that.

KEN: Yeah, I just feel like right now I have so many things to think about—I can't really deal with it. I'm trying to do a lot of different things and there's just so many things I can concentrate on at one time before I get overloaded. So I'm worried that making this commitment to make this change at this point would be very, very difficult or impossible for me.

(Now the underlying issue emerges.)

BETTY: You want me to know that you're worried about that, and you're under a lot of pressure.

KEN: Switch.

BETTY: It makes me feel better to understand why you've been somewhat distant to me. I'm glad because now we can deal with it better.

KEN: That makes you feel better.

Their conversation continues by exploring Ken's worry about his job and the difficulties that his physical condition presents. He is scheduled for an operation on his knees. The taped conversation ends with the following dialogue.

BETTY: I'm glad that you feel good about being a good high school teacher. That makes me happy.

KEN: You're happy about that.

BETTY: Yes, and it's a very hopeful sign. It makes me hopeful about your ability to feel good about yourself. That's why the operation is so important.

KEN: It makes you feel hopeful.

BETTY: Yes, and it's important to me.

KEN: It's important to you. *(He switches spontaneously. He is feeling better.)* It certainly makes it a lot easier for me to have the operation, than if you were saying, "You have to go out there and get a job, and screw the fact that it's going to hurt." So, I feel relieved because I don't have to worry about that.

BETTY: You feel relieved that I'd like you to get the operation now. *(She switches spontaneously.)* And I'm glad that you understand how I feel about it. I feel better that you feel better about having the operation.

KEN: You feel better about that.

Not only are they both relieved and closer to each other, but they are also close to solving their problem. Best of all, the change emerged from home practice, which indicates that they have internalized RE skills. With continued practice, they will maintain their skills and generalize them to their everyday lives in many new ways. Monthly sessions with the therapist also help to reinforce maintenance and generalization.

After meeting monthly for several more months, Betty and Ken returned to therapy two more times, each after a two-month hiatus, and then were seen on a "when necessary" basis.

Consultation Phase

Once couples begin home practice, therapy sessions can be scheduled less frequently. These sessions mostly emphasize maintenance and generalization, but they also offer the couple the opportunity to explore other issues such as those relating to parenting and family of origin. The role of the therapist becomes increasingly consultative: Each session is guided more by the client and less by the therapist. However, the therapist continues to reinforce and underscore the importance of continued practice. Clients continue to bring in-home practice tapes to each session for supervision.

COUPLES GROUPS

The early studies of RE therapy with couples emphasized a group model (Collins, 1977; Ely, Guerney, & Stover, 1973; B. G. Guerney, 1977; Rappaport, 1976). As couples group therapy, RE remains structured and time limited. Typically, the group therapy program includes 10 two-hour sessions, but it can vary depending on group needs (see Other Session Formats, Chapter 3). Three to four couples compose each group. The focus of the group sessions is on individual couples, not between sets of couples. Besides being cost-efficient, group therapy is valuable because couples can provide support and modeling for each other. It is important to interview each couple separately before assigning them to a group to ascertain their appropriateness for a couples group and to provide information about the therapeutic program.

The couples in each group typically are diverse, but it is useful to have couples with similar issues (e.g., couples with children with handicaps, childless couples, or those in blended families) in groups as well. Couples can model for each other, double, and support each other when anxiety and defensiveness occur. An older couple can help a younger gain perspective, while those with children share insights with those without. Couples without children may recognize issues that those with children may overlook. In the presence of others, couples are often able to see their relationship more realistically.

It is important to provide adequate time for practice and supervision with each couple. To reduce the chance that one couple garners too much attention, begin with a new couple each session (usually the couple with the least practice and supervision). If one couple is particularly stressed, suggest having a private session with them between group sessions. An intensive program (Rappaport, 1976) is described in Chapter 3.

RESEARCH IN RE COUPLE THERAPY

Relationship Enhancement therapy and the body of research supporting its efficacy have significantly influenced the field of marital therapy and research, particularly behavioral marital therapies. Jacobson and Addis (1993) believe that the active listening and expressive communication skills of RE, when used by distressed couples seeking therapy, are as successful as other approaches. This assessment is based on the research of Emmelkamp, Van der Helm, MacGillary, and Van Zanten (1984); Halweg, Schindler, and Revenstorf (1982); and Turkewitz and O'Leary (1981).

A study by Halweg, Revenstorf, and Schindler (1984) described the communication skills drawn from RE as

> (a) speaker skills, in which spouses use messages, describe specific behaviors in specific situations and stick to the "here and now," and (b) listener skills, in which spouses listen actively, summarize their partner's remarks and check their accuracy, ask open questions, and give positive feedback. Partners who employ these skills should

avoid blaming, criticizing, and sidetracking, and they should increase their mutual understanding. The CORE skills are reciprocal self-disclosure of feelings, attitudes and thoughts and accepting (not necessarily agreeing with) the speaker's utterances. (pp. 553–554)

Results from their study indicate that couples treated with RE approximated the level of nondistressed control couples. Specifically, treated couples evidenced a significant increase in the amount of "direct expression, accepting/agreeing, and positive non-verbal behavior and a significant decrease with regard to the amount of critique, refusal and negative non-verbal behavior" (p. 563). Furthermore, the treated couples closely resembled nondistressed couples in problem-solving attempts.

In the first study of RE therapy from the 1960s, Ely et al. (1973) found that couples who learned to use RE skills made use of the skills after training and displayed significant gains in the general quality of their relationship. In a later study, Collins (1977) showed that in comparison to an untrained control group, couples in group RE therapy had significant gains in marital communication and marital adjustment.

A corollary study by Rappaport (1976) compared couples to themselves following treatment and after a waiting period. The researchers found that couples made greater gains during the treatment period; furthermore, couples were more empathic toward their partners and more sensitive to their own feelings. Couples also showed improvement in marital adjustment, harmony, communication, trust, and intimacy. They were more satisfied with their relationship and more confident of their ability to resolve relationship problems.

Wieman (1973) compared RE with a reciprocal reinforcement program, an approach commonly used in behavioral marital therapy. He found that couples who participated in both programs showed significant improvements in communication, adjustment, and cooperativeness over a waiting list control group. Although the couples in the separate programs were shown to have maintained these gains at a 10-week follow-up, reports from the couples in the RE group indicated that they perceived the RE program as significantly more meaningful and worthwhile than the reciprocal reinforcement group. A study comparing group marital RE and group Gestalt facilitation found that, though the separate groups both gained in the variables being studied, RE couples showed greater gains in communication and relationship satisfaction and greater ability to handle problems (Jessee & Guerney, 1981). Brock and Joanning (1983) compared RE with the Minnesota Couples' Communication program and found RE to be more effective in improving marital communication and satisfaction, gains that were stable three months later.

In a meta-analytic study of over a dozen approaches of marital and family problem-prevention/enrichment programs (Giblin, Sprenkle, & Sheehan, 1985), RE was shown to be more effective in producing positive changes than any other program. One particularly significant study investigated the effectiveness of RE as compared to the therapist's own preferred non-RE method (Ross, Baker, & Guerney, 1985). After a three-day training program in RE therapy, therapists were randomly assigned to couples, half of whom were treated with RE and the other half with the therapist's own preferred method. The couples were tested at the beginning of treatment and after the tenth session. Couples who received RE therapy showed more gains in communication skills, relationship quality, and marital adjustment. According to the researchers, "The gains achieved through RE are due to the specific methods involved and not merely to such nonspecific factors as spontaneous recovery, placebo/suggestion, attention, thank-you and experimenter demand effects" (p. 19).

Finally, a recent research study (Griffin & Apostal, 1993) investigated RE in relation to several key psychological constructs affecting relationships proposed by Bowen (1976, 1978b, 1978c). The study posed three questions: Does RE skills training increase functional or basic differentiation? Is there a relationship between anxiety and differentiation? Does the quality of the relationship between couples improve as a result of RE therapy? Researchers concluded that RE skills training helped married couples increase their level of differentiation of self, decrease their anxiety, and improve the quality of their relationship—powerful outcomes, as these three variables are the primary objectives of most marital and family therapists. Griffin and Apostal (1993) also confirmed Bowen's proposal that there is a negative correlation between differentiation and anxiety.

PREMARITAL RELATIONSHIP ENHANCEMENT

Research in the use of RE with premarital couples strongly parallels research with married couples. A study by Steven Schlien (Ginsberg & Vogelsong, 1977; Schlien, 1971), the first study of RE therapy with premarital couples in a group format, found that couples who were trained in RE skills were better able to discuss emotionally significant topics and to express themselves in less threatening ways, and were more empathic and accepting. These RE-trained couples also showed greater improvement in the general quality of their relationship, in their ability to handle problems, and in their self-perception of warmth, genuineness, and satisfaction with their relationships. A study by D'Augelli, Deyss, Guerney, Hershenberg, and Sborofsky (1974), which used the same data as Schlien (Ginsberg & Vogelsong, 1977), supported his conclusions. A study by Ridley, Avery, Dent, and Harrell (1981) found that couples in RE skill training groups evidenced significantly greater gains in self-perception of success levels in opposite-sex relationships as compared to a non-skills-oriented relationship development program. A study by Sams (1983) showed that RE-trained couples had greater gains in empathic and expressive skills and in problem solving than couples who experienced an engaged encounter (based on marriage encounter) program.

Working with couples can be a demanding, frustrating, and difficult process. However, helping couples experience their underlying feelings for each other, improve their intimacy, and become more closely engaged can be very satisfying. Often, couples will leave a session in stress and conflict only to return the next session feeling closer to each other. Successful RE therapy doesn't happen overnight. Couples who practice and implement their relationship skills for six months to a year experience the greatest gains. Many couples who end therapy after only 10 sessions feel as if the sessions were very valuable and continue to use the skills in their daily life. Some couples return for a periodic checkup with the therapist. Even as couples continue to evolve after RE therapy, many feel grateful for the skills they have learned.

CHAPTER 8

Relationship Enhancement

FAMILY-OF-ORIGIN THERAPY

Family-of-origin therapy extends RE's emphasis on developmental processes within relationship contexts. It seems natural to follow the development of the individual and family after adolescence and young adulthood to family relations in later life. From an intergenerational perspective, development continues over the life span and across generations. Though we might separate individual and family development into stages (e.g., infancy, childhood, adolescence, and adulthood), it is a continuous process. In fact, many of the distinctions we make are socially determined, such as being a student, achieving economic self-sufficiency, and marrying. The individual as an adult closely resembles his or her younger self; the family is recognizable from one transition period to another.

Bowen (1978a) described the "multigeneration transmission process" in which the interrelated triangles, arising from the nuclear family emotional system, are replicated from one generation to the next. Of course, he emphasized the replication of dysfunctional patterns from one generation to the next, wherein self-differentiation decreased. Bowen's objective in therapy was to break the intergenerational influences that impede differentiation. Relationship Enhancement takes a more positive stance, emphasizing the need to strengthen these intergenerational influences that foster differentiation. It is likely that as family members improve their interpersonal and relationship skills, those transgenerational influences that contribute to dysfunctional patterns will naturally be undermined. The interactional system will then become more flexible (a concept important to Minuchin, 1974) and more amenable to functional change.

Framo (1976, 1992) has emphasized the influence of Fairbairn's (1954) object-relations theory on his work with couples and their families of origin. Fairbairn's object-relations theory is one of "intergenerational transmission of beliefs, attitudes, and symptoms" (Framo, 1981, p. 137), which posits the importance of relationships as the fundamental motive of life. According to this theory, infants are both unable to give up the maternal object and unable to change it to fit the reality of their experience; as a result, they incorporate frustrating aspects of their interpersonal world as psychological introjects. These introjects become part of the personality and undergo various splits. As we develop, we incorporate other people as objects for this introjection process. According to Framo (1981), these intrapsychic conflicts derived from our families of origin force us to try to fit our close relationships into these internal role models:

> One's mates or children are perceived largely in terms of the individual's own needs, or as carrying for him his own denied, split-off traits. Mates select each other on the basis of rediscovering lost aspects of their primary object relations which they had split off and which, in their involvement with the spouse, they reexperience by projective identification (Dicks, 1967). A main source of marital disharmony is that the spouses project disowned aspects of themselves onto the mate and then fight them in the mate. (pp. 137–138)

Though RE does not take such a strong psychoanalytic perspective, it acknowledges that unconscious motivations arising from intergenerational process are a powerful influence on the development of the individual and the family. RE also adds that this intergenerational transmission process includes behaviors (habits) as well. Furthermore, RE emphasizes that bringing adult members of one's family of origin together in a therapeutic context provides an opportunity to square the perceptions, behaviors, and habits of their present experience with those of their past. Since so much (perhaps all) of our experience is determined by language, RE's emphasis on communicating with acknowledgment and acceptance in a judgment-free environment limits those nonconscious actions that may perpetuate dysfunctional interactions. The client and family become more open to constructively interact with each other. Once people can experience these remnants of the past in a context of present reality, without the threat of defensiveness and judgment, it is much harder for them to hold on to old complaints and dissatisfactions. This is particularly true when these complaints and dissatisfactions are acknowledged and the feelings associated with them are accepted by the people directly responsible. It typically emerges in RE therapy that underneath all the problems, members of a family care about each other and value their relationships with each other. Long-standing hurts begin to heal and new, more positive, relationships emerge. Most significantly, each person is free to live life in more constructive ways, less encumbered by the past.

Techniques in Intergenerational Family Therapy

Family-of-origin sessions take family members back to the source of their problems. These sessions expose internal representations to the external realities of current relationships, thereby facilitating change. This loosening process can help individuals act more realistically with others, particularly with partners and children.

Fine and Hovestadt (1987) have defined family-of-origin therapy as focusing on two generations: parents and their adult children. They prefer this to "intergenerational" or "transgenerational" therapy, which implies the inclusion of three generations; however, they use all three terms interchangeably. Therapists who do family-of-origin therapy take a historical view of family functioning that often encompasses at least a three-generation perspective.

Anderson, Anderson, and Hovestadt (1988) have identified nine techniques used in intergenerational family therapy:

- Constructing a genogram.
- Examining family photographs.
- Family sculpting.
- Anthropological expeditions.
- Comparing rules, roles, and rituals between generations.
- Using assessment scales.
- Bibliotherapy.
- Family-of-origin groups.
- Family-of-origin sessions.

"A *genogram* is a format for drawing a family tree that records information about family members and their relationships over at least three generations" (McGoldrick & Gerson, 1985, p. 1). With this information in hand, the therapist can shift the family's focus from the identified patient to historical elements that are related to the presenting problem; thus, the problem is generalized. This intergenerational perspective process eases the burden (but not the responsibility) of the family members who are in treatment.

Family photographs can be used to understand family themes and to identify specific issues, such as unresolved mourning. When family members view family photographs together in therapy, they can more easily visualize the very family relationships they are discussing.

Family sculpting (Duhl, Kantor, & Duhl, 1993; Kramer, 1985), a technique derived from psychodrama, asks family members to place each other in physical space; in other words, a woman asks her husband to stand behind her chair and her daughter to sit on the couch next to her. This helps bring covert interaction patterns to the surface.

Anthropological expeditions, a technique described by Beavers (1985), encourages clients to make a field trip to visit their families of origin to observe and study the rules and patterns of the family.

Comparison of rules, roles, and rituals encourages families to look at those patterns in their families of origin that persist in the present family.

Assessment scales, such as questionnaires, help the therapist and family explore family processes and the self in relationships across generations. The Personal Authority in the Family System Questionnaire (PAFS-Q; Bray, Williamson, & Malone, 1984) was designed to measure self-perceived levels of personal authority in three generations. It can assess one's present relationship patterns as well as evaluate the self in relationship to three generations. The Family-of-Origin Scale (FOS; Hovestadt, Anderson, Percy, Cochran, & Fine, 1985) is based on a family health model and can help clients become more aware of the impact their families of origin had on them.

Bibliotherapy has available a broad range of literature dealing with adults and their families of origin. Clients who are assigned to read pertinent materials can learn about relevant aspects of their own family-of-origin experiences and become open to the possibilities of change. Harold Bloomfield's *Making Peace With Your Parents* (1983) and Maggie Scarf's *Intimate Worlds* (1995) are good examples of useful reading materials.

Family-of-origin groups focus on exploring intergenerational influences in the context of adult therapy groups or couples groups (Framo, 1976; Williamson, 1982a, 1982b). These groups are also useful in training professionals (Benningfield, 1987).

Family-of-origin sessions, conducted with adults and their families of origin, bring families together to explore the history of their relationships and establish a different, more constructive way of relating (Framo, 1992; Headley, 1977; Kramer, 1985; Paul & Paul, 1990; Williamson, 1991).

Relationship Enhancement family-of-origin therapy uses the session method. Typically, the request for family-of-origin sessions arises from therapeutic work with other relationship systems (e.g., marital, parent-child). Family history is explored at an early session of all RE therapy, and the relevance of family-of-origin issues often emerges from these discussions. At those times, the RE therapist informs clients about the benefit of a family-of-origin therapy session. The therapist emphasizes that the client is responsible to request the presence of relevant family members. Even though family members may not agree to come, the dialogue that ensues between family members and the client as a result of the invitation can be therapeutic in itself. Clients are informed of this possible benefit of taking the initiative to invite their family members. However, clients are encouraged not to consider a family-of-origin session until home practice sessions have begun. Many clients choose to have such a session after therapy has ended; it can even take place a year or two later.

OTHER APPROACHES TO FAMILY-OF-ORIGIN SESSIONS

Early Influences

Bowen (1978a) has had a significant influence on the development of family-of-origin therapy; in fact, genograms are most often associated with Bowen's approach (McGoldrick & Gerson, 1985). His article "Differentiation of Self in One's Family" (Bowen, 1972) describes his attempt to have family-of-origin therapy with his own family, an experience that influenced subsequent teaching of family therapy. According to Bowen (1978a), "Families in which the focus is on the differentiation of self in the families-of-origin automatically make as much or more progress in working out the relationship system with spouses and children as families seen in formal family therapy in which there is a principal focus on the interdependence in the marriage" (p. 545). Bowen acted as a consultant to his patients, sending them out to act in more differentiated ways with their own families. His perspective has contributed to the subsequent development of family-of-origin sessions, particularly that of Williamson (1991), discussed later in this chapter.

Boszormenyi-Nagy has influenced family-of-origin therapy with his intergenerational emphasis, which stresses the importance of intergenerational loyalties and mandates (Boszormenyi-Nagy & Spark, 1973) and relationship justice (Boszormenyi-Nagy & Krasner, 1986). Similarly, Whitaker (1976, 1989) has written about family-of-origin sessions in which three generations are included. Whitaker (1976) writes,

> The parents usually discover in this real-life confrontation that the grandparents are much different from their introject of 20 or 30 years earlier, which may enfeeble the control residing in that introject . . . I must stress here that in many years of utilizing this extended family consultation I have never seen it harmful, although occasionally grandparents are angry afterwards. Also, I have never seen it fail to be useful. Many times I can't understand why, but I grow more and more convinced it's always helpful. . . . Including the third generation increased the power of our intervention in resolving the identified patient's symptoms, as well as helping with the multiple family problems. . . . The objective of such a conference is to resolve rifts in the family . . . the discovery that one belongs to a family, and can call on blood connections makes a great deal of difference to people who feel isolated. . . . Often the discovery of the grandparents by the grandchildren may evoke forgiveness and a group spirit. . . . Each generation group may come to admit that it is only possible to belong to one's own generation, so that role expectations are eased, and new roles developed. . . . Some members may even begin to make tentative forays into a new adulthood. Roles become flexible. Teenagers can contribute wisdom, oldsters can dare to be irresponsibly childlike, men can be tender, and couples freshly loving. Grandparents may become fun playmates for the first time . . . frequently loyalty debts and covert alliances are altered. . . . Discovering that one belongs to a whole, and that the bond cannot be denied, often makes possible a new freedom to belong, and of course thereby a new ability to individuate. (pp. 188–192)

Headley's Approach

According to Headley (1977), "To include the original childhood family members in the therapeutic process is an effective means for the adult patient to resolve old family conflicts and to gain new perceptions of his relationship to that original family" (p. 37). She emphasizes the developmental change in the dependency between parents and their adult children. She believes that though adult children are intellectually aware that they are independent from their parents, they may lack emotional awareness.

Headley is methodical in her use of family-of-origin sessions. She first introduces clients to the idea of having a session with parents early in the therapeutic process to give clients time to consider the idea. Once the client is open to the idea, she explores the various aspects of such a meeting, including the fact that it can have an impact on the client's therapy and that meetings of this kind can be unpredictable. She also emphasizes that as therapist she will maintain control of the session. Before the actual family-of-origin session, she meets with the client to discuss the issues that will be brought up; it is then the client's responsibility to inform the family members of these issues.

Headley (1977) has suggested a number of strategies for therapists to use during these family-of-origin sessions. First, therapists inform the group that the meeting is for everyone. They then clarify difficulties and misunderstandings that arise, reduce condemnation, and highlight significant statements. The therapist also models emotional expression and reinforces all family members for their willingness to participate. Soon after the family-of-origin session, Headley has a follow-up session with the patient to process the experience of the family-of-origin session and to integrate it into the client's experience. She also remains open to contact with the parents after the session.

Kramer's Approach

Kramer (1985) has "family conferences" to "help both young adults and their parents explore ways to keep in meaningful contact while still maintaining their autonomy. A new framework can be established for transgenerational openness if the therapist can establish an atmosphere which allows them to hear, accept, and finally, respect each other's feelings and opinions" (p. 124). Her family-of-origin sessions may come about at the invitation of the adult child or the parents. After introductions, the therapist sets the stage for the session by introducing the rationale and framework. Then she opens the session for all the members to talk about how they see themselves as a family. She makes sure to establish rapport with each family member. In addition, the therapist stresses the importance of family members acknowledging their feelings and recognizing how much they care for each other. The therapist also is able to use the information drawn from discussion with individual members later in the session. Exploring family patterns is an important part of these sessions; these insights can lead to useful interventions.

Kramer emphasizes the importance of sibling reconnection. Siblings can be influential in family change because of their long-standing participation in family coalitions and triangulations. Including siblings in these sessions and generating an ongoing posttherapy dialogue between siblings are important objectives of Kramer's family-of-origin work.

Paul's Approach

Norman Paul's (Paul & Paul, 1990) family-of-origin therapy arises from transgenerational couples therapy. His couples therapy involves discovering the sources of each partner's identity and how the presenting problems are derived from the family of origin. He sees relational patterns that reach deeply into the past and have a profound effect on shaping the future. His objective is to free the underlying hurts and vulnerabilities that restrict the empathic capabilities of one or both partners.

Although he doesn't seem to have a formalized, routine procedure for family-of-origin sessions, he does use certain methods consistently. He first meets individually with each partner and then with the couple together. Before couples begin the process of therapy, he has them complete a comprehensive questionnaire and three-generation genogram. He also video- and audiotapes the session so that the client and other family members can review it for feedback. The video camera focuses on each person alternately, paying more attention to the listener to enhance empathic skills. The couple is asked to review the tapes between sessions; this emphasizes the collaborative nature of the therapy (much like RE). After termination, the couple is asked to review session tapes to reinforce what they've learned about their relationship; this also undermines regression. After two to six months, each partner is seen with his or her family of origin. In sessions with the couple and family of origin, Paul uses "enabling tapes," which elicit a wide range of emotion and provide a vivid example of universal human experience. Clients are asked to empathize with and match the experience portrayed on the tape. These reactions are also videotaped for playback at a later time.

Paul's objectives in family-of-origin therapy are to elicit the multiple truths contained in all families, which help the family create a self-image that more closely approximates reality; to bring to light hidden sources of anger so the distortions they can create will be reduced; and to foster the emergence of new relationships through empathic understanding of old hurts and current needs. As a result, both partners can bring new awareness to their relationship. Past issues remain in the past, and the constriction resulting from unexpressed anger and grief, projected feelings, and compulsive behaviors is eased. This naturally leads to greater empathy for each other.

Williamson's Approach

Williamson (1991) asks the question, "How does the adult leave the parental home psychologically in a very complete sense and still belong emotionally with the family-of-origin?" (pp. 4–5). The resolution of this "intimacy paradox" will mostly determine how one handles this issue in all one's intimate relationships, particularly committed relationships. Williamson feels that "intergenerational intimidation" is the most difficult problem children face, and "the major obstacle in the way of the renegotiation of family politics and the establishment of personal authority in the family and therefore in life" (p. 8). At the core of intergenerational intimidation is the primitive fear of either personal death or parental death, which arises from the unconscious fear of challenging the established social and political order (power) in the family. Developing a peer relationship with parents and terminating the intergenerational hierarchical power boundary with the parents (Bray, Williamson, & Malone, 1986; Williamson, 1991) are the twin objectives of his approach.

Williamson's work on personal authority focuses on what he calls the "primary triangle" (1982b), composed of the individual adult and the parents. While he doesn't ignore the influence of siblings and grandparents and their importance as sources of information, his family-of-origin sessions are limited to this primary triangle. The client is encouraged and prepared to deal directly with the parents, the original source of feelings, nurturance, and personal needs. "In this way, both the ongoing relationships with the actual parents, who get a face-to-face opportunity to declare and reveal their own current psychological and social reality, and the inner relationships with the parental introjects change more or less simultaneously as they interact with each other" (Williamson, 1991, p. 13). The value of dealing directly with parents to change parental introjects is reminiscent of Framo's object-relationship perspective (1980).

Williamson developed Personal Authority in the Family System (PAFS) as a synthesizing construct connecting differentiation and intimacy (Bray & Williamson, 1987; Bray et al., 1984; Williamson, 1982a). PAFS can be summarized as:

1. Consistently knowing and directing one's personal judgment even in the face of familiar and/or social pressures.
2. Valuing one's personal judgment and being able to act on it.
3. Being responsible for one's experiences, decisions, and actions and their consequences.
4. Being able to connect emotionally with other people based on one's desire for intimacy.
5. Being able to relate to all others as peers, beginning with one's parents.

These themes include a number of family therapy concepts, chiefly

> detriangulation, differentiation of self, and establishment of a strong "I" position (Bowen, 1972); the achievement of "a balance of fairness" and "relational justice" in the family and the resolution of covert family loyalties (Boszormenyi-Nagy & Ulrich, 1981); the resolution of unmourned loss experiences in the family (Paul, 1967); the settling of intrapsychic conflict generated by negative aspects of transgenerational introjects and the subsequent experience of mutual forgiveness (Framo, 1981); the realignment of the family's basic functional structure (Minuchin, 1974); and open acknowledgement of powerful family dynamics moving backward and forward across the three-generational cycle (Whitaker & Keith, 1981). (Williamson, 1991, p. 42)

Williamson's family-of-origin method (Bray et al., 1986; Williamson, 1991) is consultative. A small group of clients (four to five members) meets for 90 minutes weekly, for 9 to 12 months. During this time, each client is helped to prepare for the meeting with his or her parents. The group experience includes autobiography, audiotaped letters and phone conversations to parents, consultation with siblings and extended family members, and informal conversation with parents in their home. This forms the basis for an agenda of items for the face-to-face discussion with the parents. With the help of the group and the consultant, the client prepares himself or herself to approach the parents from an adult posture and to avoid the intense emotionality that such parental relationships can engender. In the therapist's office, the client meets with the parents for two or three 105-minute sessions, with at least one night in between sessions. Generally, the therapist will give the family assignments to be completed before the next meeting with the therapist. The client and parents are encouraged to spend time with each other between sessions, either doing serious work or just being playful.

The consultation that takes place in the therapist's office can be divided into six stages. In the first stage, all parties agree to conduct the session. At this time, the therapist establishes a relationship with the parents and conveys the message that the client is taking charge of future sessions. During the second stage, the client extensively questions the parents according to a prepared agenda. The client tries to be compassionate and empathic during this time, frequently acknowledging the information received. The third stage, the most emotionally difficult period, requires sensitivity and gentleness. With the help of the therapist, the client clarifies and expands upon the information received to date. The client uses prepared and spontaneous questions and tries to remain nonjudgmental and nonblaming. During this stage, the client provides feedback to the parents, and reports on what he or she has felt and thought about a particular behavior or historical event. The client's experience of giving feedback is particularly important to this method of therapy. During the fifth stage, the client assumes a new level of personal authority. This is when an atmosphere of acceptance and mutuality emerges, in which no one tries to control anyone else. The last stage emphasizes the value of becoming a peer with one's parents and its generalization to all relationships, including those with other important parental figures and one's partner.

Framo's Approach

According to Jim Framo, who has conducted many family-of-origin therapy sessions since he first published on this subject in 1976, "One session of an adult with his/her parents and brothers and sisters, conducted in this special kind of way, can have more beneficial therapeutic effects than the benefits derived from the entire length of a course of psychotherapy" (Framo, 1992, p. 1). He has been particularly instrumental in bringing family-of-origin therapy to the attention of the therapeutic community. His orientation is drawn from object-relations theory (Fairbairn, 1952) and its application to marital relationships (Dicks, 1967). His family-of-origin work derives from four therapy contexts: family therapy, marital or divorce therapy, couples group therapy, and individual therapy. Although most clients for family-of-origin sessions come from one of these four groups, he also sees clients who approach him for family-of-origin sessions only.

Framo typically explores family history, roles, and relationships early in therapy. Many of the couples he sees for conjoint marital sessions he then refers to his couples group. These couples groups are composed of three couples with a male/female cotherapy team; sessions last for two hours. He approaches his couples group therapy as marital therapy in the context of a couples group. The therapist focuses on each couple separately, and after they have been engaged for a period of time, other group members are invited to give feedback to the couple, as in RE couples therapy. The emphasis is on transference distortions between the marital partners, not across couples. In the early phase of therapy, family-of-origin issues are acknowledged but do not become the primary focus of treatment; rather, the marriage is the focus. As therapy progresses, family-of-origin issues are brought in more often and the value of family-of-origin sessions is emphasized. Framo believes family-of-origin sessions are most useful toward the end of therapy because clients trust the therapist more, have already made therapeutic progress, have come to recognize the influence of past experiences on the present, and are better prepared to deal with the hard issues having to do with their parents and siblings. Similarly, in RE therapy, family-of-origin sessions are most effective after clients have become more familiar with and skillful in using RE.

Framo typically suggests that clients invite both parents and siblings. He believes it is crucial that siblings attend and usually will not hold a session unless they are present. From an RE perspective, the inclusion of siblings allows for the natural coalitions and triangulations to enter the therapy, thereby encouraging clients to change. Framo's family-of-origin therapy sessions last for four hours. The family usually meets for two hours on a Friday evening and two hours on Saturday morning. If the four-hour session takes place on one day, there is a break for several hours. There are advantages to breaking the family-of-origin therapy into two segments: Family members may risk more knowing there is a second session; they have an opportunity to deal with issues they couldn't bring up in the first session; and they are more able to trust the therapist after a get-acquainted session. Framo has been exploring a third two-hour meeting for some families.

The first goal in these sessions is to help reduce the family's anxiety. Therapists can accomplish this by taking time to get to know the family members and by stating the purposes of the session soon after it starts.

Therapists also emphasize that the focus is on everyone—the entire family—not just the client, and that the therapists' role is not to treat but to function as facilitators who will keep the session safe for all family members. As the session proceeds, the therapists try to help the adult children understand the extenuating circumstances present in the parents' lives that pertain to any alleged mistreatment or indifference. During the middle phase, the therapists intervene only enough to keep the discourse going; they exchange views in front of the family, one taking a supportive and the other a confrontative role.

In the second segment, families are primed to deal more honestly with the real issues. During the final phase, the therapists attempt to weave together the apparently disparate themes. They also encourage each dyad combination to face one another and talk about their relationship. (This is reminiscent of RE.) At the end of this second two-hour session, therapists try to create mechanisms the family can use on their own to restore and improve their relationships. They urge the family to listen to the tapes of the session and to send copies to any absent members.

After the family-of-origin sessions, the client is debriefed in couples, couples group, or individual sessions. Clients typically express relief that the process wasn't as bad as they thought it might be, and that they feel a stronger connection to their therapist(s). The therapists are open to contacts from other family members, but the members rarely make further contact.

Dail's Approach

Relationship Enhancement therapy's family-of-origin work bears many similarities to Dail's (1984) concept of intergenerational relationships. He believes communication forms an integral part of intergenerational relationships. In his view, communication necessitates three components—a sender, a message, and a receiver, the message providing the bond between sender and receiver. His concept of message is closely related to the conversive skill used in RE therapy. Dail's concept of horizontal or vertical conversational planes also has relevance to RE. He describes vertical/communication/interaction as a phenomenon whereby speakers move away from one another. In RE therapy, this is identified as a form of distancing, judging, questioning, being observational, hierarchial, or speaking in only past or future terms. The horizontal flow of communication/interaction is more positive in Dail's view, and suggests that people are equal in their relationship, a concept that echoes the core

RE concept of equivalence. In RE therapy, people are taught to respect this value and to learn the skills to maintain this horizontal plane without disrupting the hierarchy or roles within the family. As a result, the plane is infinite with no barriers at either end (Dail, 1984). The elements of nonjudgment and acceptance combine to help create equivalence. Keeping conversation on a horizontal level helps to reduce defensiveness, heal past hurts, and create the possibility that family members will build more constructive relationships with each other in the future.

RE FAMILY-OF-ORIGIN THERAPY

Although RE family-of-origin therapy evolved out of the author's own intergenerational perspective, it draws heavily on the family therapy perspectives and methods used in other family-of-origin therapies. In fact, RE family-of-origin therapy shares many objectives and techniques of these other approaches.

The RE model emphasizes the importance of differentiating past from present through family-of-origin therapy. RE's communication approach keeps families talking in the present and puts boundaries on past references, differentiating past (childhood) from present (adulthood). The RE method also emphasizes equivalence in relationships (no matter what the family hierarchy) and the importance of maintaining intimacy while keeping a strong "I" position. This method looks at the formation of self and family as a process of increasing differentiation over time. At the same time, this approach acknowledges that we never lose the need for intimate primary relationships and the "security" they provide. Therefore, the RE family-of-origin session helps family members achieve greater levels of autonomy as part of their ongoing developmental process.

Most significantly, the healing that occurs in the RE family-of-origin method arises when members of a family acknowledge and accept that they remain important to each other despite their separateness. This acknowledgment has the potential to engage all family members in an evolving constructive process, which is the objective of RE family-of-origin therapy.

What is unique about RE, however, is that these skills are learned. By adopting a systematic and structured teaching method, the RE therapist creates a nonjudgmental, accepting environment. This helps ensure that the family-of-origin sessions will be constructive and positive. It also allows family members to be acknowledged and engage with each other.

Clients in RE learn to recreate this secure context in their own relationships (generalization and maintenance).

Relationship Enhancement family-of-origin therapy typically arises from therapeutic work with other relationship systems, most commonly with a couple relationship. Bear in mind, however, that all families seen for therapy are interviewed about their family histories on both sides. This exploration usually traces family history back as far as the client can go, in cases to the date of emigration to this country and, if available, to the countries of origin of the ancestors. Clients are urged to ask knowledgeable family members for information to fill in any significant gaps. Often, the implications of this family-of-origin information, particularly those facts pertaining to the presenting problem, are shared with the clients. Typically, this is when the therapist would raise the issue of the importance of family-of-origin therapy. Therapists are encouraged to wait, however, until the issues pertaining to the presenting problem have been eased and the family has begun to generalize the therapy to their everyday lives. By that time, most clients trust the therapist and are beginning to apply the skills they have learned.

On those occasions when the nuclear family is overly involved with their families of origin, the therapist may decide to include the extended families at an earlier phase of the therapy. Both sides of the family need not be seen. Sometimes, one partner's issues with his or her family of origin predominate and/or the other partner is reluctant to bring his or her family of origin into the therapy. These choices are respected: The therapist makes it clear that the invitation must issue from the client. This is consistent with the person-centered orientation of RE therapy. The client then chooses or agrees to participate in the therapy in the true spirit of the important RE principle of collaboration between client and therapist. Thus, when a client invites his or her family of origin to participate in therapy, the therapist remains more independent of the emotional field and family transactional process.

When a client chooses to invite his or her family of origin to participate in therapy, the partner usually is not included, though he or she is included in all the preparations for the family-of-origin sessions. This reduces the possibility that the couple relationship will be the focus and thereby further triangulated. It also emphasizes the distinction between the past (family of origin) and present (couple/family). Framo (1976) speaks of the importance of not inviting the partner. Only on those occasions when the couple relationship is already triangulated by family-of-origin issues is it advisable to include the partner in the family-of-origin sessions; this allows the therapist to directly facilitate differentiation and boundary setting between generations. It also helps to free the couple relationship from the constraints that arise from leftover family-of-origin issues. Finally, it helps to improve the autonomy of the couple and subsequent family life.

Family-of-origin sessions usually take place at the convenience of the family. It is important that all family members feel comfortable in the setting, which can be the therapist's office, client's home, adult client's parents' home, a sibling's home, or a convenient place such as a hotel or restaurant. The choice of place is always significant and it is useful for client and therapist to explore its meaning.

The client arranges a convenient day and time for the meeting and invites all family members, no matter how far away they live. If some family members cannot attend, the meeting is held with whoever is available. The therapist informs the client that these absences may reduce the effectiveness of the meeting, but that a session can nonetheless improve the family's dynamics. Family absences need to be explored in the actual family-of-origin session. If even parents are unwilling to come, the session can still proceed. These parentless meetings often prove useful, because the sibling relationship usually recapitulates the dynamics of the parents' own relationship. In addition, a shift in the sibling system can be very constructive since this relationship system will likely continue after the parents are gone.

Before the family-of-origin meeting, the therapist informs the client of the basic format of the session(s). The meeting is scheduled to last for three to twelve hours and is divided into three-hour periods with breaks for meals; it can also adjourn until the next day. Often families come together for a weekend. For some families, a second family-of-origin session is scheduled within the next several months to build on the benefits of the first session. The meeting and follow-up are divided into six basic components (see Table 8.1).

Table 8.1 Basic Components of RE
Family-of-Origin Therapy

1. Introduction/Engagement.
2. The Review of Family History.
3. Family Interaction (Relationship Enhancement Therapy).
4. Sharing/Review.
5. Suggestions for Future Interactions.
6. Processing the Family-of-Origin Session.

1. *Introduction/engagement* is very much like any first family session. After introductions, the family member responsible for inviting everyone (client) talks about the purpose of the meeting. All family members explain their reasons for coming. Therapist talks about himself or herself and relates the orientation to RE family-of-origin sessions.

2. *The review of family history* is therapist-directed. All family members participate. Most often, this is a warm, productive, and often revealing interlude during which the family relationship system is affirmed. It can, however, be a painful and difficult stage for those families whose histories contain painful secrets, such as incest.

This is an important time for learning. Therapists can convey their ideas about family development as an evolving and essentially normative functional process. Families who understand this concept tend to have a less judgmental (less pathological) view of their family development, which creates a bridge to the introduction of RE therapy.

3. *Family interaction (RE therapy)* arises from the material explored while obtaining a family history. This is the focal point in the therapy. Family members engage each other and relate to each other within the structure and limits imposed by RE therapy. The therapist integrates systemic and structural concepts into the session to facilitate the expressive, acknowledging, and mode-switching (conversive) skills in a nonjudgmental context. The content of the family's interaction arises from their own dynamics. Each speaker is responsible for initiating the conversation with his or her own topic.

This is an enactment stage (Minuchin, 1974) whereby the therapist functions as a facilitator helping the family process their experience with each other in a safe, nonjudgmental context. First, the family as a whole is informed of the principles, skills, rules, and therapist's role/responsibility. The person who has invited the family is already familiar and skilled in this approach; therefore, that person begins the process by being the first speaker and choosing the person to be the listener. The process begins with this dyad and continues until all the members of the family have initiated a conversation with at least one other member of the family; if possible, all potential dyads take a turn. In this nonjudgmental, accepting atmosphere, the habits of the past—old metaphors, attributions, and triangulations—become blocked and the present emerges, in which children are now adults who can acknowledge the differentiation and "I" position of the adult children. (Their parents undergo the same process.) At the same time, family members can acknowledge the intimacy and importance of these relationships. In addition, the sibling subsystem shifts, enabling siblings to differentiate their childhood interactions from their mature, present-day interactions. Often, family-of-origin sessions move the sibling system to a more productive, present- and future-oriented level.

4. *Sharing/review* follows the interaction phase and allows the participants to step outside their emotional family field to understand the process. During this phase, family members can observe their dynamics and behaviors. This helps to keep the emotionality of the session within certain bounds and fosters further differentiation. It also allows family members to share the emotional experience of being together in therapy, which enhances their closeness and intimacy.

5. *Suggestions for future interactions* is the generalization and maintenance phase, which allows the family to see how they can apply what they've learned in the session to their regular lives. A portion of the session is set aside to discuss ways to build on this experience in future interactions together. The therapist emphasizes how the family can draw on this session to facilitate further differentiation while recognizing the meaning and importance of their relationships. Sometimes, a subsystem of the family (parents or siblings) meets with the therapist at a later date.

6. *Processing the family-of-origin session* takes place with the client, partner, and/or children. At this time, therapist and client integrate the family-of-origin session into the ongoing therapy.

Usually, the client initiates ending therapy shortly after this debriefing and integration session. The therapist then meets periodically with the client, couple, and/or children to help generalize and maintain therapeutic gains. Informal follow-up continues usually for a six-month to two-year period, during which the client ascertains that the family-of-origin session caused a significant shift in family life and that continued therapy is no longer necessary.

Preparing Clients for Family-of-Origin Sessions

Other therapists, particularly Williamson (1991) and Framo (1992), take a long time to prepare clients for family-of-origin sessions; in RE, however, this isn't necessary, because the family-of-origin session is presented as an option, not an expectation of therapy. Clients are encouraged to consider the value of these sessions, but they understand that the decision to invite family members to therapy and when to do so rests squarely with them, not with the therapist. The therapist is patient and waits for the client to indicate readiness. In fact, clients are usually encouraged to defer a family-of-origin session until they are in at least the home practice portion of RE therapy. Frequently, clients choose to have a family-of-origin session some time after therapy has ended.

When clients indicate their readiness to invite their family of origin, a session (or part of one) is scheduled to discuss organizing the meeting. Partners and children, particularly adolescents, typically take part in these discussions, even though they won't attend the session itself. Partners appreciate being included, and children feel they are equivalent members of the family, have a chance to see their parents more realistically, and can more clearly understand the intergenerational influences affecting them. Including the children in this discussion may also make family members more aware of the triangulations that exist between child, parent, and grandparent, and more amenable to changing them.

The discussion includes whom to invite and what to do in the event that certain family members are not willing or able to attend, or that no one is. It is often helpful for clients to role-play inviting each family member, particularly those about whom the client is most anxious. A discussion of how the family-of-origin session is organized and what the client can expect is essential to gain the client's confidence about having such a session. The therapist should also attend to those issues that are of concern to the client and explore how they will be handled. If family members agree to come, the therapist emphasizes what a positive step this is, and helps the client acknowledge how important he or she is to the family and to the cohesiveness of the family of origin. When family members refuse to come, the couple or family sessions can be used to support and help the client cope with the hurt of the refusal. This discussion with partner and children can foster increased differentiation. Even though members of the client's family of origin opt not to attend a meeting, the invitation can stimulate further dialogue among them. At such times, clients should be encouraged to use their RE skills to maintain involvement with their families of origin while maintaining their differentiation and the privacy of their current relationships.

When, Where, How Long, and How Often

The therapist needs to remain open and flexible when it comes to scheduling a family-of-origin session. These meetings are very hard to coordinate, and the therapist may have to cancel appointments and rearrange schedules several times until all the members can be accommodated. This is particularly important when members live far away. Often, clients want to schedule a meeting to coincide with a far-flung member's visit, which all too often takes place at the last minute. Often, whether a family-of-origin session takes place hinges on the therapist's commitment and willingness to help make it happen.

Weekends are often the best times to schedule these sessions; holidays are also popular. Some families find that an evening during the week is most convenient. Coordinating a date and time is the client's responsibility; the therapist need only be as available as possible.

A typical format is to begin a three-hour meeting on Friday evening, reconvene for two three-hour sessions on Saturday (with an intermission for lunch), and conclude with a summing-up and evaluation session on Sunday following breakfast. This Sunday session is optional; however, if the family and the therapist agree not to meet on Sunday, the family is encouraged to get together on their own and spend time together.

A single three-hour meeting is the shortest period of time that has been scheduled for a family-of-origin session. Three hours seems the optimum amount of time that families can tolerate the energy and emotionality these sessions generate. Breaking after three hours maintains energy and motivation. Typically, a second three-hour session is then scheduled for a later period. It is essential that the therapist remain flexible regarding the length of the session, the stopping point should be determined by the dynamics within the family. Therapists make themselves available for the maximum time agreed on, with the family understanding that the session may be cut short. This person-centered posture leaves the process more under the control of the family, thereby meeting their needs and respecting their tolerance for emotional intensity.

Most family-of-origin sessions are conducted on a one-time basis, no matter how many hours it may take. Some families, however, choose to have another session at a later time to continue or process the first meeting. Occasionally, when one or more members are unable to attend the first meeting, another is scheduled. In one family, a sibling who was unable to attend the first session because of travel constraints requested a second session a couple of months later because he wanted to participate. Sometimes the siblings want to meet by themselves while parents have a session with the therapist. All family-of-origin sessions are followed by a couple and/or family session to process the meeting with family-of-origin members. Sometimes, family members who have participated in the meeting request their own therapy with their partner and/or children. In all cases, the decision to meet is initiated by the client(s).

Probably the best place to meet for family-of-origin sessions is the therapist's office because of its neutrality. Some families prefer to meet in the home of the parents; this can be seen as a metaphoric homecoming and subsequent leave-taking. It's also possible to meet in the home of another family member if doing so is more convenient. When the meeting is held outside the therapist's office, the adult client responsible for convening the meeting should drive the therapist there. This is consonant with the client's assuming responsibility for bringing everyone together and also underscores the fact that the therapist's role is facilitative, not instrumental. This travel arrangement may ease the client's anxiety before the session and may also allow an opportunity for client and therapist to process the session on the ride home.

The Role of the Therapist

In many ways, family-of-origin therapy is similar to other forms of RE therapy. The significant difference is that the therapist has no opportunity to develop trust with family members other than the client. The success of a family-of-origin session depends greatly on the degree to which the client has confidence in both the therapist and the therapeutic approach. In fact, what typically motivates clients to schedule a family-of-origin session is their own positive experience with RE therapy. Some clients begin the family-of-origin session by explaining their enthusiasm for RE therapy and how successful their experience has proven.

Until the family-of-origin session is held, the therapist is primarily an agent for the client and his or her family. During family-of-origin sessions, however, the therapist's role changes significantly in that the therapist is responsible for keeping the conversation safe and maintaining a nonjudgmental, accepting attitude not only for the client but for all participants.

This new role profoundly changes the client's relationship with the therapist. Most clients find that the relationship with their therapist is enhanced after a family-of-origin session, and they report feeling both more trusting of their therapist and more inclined to open up. It's as if the therapist has become a member of the family. The therapist-client relationship is further changed by the fact that family-of-origin sessions enable the therapist to have direct contact with the client's family. Thanks to this reality testing, clients are no longer the sole source of information about their family. All subsequent sessions with client, partner, and children are enhanced by this new awareness.

During the session, therapists can use their own curiosity about the family history and its effect on current familial relationships to model and enhance the family's interest in family-of-origin issues. For example, by recognizing and articulating the family's development and the struggles it has undergone to cope and survive, the therapist models acknowledgment and acceptance. The therapist's hypotheses regarding events in the family's past and their connection to present-day concerns reinforce the family's understanding of intergenerational influences. Most important, when family members recognize that issues have evolved from previous generations, they feel less judgmental about present-day concerns. This perspective underscores the importance of coming together in the present to change and improve these issues so influenced by the past.

Another role of the therapist is to keep the family process generalized without focusing on one person, coalition, or triangulation. Relationship Enhancement communication skill practice accomplishes this very effectively: Because only two persons in a family can speak at one time, triangulation doesn't occur. By making sure that each family member initiates a conversation before the session is over, the therapist generalizes issues to all family members.

The centerpiece of the RE family-of-origin session is practice of the RE core skills. Keeping family members engaged in this process elicits a new understanding of family dynamics and of individual members. Skills practice also elicits present-time expressions rather than expressions about the past or future, which are distancing and disengaging. For example, consider the following dialogue:

SPEAKER: The situation was thought out and manipulated by this other person. *(This statement is descriptive, disengaged from self and past-focused.)*

THERAPIST: Why do you want them to know that? *or* How does that make you feel? *(The therapist focuses on present feelings.)*

SPEAKER: It makes me feel sad that I let that happen. *(The client acknowledges and owns present feelings.)*

In essence, asking clients to focus on their present feelings about past or future events maintains a present-day orientation and keeps people engaged in the present. In family-of-origin sessions, the impact of past experience is profoundly changed when clients acknowledge the meaning (their feelings) of their past experiences in light of their present experience. This creates a boundary between past and present, which further differentiates the family and its members from the past. As a result, the family becomes more flexible and open to functional, positive change. When clients engage in an RE conversation, the underlying positive message tends to emerge; this fosters ongoing healing in the family. Of course, these changes occur over a long period of time, typically six months to a year from the initial family-of-origin session.

Therefore, RE therapists use all their skills to keep the conversation within the boundaries of RE principles, to use RE skills, and to keep the four pillars of RE in mind. In family-of-origin therapy, the RE therapist often needs to structure, model, and troubleshoot more than in individual sessions, because other family members are not familiar with the process and because the sessions can become so intense.

CASE EXAMPLE OF RE FAMILY-OF-ORIGIN THERAPY

The following case example illustrates the process and value of RE as a therapeutic approach and of family-of-origin therapy itself. April and her family met for a single six-hour session on an Easter Sunday. The children, spouses, and boyfriends of the immediate family were at one sibling's home preparing Easter dinner and waiting for the session to end. This family-of-origin therapy evolved out of April's marital therapy with her husband, Steve. The family-of-origin session took place after April and Steve had begun home practice of RE skills.

April and Steve, an affluent couple with a five-year-old daughter, initiated therapy because they were unhappy. They had been married for seven years and had lived together for eight. At the time of their first visit, they expressed a sense of emptiness in their relationship but were unable to express any understanding of its etiology. In the beginning of therapy, their affect was constricted, and they denied intimation of their underlying experience. Talking to the therapist and to each other, their affect was flat and their expressions superficial.

Steve, a middle child with two older and two younger sisters, was born into an affluent and influential family in an East Coast community. His family, on whom he depended, had such a strong influence on his life that he moved back after graduate school even though he loved the West Coast. During therapy sessions, he acknowledged his nostalgia for the West and the friends he left behind and his unhappiness over not remaining there to pursue his career. Nevertheless, he maintained a close relationship with his family, playing the role of the perfect son. Of late, however, some formality and distance had entered into his relationship with his father, who was seriously ill at the time Steve and April began therapy. Steve was unhappy in his work as well, although no one suspected this, so great was his effort to please those around him.

April was the second oldest of five children. She left home when she was 16 years old (all her siblings left home as teenagers), had many heterosexual relationships, and lived with several men before marrying Steve, who, for his part, had only one romantic relationship before marrying April. April's growing up was unhappy. There were many conflicts in her family. Her father was relatively noncommunicative and often verbally harsh. Her mother was depressed throughout April's childhood and overly dependent on her children to meet her unmet marital needs. Nevertheless, they were a close-connected family by the time all the children reached adulthood. Though not overtly intimate with each other, the family compensated by joking around together; their sarcasm with each other created a kind of uncomfortable intimacy.

April and Steve began RE couples therapy and practiced RE skills for five sessions; after the sixth session, they began home practice. At this time, they became aware that there was little left in their relationship and agreed to get a divorce. They continued the home practice to help them work on their separation and divorce and because of their concern for how their daughter would be affected. After the family-of-origin session with April's family, they continued home practice on their own and decided to learn filial therapy to help their daughter.

Throughout the couple therapy, their family-of-origin issues played an important part. The value of a family-of-origin consultation, which had been explained to them in the early stages of the therapy, was reintroduced when they began the home practice session. April thought she would find such a session helpful and that her family would be open to it. Steve was reluctant to ask his family because his father was so ill. This was unfortunate given his continued attachment to and dependency on his family of origin. April invited her family and they agreed to come. The marital and filial sessions continued during the time that the family-of-origin session was held.

The following transcript is taken from April's family-of-origin session. April invited her entire family, and only her youngest brother was unable to attend, as he, his wife, and child had recently moved to California. The family consists of Roberta, the mother, age 56, and Elliott, the father, age 57, who have been married for 38 years; David, age 35; April, age 32; Nancy, age 29; Mary, age 27; and Frank (not attending), age 25. David lives in the home of Roberta's mother, who died a year or two before. Nancy is married for the third time. She has a 13-year-old son from her first marriage; she was 16-years-old when he was born. She also has an eight-year-old son from her second marriage. Mary is living with a man and has a seven-year-old child from her estranged husband.

   In the therapy session, the family took seats while the therapist was out of the room, leaving one seat free for the therapist. The seating arrangement was as follows:

THERAPIST: I have to tell you that, as I told April, it says something about a family that agrees to do something like this. After all, when you have grown-up kids and so on, and everybody gets invited, and then everybody comes, I always find that significant. There are lots of people who don't invite their families, and lots of families that don't agree to come. *(To April)* So, as I told you, and as we discussed, I thought it might be good to talk about how you came to invite everybody here, what you said to them to get them here, and . . .

APRIL: Right, well . . .

THERAPIST: . . . what we anticipate from this time together. Then it will be everybody's turn to talk about that.

APRIL: Well, that was through one of our sessions where we were talking about how the ways Steve and I relate to our families has a lot of influence on how we relate in our marriage. And then we got on the subject of maybe bringing in our families for therapy, too—for family counseling, a family therapy counseling session. And Steve just said, no way, he couldn't imagine bringing his family in, and I just thought, oh, I bet my family would love it.

THERAPIST: Uh huh.

APRIL: And, actually, most of us do. Most of us think it is a good idea, but we are just a little nervous.

THERAPIST: Oh, probably a lot nervous. Me too.

MARY: I'm really amazed, I thought I was just going to cruise in here and just have a great time.

THERAPIST: It puts a little pressure on you. It's hard to know what this kind of session is about. You've never done it before, so I'm sure you have a lot of curiosity about this. Let's start with you. *(The therapist arbitrarily chooses Mary.)* How did you feel about coming in? You said you felt good about it.

MARY: I thought it was a great idea. I mean, you know, we've seen, at least I have, seen a couple of therapists, and I think that basically the family has been involved in therapy throughout the years, and they have always been trying to get us in one room together at the same time, and nobody has achieved it yet.

THERAPIST: Wow.

APRIL: Until you, so that's really saying something.

THERAPIST: An opportunity, that's terrific.

APRIL: I had no real image of what I thought would take place or what would go on, you know.

THERAPIST: Well, I'm glad you feel that way.

APRIL: Yeah.

THERAPIST: Good. *(to Elliott)* How about you? How do you feel about being invited?

ELLIOTT: Well, truthfully, it's the same thing. We've had therapy before, for different problems in the family, and it's interesting to me. I have nothing to hide and that's the way I feel about it. I'd like to find out, you know, I'm always open to suggestions.

THERAPIST: Uh huh. Well, that's neat. *(To Roberta)* How about you? How do you feel about coming in?

ROBERTA: Well, I thought it would be all right as long as I was out of your line of vision.

THERAPIST: All right. Make sure I look out that way.

ROBERTA: And you didn't say anything directly to me. *(Laughter)* I can't handle that, you know.

THERAPIST: I understand.

ROBERTA *(to Nancy)*:   I should have clued you in yesterday when you said, "Why don't we all come in a different character?"

NANCY: I wanted to come in disguise.

APRIL: And have a little masquerade therapy session here.

ROBERTA: Yeah.

MARY: We could call it, "Guess Who?"

THERAPIST: Well, of course, I understand that you are a little bit anxious about coming in, and I'll try to remember to keep that in mind.

ROBERTA: Okay.

APRIL: Go easy on her.

THERAPIST: Okay. *(To David)* How about you?

DAVID: To tell you the truth, like the rest of the family has been saying, they have been in counseling, but this is the first time for me. So it's completely new to me. I'm just nervous, that's all, to see what happens.

THERAPIST: Good.

DAVID: Just worried they are going to tear me apart or something.

APRIL: That's one thing I was a little worried about.

NANCY: Me too.

APRIL: I didn't know exactly how it works and actually what our goal is, I'm not quite clear.

THERAPIST: Yes, exactly.

APRIL: And I started to get a little nervous about, was wondering whether or not we were going to have attack parties.

MARY: Wreak havoc on each other? Attack parties.

APRIL *(to Therapist)*:   You wouldn't let that happen.

MARY: And/or let somebody get emotional, please don't do that.

THERAPIST: I'm hoping that that will happen.

MARY: No feelings now, okay?

APRIL: God forbid.

THERAPIST: I think I'll leave now. If that's the case maybe I should leave now. If you say no feelings, I don't know what to do. *(To Nancy)* What did you think when you were invited to come?

NANCY: I wanted to come. I've had a lot of therapy.

THERAPIST: You have.

NANCY: Yeah, my husband and I, and my kids and I.

THERAPIST: Uh huh.

NANCY: So, I kind of like it. It's done me a lot of good.

THERAPIST: Uh huh.

APRIL: Nancy and Mary have both had the same therapist for quite a while.

ROBERTA: Yeah.

NANCY: Although you don't feel the same about him anymore, I understand, right?

MARY: No.

NANCY: I do. He's helped me through a lot of hard times.

THERAPIST: You appreciate that.

NANCY: Yeah.

At the very beginning of the session, the therapist inquires how the family was invited and how they feel about it. The family's anxiety is evident, and the therapist accepts it. Roberta immediately acknowledges her discomfort and insecurity, and April supports her. The therapist now knows that Roberta is someone with whom he must be careful. David is anxious because he is the only one who hasn't experienced therapy. April and Mary become playful and joke around, but their anxiety is also high.

THERAPIST: Well, therapy works in varying ways, and a lot depends upon the combination of therapist and client. Also, at some point in the process, you could realize that you like your therapist and find that you are being helped, and at another point discover that maybe that it's not helping you so much. I tend to work mostly with people in their primary important relationships, because I think that that is where the resources are, and that's where some of the issues are. If we could address some of those issues with one another in a constructive way, oftentimes we can be freed of some of the difficulties that not addressing them creates. Oftentimes, that alone helps. Now, for this. This works from my point of view in two ways, really; First, I would like to get all your names and ages, if you don't mind, and a little bit about the family background and history. Sometimes it's really interesting to review some of that; it's like a different kind of talking. I think, April, you told the others that I ask people to talk in a particular way. So, when we do that, we only do that. If we are going to work together, for the most part, only two people really can talk at a time, if you think about it. If a third person comes in, then we have more than one conversation going. So, what I would do is ask two of you at a time to talk in a particular way during our time together, depending upon how much time you want to spend together today. I would like to get everybody involved in that process. That doesn't mean that everybody will have a chance to talk with everybody else, but at least we will begin to process some of the feelings and thoughts. Under these conditions, one of the ways I ask people to talk is that they are not allowed to make accusations or judgments or ask questions. And I monitor that and see to it that those rules are maintained. And out of this process, oftentimes a lot of meaningful things can emerge. Now, one of the benefits of this is that you go away a little bit different, in a positive way, in terms of recognizing who each of us is, or who we are today, and not being quite as tied to old habits that come from our growing up together. And this recognition builds over time. So it's not as if we expect a concrete kind of "Ah, we got this," out of us today, but more that somehow there is subtle change emerging within ourselves. And this little bit of a difference helps us be more secure or more focused, or be freed of some of the constraints that perhaps we had before we came in. So, let me just take down basic information, if we could. *(To Elliott)* Your first name is?

Here the therapist is taking some time to structure the session, and to inform the group about some of the values, rules, techniques, and objectives of the session. He then takes charge of the session by talking to each member, one at a time, getting information about each of them and the family. The therapist begins with the father and then moves to the mother. This acknowledges the hierarchy of the family and prepares family members for their upcoming work on differentiation.

Review of the Family History

The therapist begins by asking Roberta and Elliott how they met and married. Intrigued, the children make comments and ask questions. Then the therapist speaks to David, the oldest child, and asks why he's never been married. Next, the therapist questions April and then Nancy. The issue of her having a child at age 16 surfaces, and the therapist asks why this happened and if family pressures contributed to it. The father responds first.

ELLIOTT: I really don't. Maybe Roberta does, but I don't. I don't see why she would feel trapped. We were living in Chalfont. I don't, do you?

ROBERTA: Well, yeah, I think in a way, um, it was probably Nancy's reason that they all left very, very early.

THERAPIST: They did?

ROBERTA: Yes. And, um, there wasn't a lot of joy in our house. Elliott earned a good living and he provided for us very well. I mean we had everything we wanted. But we just as a family were not very loving.

THERAPIST: Uh huh.

ROBERTA: Um, I don't think any of us understood each other. We all had problems that we kept inside. All of us were kind of self-centered. I was.

THERAPIST: You were?

ROBERTA: Yeah, yeah, to a great degree. Um . . .

THERAPIST: You know why that was so?

ROBERTA: Yeah, I guess I do. You know, I felt the lack of a perfect family. I wanted, I wanted to do it right.

THERAPIST: Um huh.

ROBERTA: And, and I just couldn't.

THERAPIST: You couldn't.

ROBERTA: I couldn't do it right, and I didn't know why I couldn't do it right.

THERAPIST: So you were unhappy with yourself because . . .

ROBERTA: Pretty much. Yeah, and I still am because of that.

THERAPIST: I hear some noises over here.

DAVID: It doesn't matter. It just matters how everybody ends up, Mom, not how we were when we were, when . . .

ROBERTA: In your perspective, not in mine.

DAVID: Okay. Well, I don't think that's all that matters, but I do know . . .

ELLIOTT: As long as everybody turned out all right.

ROBERTA: All, most of the children had a serious problem.

THERAPIST: Um huh.

ELLIOTT: Either while they were at home, or when they left, as soon as they left home, or the reason they left home. But, in my opinion they did, all of them, turn out fine.

THERAPIST: Um huh. So, you're pleased about that.

ROBERTA: That's true.

MARY: So to speak.

APRIL: Relatively.

NANCY: So to speak, yeah.

THERAPIST: But David was uncomfortable that you were . . .

DAVID: I feel bad that Mom's been that way.

APRIL: I do, too. I feel very bad.

NANCY: And you know what, Mom, I mean your life at home as a kid was not a bed of roses either, and neither was yours *(to Elliott)*. I mean, everybody's got a serious problem.

DAVID: Worse than Mom's at home.

ROBERTA: Yes, it does.

ELLIOTT: I adjust to that. I feel that just about all families, especially large families, have problems.

THERAPIST: Uh huh.

ELLIOTT: And to find a perfect family I think you are going to have to do a lot of looking, you know, especially a five-children . . .

ROBERTA: They didn't feel much, though, and you know, none of you felt loved. Is that so?

NANCY: I would say that's true.

APRIL: I have to agree with that.

ROBERTA: Yeah, and they were but we, we couldn't, we couldn't . . .

THERAPIST: Convey it.

ROBERTA: Communicate it.

THERAPIST: Right, and you feel bad about that. It is interesting, too, how quickly people had to reassure you. You all must feel bad about this. As soon as you started to talk about your unhappiness, everybody—David, April—they all came out to reassure you because of how bad you might be feeling. I would like to understand why you would think that you wanted to have a perfect family. You felt somehow that you weren't doing that, and you were unhappy with yourself. That's where we left off.

ROBERTA: Well, because I could feel their unhappiness. It was verbalized.

THERAPIST: Uh huh.

ROBERTA: I guess April started first. When April was 11 or 12 or 13, we were already at Catholic Social Services because things were just not going right. And . . .

The underlying, deep-seated unhappiness in the family surfaced when April entered adolescence. It is interesting that April was the first child to bring the family into therapy years ago, and that she brought them to family-of-origin therapy. When Roberta expressed that she felt bad, other members of the family, initially David and then Elliott, became uncomfortable and tried to reassure her. Clearly, David—the oldest child, a male, the only one never to have married—is very attached to his mother. Family loyalty—that someone has to take care of Mom—emerged as a family theme. (Roberta's depression is the metaphor that changes by the end of the session and fosters increased differentiation.) David felt compelled to reassure his mother after she voiced her concerns; when the therapist acknowledged David's efforts, David was able to acknowledge how bad he felt, then elicited more reassurance from the others. Roberta, however, maintains that her children didn't feel loved. Nancy and April agree. This unhappiness played a part in the decision of each child to leave home by age 16, and has not been resolved up to the time of this meeting. Yet this family clearly cares about each other.

The discussion resumes around the issue of the children's going to Catholic schools and Roberta's Catholicism. Elliott, raised a Protestant, had to take catechism in order to be allowed to marry Roberta. The discussion turns to family-of-origin issues.

Elliott spoke about his difficult childhood, his resentment about his mother's rejection, and his sister's caretaking. All this has affected his relationships with his wife and children. He tends to be reticent, unable to acknowledge his feelings, and critical to the point of acerbity when any hint of intimacy emerges. It's clear to everyone in the room that his growing up was as unhappy as his wife's; their children understand and share their sadness. The theme of leaving home at 16 is linked to Elliott's teenage experience. Living with his family for the first few years of their marriage was also difficult and took its toll on David, who was born during this time, has had sleeping difficulties, and is uncomfortable to this day.

Elliott continued talking about the hurt and anger he experienced in his relationship to his mother. The discussion about Elliott's parents' intimacy led to a discussion of his own difficulties in this area. Elliott acknowledged the truth of the therapist's hypothesis that he feels closer to his sons than his daughters. The therapist wanted Elliott's children to understand their father's difficulty being intimate, and to see that this difficulty stemmed from his upbringing. This would enable the children to accept their father—and ultimately themselves. But it is Roberta who picks up the cue and talks about the lack of intimacy in her relationship with her husband and its effect on the children.

ROBERTA: Um, Elliott always provided us with the creature comforts and the physical things, but I just always felt like I was all alone.

THERAPIST: Uh huh.

ROBERTA: Raising the family. And I think I took a lot of the frustration out on the kids, because I know they all felt that they were in the way.

THERAPIST: In the way?

ROBERTA: Yes.

THERAPIST: Of what?

ROBERTA: Well, just in our way.

THERAPIST: In your way?

ROBERTA: Yeah. We didn't really want them.

THERAPIST: That's the way they felt.

ROBERTA: Yeah.

THERAPIST: How do you know that?

ROBERTA: They told me.

THERAPIST: And how do you feel about that?

ROBERTA: Well, I sure wish I could go back and do it again.

THERAPIST: You're unhappy about that?

ROBERTA: Yeah, I am, very unhappy.

DAVID: Look at it all. They all have heartaches. Mom and Dad stayed together, but it was a rough time. I just don't see any benefits in it. So I guess what you are saying is true, Mom, you know.

ROBERTA: I mean, what I meant . . .

DAVID: But I don't hold it against you, or anything, you know . . .

ROBERTA: Yeah, I know you don't.

THERAPIST: You're worried about that, though.

DAVID: Yeah, she only . . .

ROBERTA: And there's a fear there, of getting into the same kind of relationship that Dad and I had. *(The intergenerational influences are being acknowledged.)*

DAVID: Yeah. There is.

ROBERTA: I mean, some men see their mothers as significant, positive personalities, and I don't. I don't think any of my kids have seen me as a positive force.

THERAPIST: You must feel bad about that.

ROBERTA: Well, I . . .

DAVID: We do, we see you now, I do personally, as a positive force in my life.

NANCY: Yeah, Mom, I do too.

THERAPIST: I want to point out to you something about your son, David. Every time you show some signs of distress, he wants to reassure you.

DAVID: Yeah, she takes things too hard.

   (Laughter)

THERAPIST: I want to point that out to you.

ROBERTA: Why should they have to?

THERAPIST: Why should they have to?

ROBERTA: Yeah.

THERAPIST: Because you still feel so unhappy.

DAVID: Yeah, you make us feel guilty.

MARY: Absolutely.

DAVID: Like we did something wrong.

ROBERTA: All right.

NANCY: Yeah.

THERAPIST: And today might be a chance to . . .

APRIL: It's true.

THERAPIST: To do that. In our talk session.

Here the therapist focuses on the primary theme of the mother's unhappiness and its effect on the children. David concurs and the others acknowledge this as well. To help Roberta cope with her discomfort, the therapist suggests that this be addressed in the RE portion of the session.

MARY: Oh, this is getting good.

THERAPIST: It's upsetting to you a little bit; it's hard, I understand. But that's . . .

DAVID: She's the central figure in the family. In the family structure.

THERAPIST: Absolutely.

ROBERTA: No, we both are.

DAVID: Well, but still you're the mom, so it's basically that.

Elliott shifts the focus onto him to help relieve Roberta's discomfort. The therapist's acknowledgment of him enables him to explain that his discomfort as a disciplinarian arose from fears about his own anger. Roberta feels relieved. Elliott continues to talk and becomes increasingly self-explorative. This is followed by Nancy's expressing her worry that her son might be affected by these same forces.

The family is deeply sad. The therapist employs structuring to help keep the session safe. He also becomes didactic. He continues to inquire about each of the members, including the youngest son, who is not present.

Family Interaction

After the review of family history is complete, the therapist introduces the next phase of the session.

THERAPIST: I would like to proceed. The next phase of what we'll do today needs an explanation. Of course, April, you've had some experience with this. I think you've shared it with them, have you?

APRIL: No, I don't think I've told everybody.

THERAPIST: Maybe you might talk about that a little before I talk about what it is, in fact, we do. Would you?

APRIL: Well, I just want to say, first off, that I've found it very effective, the technique that you use. It teaches a person how to communicate, how to express themselves in a positive way, in a way that that helps the other person really understand how you feel, and then on the other side of it, it teaches you how to listen, without judgments or questions or changing the subject, so to speak, to really just be open and listen to what the other person is saying. By following the process, you find that you really do discover things that you wouldn't have discovered if you spoke just the way we do every day. There are just so many defenses and there are so many other things going on. You learn how to not allow yourself to fall into these traps. It works.

THERAPIST: Uh huh.

APRIL: You find out about each other.

THERAPIST: And yourself.

APRIL: And yourself. That's true.

THERAPIST: A lot of self-learning in the process. I'm pleased that you perceive it that way.

APRIL: Yeah, I do.

The therapist then explains the rationale, structure, rules, and process of RE. He also explains that two people will converse in this way at one time and that each person will have an opportunity to initiate a conversation.

THERAPIST: Okay, so, since April invited all of you, April's agreed to be first. And she has some experience with this, so that helps.

APRIL: I just got nervous.

THERAPIST: Uh huh.

MARY: Yeah, 'cause you're on now.

THERAPIST: Yeah, well it does. It makes you anxious 'cause you know what you have to do is you have to give up some of your defenses. It makes you much more vulnerable.

APRIL: Yeah.

MARY: Uh huh.

THERAPIST: And the only reason it can be safe to do that is because the other person you are talking to must be nonjudgmental also.

NANCY: Uh huh.

THERAPIST: That's why I hope that you will find that this is more secure than it would be if we had a normal conversation. And my presence adds, for now, a certain benefit because this is my office and I will insist on your keeping within those boundaries that I've just described. So, April's first, and she'll be the first speaker.

APRIL: Okay.

THERAPIST: And you have to pick someone to talk to first.

APRIL: I'll talk to Mary.

THERAPIST: Okay.

The theme of April's conversation is that she cannot be open and affectionate in her marriage or in her family of origin. She decides to speak first to her sister, who may appear a "safe" choice. April and Mary continue their conversation. At the end they and the family talk with the therapist about this first RE conversation. April and Mary feel good about it. Nancy thinks "It's terrific," and hopes that she can incorporate this into her life outside of the session. Roberta also hopes that RE techniques can be used in other places. Elliott struggles to understand the process and says so. He feels anxious and defensive. He asks Roberta if she understands and she says "Yes." Then Elliott asks, "Am I stupid or what?" The therapist responds.

THERAPIST: Well, you're worried about that. I mean you're concerned about that. I understand what's making you uncomfortable because you're not used to it. It all fosters a little bit more openness and vulnerability than you're accustomed to. I think your not understanding it is more like just being uncomfortable about that. And I would never force you to, uh, go further than you would feel comfortable with. I want you to understand that, and I want to help you too. I'll give you words and guide you, to help you to be able to do this more. Because I recognize that this is not familiar to you, and what makes me feel good is that you raised it, you didn't hide it.

ELLIOTT: Yeah.

THERAPIST: That makes me feel good because I think that you have a lot of emotions that you just don't let yourself show.

ELLIOTT: Can't express it.

THERAPIST: Right. And I'm hopeful that maybe through this process you will be able to express some of it. In fact, I was going to ask Mary to be next, but maybe you would like to volunteer to be next.

ELLIOTT: Well, if I volunteered I really don't know what I'm volunteering for.

THERAPIST: Okay. Well, it would just be to pick somebody here to talk to about something. It doesn't matter what as long as it's important to you.

ELLIOTT: Well, uh, I'll pick David.

DAVID: Oh no.

   (Laughter)

THERAPIST: All right. Good.

Elliott's willingness to initiate a conversation even though he seemed defensive and resistant was a surprising development. It is also interesting that he picked David to speak to. Perhaps he was motivated to overcome his defensiveness because the conversation between April and Mary affected him so deeply. He stated earlier that it was easier for him to talk to men than women. However, here he chooses to talk with his son about a deeply sensitive topic, abandonment, that acknowledges the depth of his feeling. Most men have difficulty talking about their feelings, especially with their sons and fathers. How moving it was for Elliott and David, two family members who have the most trouble expressing their emotions, to have the opportunity to engage in such a touching and meaningful conversation.

As they continue to share their feelings about this, they become more comfortable. At the end of the dialogue, they both talk about how hard it is for them to express feelings. The therapist reinforces their effort and encourages them to continue to practice talking this way.

The therapist then says, "Well, there are two people who haven't talked yet" (referring to Nancy and Roberta).

NANCY: I'll do it.
THERAPIST: Who do you want to talk to?
NANCY: I want to talk to Mary.
THERAPIST: Okay.
MARY: I knew it.
NANCY: I'm not sure how to start off.
THERAPIST: All right. Tell me what you'd like to say. Do you know what you want to talk about?
NANCY: Yeah. I want to say, should I just tell you what I want to say? Or say it?
THERAPIST: You could say it to her, if you want, or I could model it for you. Either way.

In this segment, Nancy brought up a critically important and emotional subject that had caused great hurt and created great distance in her relationship with her sister. Since it was also the first time that both Nancy and Mary met with the therapist, he had to stay very involved in their conversation. In effect, he controlled the structure of the interaction, modeling specific expressions for both speaker and listener. If at times it seemed as if he was putting words into their mouths, he was, in fact, merely structuring the deep-seated feelings that arose from the sisters themselves. Generally, clients feel comfortable correcting a therapist if he or she inaccurately models a feeling. The therapist then explores this misunderstanding with the client until the therapist can model the feeling correctly. In fact, the sisters appreciated the degree to which the therapist was involved; his use of the principles, rules, and structure of RE kept them engaged in a safe conversation. At its end, they were both able to affirm their mutual caring and the importance of their relationship.

The sisters' conversation had a profound impact on the family. Up until this moment, everyone had been sensitive to Roberta's discomfort and tried to protect her by not engaging in a conversation with her. Now, Nancy senses that her mother is upset and turns to her. The therapist responds by encouraging Roberta to move closer to the group.

THERAPIST: It's Mom's turn. During that time you were crying some. So, if you could move your chair in a little bit, 'cause, uh, you're not in the video, and it would be good to, you know, since you're going to get a copy of this to have. Move in a little bit more.

MARY: She can have my spot.

(Laughter)

APRIL *(to Roberta)*:   Interesting how you got rid of that smile.

(Laughter. The others are anxious.)

THERAPIST: Move just a little bit closer, that would be good. Now, you're free to pick anybody you want to talk to. The choice is yours.

ROBERTA: Well, this, this is a hard decision because I have things to say to everybody, but . . .

THERAPIST: Well, we could try to do that. I mean, I'm here as long as we're comfortable doing this. But it would be good for you to pick somebody first, and perhaps proceed from there.

ROBERTA: Okay, um, I guess I'll speak to Nancy.

This conversation forms the nucleus of the session. Up until now, everyone was deferring to their mother. Recognizing her sensitivity and bad feelings, her family was reluctant to encounter her. However, the emotionality of the session, the security of the therapeutic context, and the therapist's acceptance all helped Roberta initiate a conversation. She chose Nancy to converse with, sensing that Nancy was the family member with whom she could most naturally form a strong coalition. In the past, Roberta had turned to Nancy to meet some of the needs that weren't being met by her husband.

Nancy then drew her mother deeper into the process by asserting that she had a different view of her mother than Roberta assumed. Nancy was able to acknowledge Roberta's suffering, but at the same time assert that she felt good about herself and her relationship with her mother. By the end of this conversation, Nancy said how bad she felt that her mother couldn't talk to her about this before, and asserted that she wanted Roberta to try to say what was on her mind. In effect, Nancy acknowledged and asserted her own adult status and her equivalence and peer status with her mother.

Now Roberta's depression, bad feeling, and shame for how she treated her children were all on the table. That her negative feelings have been the force keeping her children emotionally attached to the family and unable to establish secure, intimate relationships with peers and siblings is no longer a "family secret," something everyone knows and nobody can talk about. Most likely, this family secret has been instrumental in keeping the family and its members trapped in the past.

April wants to talk with her mother about how bad she feels. Her dilemma, from which she has suffered since adolescence, revolves around not being free to fully pursue her own direction because of concern regarding her mother's unhappiness.

April asserts that she sees her mother differently than Roberta sees herself. April takes responsibility for (owns) her own feelings of how much she appreciates her mother and believes her to be a good mother. By taking responsibility, April also establishes a boundary that challenges her mother. This is a move toward differentiation, freeing Roberta from ruminating on the past and opening up a relationship with her daughter based on present-day realities. Making a move toward equivalence, April continues to talk about feeling bad and angry with herself for the pain her actions caused her mother, and Roberta responds.

APRIL: Switch.

THERAPIST *(prompting)*:   It makes me feel to know that . . .

ROBERTA: That makes me feel real good to know that. I guess I wanted to hear that. I think I needed to hear that, and was afraid or something. It was too difficult to talk about it.

THERAPIST: And now I feel . . .

ROBERTA: And I feel good that I, that you said it.

APRIL: You feel good that I've said what I have because you did need to hear that, and it helps you to know how I feel now.

ROBERTA: Uh huh.

THERAPIST: She feels good because it's been so difficult to say that.

APRIL: You feel relieved that you have said what you have. It's been very hard for you to say that.

ROBERTA: Uh huh.

APRIL: And you want me to know that.

ROBERTA: I want you to know that what you think is important to me. I'm upset to think that, I'm sad to think that you're upset that you might have caused me to feel bad about myself. I don't want you to entertain thoughts like that.

THERAPIST: Why shouldn't she?

ROBERTA: Because it's just . . .

THERAPIST: That's a judgment.

ROBERTA: Because . . .

THERAPIST: It's not true, or it is true.

ROBERTA: No.

THERAPIST: If it's true, you've got to tell her.

ROBERTA: It's not true.

THERAPIST: It's not true. You're sure? It's not true.

ROBERTA: Well, I don't blame you for anything you did. It hurt at the time you did it.

THERAPIST: It's important you treat her like an adult. Face-to-face. It did hurt you, and you want her to know that. Isn't that right?

ROBERTA: Yes.

THERAPIST: You can tell her that.

APRIL: I did hurt you.

THERAPIST: No, no. She hasn't said it to you yet.

ROBERTA: It, yes, it did hurt.

THERAPIST: And I want you to know it.

ROBERTA: I want you to know it.

THERAPIST: Good.

APRIL: You want me to know that I did hurt you.

ROBERTA: Yes. And I also want you to know that, I don't want you to feel that you've done anything to me. I mean it.

THERAPIST: Why not?

ROBERTA: I don't . . .

THERAPIST: It's important to me that you know that I don't harbor any resentment.

ROBERTA: Right.

THERAPIST: To you.

ROBERTA: It's just . . .

THERAPIST: It's important to me that you know that because I want to be close to you.

ROBERTA: Yeah, I love you and I want to be close to you, and I don't want you to feel that you've done me any . . .

THERAPIST: No, you can't say it that way. She has done you harm. You were hurt.

ROBERTA: But it's over.

THERAPIST: No, it's not over. It still hurts you, some of those things. But you don't harbor resentment towards her. Is that right?

ROBERTA: That's true, because I don't feel it was her fault. It wasn't your fault.

THERAPIST: Why not?

ROBERTA: Because I was the responsible party.

THERAPIST: Why?

ROBERTA: I was her mother.

THERAPIST: So?

ROBERTA: That's my role.

THERAPIST: So? She's not entitled to be a bad girl maybe some of the time? to be a person? And be responsible for that to you? She's not entitled to that because you're the mother? That's what you are telling her.

ROBERTA: All right. That isn't what I mean.

THERAPIST: I didn't think so. But that's in a way what you're telling her. It's like, she can't be grown up. She can't be a person to you unless she can own her responsibility to you as your daughter. And she hurt you. Let her know that.

ROBERTA: The hurt. I forgive the hurt. It's not important anymore.

THERAPIST: I want you to know that.

ROBERTA: I want you to know that.

THERAPIST: But I was hurt.

ROBERTA: I was hurt, but our relationship now is more important to me than anything that went in the past.

THERAPIST: And I want you to know that.

ROBERTA: And I want you to know that.

THERAPIST: Good.

APRIL: You want me to know that you were hurt by me, and that I did make mistakes but you forgive me, and our relationship now is very important to you and you don't want anything that happened in our past to get in the way of that.

THERAPIST: That's important to her.

APRIL: That's important to you.

ROBERTA: Right. Yes.

THERAPIST: How does it make you feel to say that to her?

ROBERTA: I feel good about that. I mean there's something very painful going on here, but I, yeah, I feel good about it.

APRIL: You feel good that you've told me these things.

ROBERTA: Yeah.

THERAPIST: Even though it hurts her to . . .

APRIL: Even though you know it's painful.

THERAPIST: Yeah. Her turn. Do you want to switch?

APRIL: It makes me feel good that you told me these things. It makes me feel good that you trusted me enough to tell me. That, that makes me feel very good. It's important to me that you know that.

ROBERTA: It's important to you that I trusted you enough to tell you that.

APRIL: I feel good, I'm hoping, I feel hopeful that you'll feel better now that you've told me this.

ROBERTA: You're hopeful that I'll feel better after telling you this.

In this sequence, Roberta again tried to take responsibility for April's feelings and to protect her daughter. The therapist challenged her to openly acknowledge the hurt. This is an important part of the healing process. If she had continued to deny her hurt and keep it to herself because she is the mother and should be responsible, she would have been in danger of maintaining her sadness and depression, and of not giving her children a chance to confront her and resolve it with her. The therapist said, "It's important that you treat her as an adult. Face-to-face. It did hurt you and you want her to know that. Isn't that right?" Roberta responded, "Yes," and began to tell the truth about what April knows but hadn't been able to talk about openly. Roberta finally recognized the significance of this conversation. As a result, April appreciated being trusted as an adult daughter.

After the conversation, the therapist asked, "Who's next?"

DAVID: Not me.

David was very emotional and had difficulty speaking. The therapist accepted this and turned to see if anyone else wanted to talk. Mary responded; she had a lot to say.

MARY *(to Roberta)*:   It will be brief. I just wanted to tell you that it is really very painful to know how hurt you've been, and that I have hurt you also. I know that we all have hurt you growing up. And it really hurts a lot to know that you feel that much pain. And it makes me very sad to realize exactly how you feel.

THERAPIST: I want you to know that.

MARY: I want you to know that.

THERAPIST *(to Roberta)*:   Tell her that.

ROBERTA: It makes you very sad to know that I have these feelings. You feel you've hurt me in growing up and that you're upset that I feel like this.

MARY: It makes me very, very sad to know that you feel this badly. Okay. I want you to know that.

THERAPIST *(to Roberta)*:   It makes her feel bad. *(The therapist maintains involvement to keep what is a very emotional conversation engaged and safe.)*

ROBERTA: You want me to know that it makes you feel bad.

MARY: I also want you to know that I forgive you completely, and I want you to forgive me also. I want you to know that.

THERAPIST: Why do you want her to know that? *(Therapist elicits underlying positive feeling.)*

MARY: I want you to know that because I feel like what you meant to me in my life is priceless, and it's one of the most important things in the world to me, and to think for a second that you don't know that makes me feel terrible.

THERAPIST: It's important that you know that.

MARY: And it's important that you know that.

ROBERTA: It's important to you that I know that I'm valuable to you, and you are surprised, I guess, that I didn't know it.

THERAPIST: And it hurts her that you don't know it.

ROBERTA: And it hurts you that I don't know it.

MARY: And I want you to realize how important you are, and how much I do love you, and that I forgive you, and it would mean a great deal to me to know that you understand that.

ROBERTA: You want me to understand that you forgive me and you want me to forgive you and that I am valuable to you.

THERAPIST: And it's important that I know that.

ROBERTA: And it's important to you that I know it.

MARY: Okay. Switch.

ROBERTA: Um . . .

THERAPIST *(prompting)*:   It makes me feel to know that . . .

ROBERTA: It makes me feel good to know that.

THERAPIST *(to Mary)*:   It makes her feel good to know that.

MARY: It makes you feel good to know that.

ROBERTA: And I want you to know that I do forgive everything that happened, and I'm glad you forgive me because I want that. I just want to be real careful about our relationship, because it's very valuable to me, too. You mean a lot to me.

MARY: You want me to know that, uh, I mean a lot to you and that you forgive me and you're glad that I forgive you, and you want to be very careful with our relationship because it means that much to you.

ROBERTA: Yes.

THERAPIST: It's important that I know that.

MARY: It's important that I know that.

ROBERTA: And I want you to trust me that I can deal with these feelings and these things that are coming out today. It may not look like it now, but I will be stronger and understand more about what went on between us all.

THERAPIST: That makes me feel . . .

ROBERTA: And it makes me feel good and it makes me strong and it makes me feel different, or, yeah, it makes me feel more capable.

(No longer depressed, Roberta asserts her strength and independence to her daughter, which will help them differentiate.)

THERAPIST: And that makes me feel . . .

ROBERTA: And that makes me feel good about myself, and I'm glad you feel that you're telling me the truth, in the things you say to me. That's very meaningful to me. I want you to know how important it is that we are talking like this.

MARY: You want me to know how important it is to you that we have been open like this and been telling each other how we feel. You believe what I say is true, and you feel that you want me to know that you can handle the feelings and the emotions that have come out, and you will feel better, and you're happier.

ROBERTA: Yeah.

MARY: And you feel more in control of your life and yourself. You just feel a lot better.

THERAPIST: It's important that you understand that.

MARY: It's important that I understand.

THERAPIST: Because she can believe what she's been told.

MARY: And it's important that I understand that because you can believe what you've been told.

THERAPIST: And that makes her feel stronger.

MARY: And that makes you feel stronger.

THERAPIST: And that makes her feel good.

MARY: You feel good because the things that I have said to you have been meaningful and truthful and you believe them, and you want me to know that you feel much stronger and you are capable of handling this and you want me to know that.

THERAPIST: It makes her feel good.

MARY: And it makes you feel good.

Here Roberta is taking responsibility for herself, asserting that she can cope. This frees the children from feeling so responsible for her. Mary responds with great emotion. There are tears in her eyes, but it is hard for her to let it show.

ROBERTA: Switch.

THERAPIST: Good.

MARY: Um.

THERAPIST *(prompting)*:   It makes me feel to know that . . .

MARY: It makes me feel wonderful to see this come out of you, because now I feel like you're going to feel so much better, and that so much of this pain will subside. It's been very painful all these years watching this in you.

THERAPIST: So I feel . . .

MARY: So, I feel really sad, but very happy because I feel like it's one of the most wonderful things that could have ever come out of this. And it's like a rebirth or something, I don't know.

THERAPIST: And that makes me feel . . .

MARY: And that makes me feel really happy.

THERAPIST: Good.

ROBERTA: So, you're happy that these things have come out and that I feel more clear about myself. It was important to you that this happen, and you feel good now that it has, and it's important to you that I know that.

MARY: Switch.

ROBERTA: It makes me feel not surprised. It makes me feel relieved and glad and grateful that we are where we are today with each other.

MARY: You feel relieved and grateful that we are as open now as we are today.

ROBERTA: I want you to know that I have always been proud of you. I guess I wanted to be close to you, because I think you are a very worthwhile person, and I wanted you to feel the same about me. I was always a little worried that maybe you didn't because I didn't have very good feelings about myself so I didn't know how you could have good feelings about me either. But you have had good feelings about me anyway.

THERAPIST: And that makes me feel . . .

ROBERTA: And that makes me feel good.

MARY: You feel good because you were afraid that because you felt badly about yourself that I didn't feel this way about you. It makes you feel really good to know that we can have this kind of relationship, and that I never stopped respecting you or loving you, all the time you thought that—how could I?

THERAPIST: It makes her feel good.

MARY: It makes you feel good to know that. And that you feel that I'm a very worthwhile person, and you've always been proud of me, and you want me to know that.

ROBERTA: Switch.

MARY: That makes me feel very good. I'm glad, I feel relieved, and more at peace that I know that you know how I feel now, and that it's out in the open. It's something I've always wanted to say but never felt able to do it. And it just makes me feel a lot better knowing that you know.

ROBERTA: You feel good because you've let me know what your feelings are, and I feel good about what I've heard from you. So you feel good about that because we've been open for the first time.

MARY: And it makes me feel really happy that you believe them, and that you know that they're true.

ROBERTA: It's important to you that I believe them and know they're true.

THERAPIST: That makes her feel good.

ROBERTA: And that makes you feel good.

THERAPIST (*to Roberta*):   Do you want to say anymore?

ROBERTA: You mean to Mary or to everyone?

THERAPIST: Whatever.

ROBERTA: I just want you all to know that you are all very important to me, and I guess about the most important people in the world, and I have always been very proud of you, and I don't want you to think that I'm concerned about your success as people because I figured I did a bad job. I mean, I think you've turned out great, despite the nonsense that went on.

THERAPIST: And that makes me feel . . .

ROBERTA: And, yeah, that makes me feel real, real good and real lucky. Real lucky.

THERAPIST: She wants you to know that.

NANCY: Yup. You want us to know that.

APRIL: You want us to know that.

DAVID: All right.

MARY: You feel lucky.

THERAPIST: How does that make you guys feel?

APRIL: Makes us . . .

   (Laughter)

THERAPIST: Glad you caught that.

APRIL: It makes me feel good.

This dialogue captures the essence of the therapy. The family's underlying positive feelings for one another emerge, and the family secret is out and discussed. Mom is strong, not depressed, and capable of taking care of herself. She feels good knowing how her children feel about her. The daughters and mother are developing more of a peer relationship with each other. David isn't ready for this yet, but the therapist suggests a future meeting with him and his parents when he is ready. Only one person, Elliott, has not expressed himself. It became clear to the therapist and the family that Roberta and Elliott would not have a conversation this session; in fact, they actually initiated conversations that ensured that they wouldn't speak. Nevertheless, this fact has been unacknowledged during the session, so the therapist now tries to bring Elliott into the conversation.

Sharing/Review and Suggestions for Future Interactions

These two components of the family-of-origin session are combined at the end of this session. The therapist first turns to Elliott to elicit his response. He says, "I think it was a good idea to get it all on the table." David expresses himself next.

THERAPIST: Well, I appreciate that you shared your time with me.

DAVID: It's an Easter Sunday I'll never forget, I'll tell you that.

MARY *(to Therapist)*:   And I appreciate you, too. *(To David)* I think you helped us a lot, and I'm grateful.

ROBERTA: Wonderful.

THERAPIST *(to Roberta)*:   Well, sure. Look, you were brave, I thought. I was proud that you did that. Because it was hard.

MARY *(to Roberta)*:   And you were going to be held responsible for this, too.

NANCY *(to Roberta)*:   I told you that just to get you here.

DAVID *(to Roberta)*:   It's for your benefit; Mary told me it was for you.

ROBERTA: Ah hah, you did that for me? Thank you. I'm touched.

MARY: No, no. Originally I did. He had something about it, and he said, "I don't have any problem with the family, I don't want to go, I don't need to go."

ROBERTA: Ah!

MARY: And I said, "Well you've got to look at it this way: April's therapist would like some insight into the family to help April in therapy. I think you owe it to her to come."

DAVID: I've got something to say.

MARY: It got you here, didn't it?

THERAPIST: And it was important that you were here.

DAVID: Yeah. I learned a lot today.

THERAPIST: I appreciate that.

The shift in Roberta's demeanor was significant. Though she came to the session depressed and vulnerable, her mood began to improve as the session progressed until finally she was able to assert her confidence in herself. Witnessing this change in mood and confidence level, her children realized how much they had been concerned about her and the degree to which they now felt free to pursue their own individual directions.

It had been a long day. The family members and therapist were tired. Before ending the session, the therapist took time to allow everyone to express and acknowledge each other's feelings about this experience. This helped to provide closure.

Follow-Up Session with April and Steve

The therapist met with April and Steve a week after the family-of-origin meeting. It is important to meet with the client who brought the family together for therapy to process the impact of this experience on the couple. Steve was involved in the family-of-origin session, for he was back at Roberta and Elliott's house waiting for the family to return so they all could have Easter dinner together. Steve comments on his experience.

STEVE: Well, it was interesting because I sat with one spouse and an intended spouse, who were very apprehensive.

THERAPIST: Uh huh.

STEVE: And I tried to reassure them that nothing but good could come from it.

THERAPIST: Uh huh.

STEVE: And then to see their faces when they came back in was truly an experience.

APRIL: Yeah.

STEVE: They were drained.

THERAPIST: Uh huh.

STEVE: They were mentally and physically . . .

THERAPIST: Yeah.

STEVE: You could see it.

THERAPIST: It was . . .

STEVE: It was not the normal family gathering.

THERAPIST: Oh?

STEVE: No . . .

THERAPIST: Oh, you mean afterwards.

STEVE: Afterwards.

THERAPIST: What was different about it?

STEVE: First of all, they sat down to eat. I know it sounds funny.

APRIL: We actually sat down while we ate.

STEVE: Usually, at these functions . . .

APRIL: Like civilized people.

STEVE: No, they, it's more of a smorgasbord style. People are usually walking around talking with their plates, and carrying on, and I noticed that because that was unique from my family.

THERAPIST: Uh huh.

STEVE: Different. My family's always very staid; they sit at a big long table, and my mother crowds them in whether they're comfortable or not. I've always disliked that. But this time, they (April's family) all found seats.

THERAPIST: Hum.

STEVE: Well, they were talking about the session.

THERAPIST: Uh huh. They were.

STEVE: Sure.

APRIL: Yeah, everybody liked it. Everybody wanted to go back and have another one, except for my father.

THERAPIST: Uh huh.

APRIL: And he, he said, "Well, that guy, I've got to have a lot of respect for him. I know he's really good at what he does. But I just don't see the point in repeating things over and over and over again."

THERAPIST: Uh huh.

APRIL: So I asked him, "Didn't you think, though, a few times, the things that a person ended up saying were different from what they started saying, even though they kept repeating?"

THERAPIST: Uh huh.

APRIL: And he said, "No, I don't get it. I heard the same thing over and over again." I don't know what that means. Whether he is defensive because he doesn't want to face up to what he might have to do at the next session, or . . .

THERAPIST: I think it makes him anxious.

APRIL: Yeah.

THERAPIST: Because he was feeling anxious. But I have to say that you know, he volunteered.

APRIL: Uh huh.

THERAPIST: To do it, and he did it. And so, I was really pleased.

STEVE: At one point . . .

APRIL: Yeah, he did. That was a big step for him.

THERAPIST: Uh huh. He did well.

APRIL: Yeah, I feel a difference. I don't know if it's just me or if it's the rest of the family, but there is a difference there, somehow. I don't know if I can put my finger on it. There's less, I guess, less of a distance.

THERAPIST: Uh huh.

APRIL: Less of a coldness.

THERAPIST: Uh huh.

APRIL: Between us.

THERAPIST: Uh huh.

Obviously, the family-of-origin session had an impact on the family and on April and Steve. They continue to talk about it for a while and then the therapist engages them in RE practice. During the conversation, April brings up their separation.

APRIL: I feel good that I'm comfortable with the prospect of a split in our relationship. I'm comfortable now, more comfortable because I feel like Melissa [daughter] and myself will be all right. That without you in our everyday lives we can still go on and we can live a good, happy, fruitful life. And that makes me feel hopeful. That makes me feel good. Relieved.

STEVE: You feel relieved and hopeful because you feel that if there is a split in our relationship you and Melissa will both be okay, and you'll lead good productive lives.

APRIL: Switch.

STEVE: Well, that makes me feel good to know that you feel that way. Because it gives me a sense of assurance. And it relieves me, that you feel that way.

APRIL: You want me to know that you're relieved that I feel that way.

April and Steve separated. They continued to use RE to help them cope with the many difficulties that separation and divorce engender. After their couple therapy meetings, they began filial therapy sessions and initiated home play sessions with Melissa. Both believed that the sessions helped Melissa. After the separation, April opened her own business, it was a success and she invited her sister Mary to join her.

Eight months after the family-of-origin session, Roberta joined the Peace Corps. Elliott was hurt and angry and insisted on selling their home. He purchased a trailer to live in by himself. Roberta kept in touch with her children and Elliott during the two years in the Peace Corps. Elliott grew closer to his daughters and spent more time with them. When Roberta returned from the Peace Corps, she moved back in with Elliott.

For two years after the family-of-origin session, the therapist saw the other children who attended the session. Nancy was seen first, with her husband and children from her earlier marriages. Eventually, she left her husband and established a more stable relationship with her present husband. Mary also was seen with the man with whom she and her son were living. After three months of therapy, they decided to separate. A year later, she returned with the man with whom she is presently living. This is a stable relationship that has lasted two years. David was seen with a woman ten years his senior with whom he was involved, a relationship that reflected in some ways his dependent relationship with his mother; after six sessions, however, this woman decided not to continue therapy. Two years later, David married a woman his own age and seems to be happy.

What does all this mean? Are these changes due to the family-of-origin session? It's hard to be sure. It is clear, though, that the family-of-origin session had a lasting impact on all of them.

CHAPTER 9

Relationship Enhancement in the Twenty-First Century

BRIEF THERAPY AND MANAGED CARE

Relationship Enhancement is a versatile therapy with many applications. This is particularly relevant in light of today's emphasis on brief therapy and managed care. Contemporary psychotherapy has to be formulated to meet the demands created by the new and multiplying forces in healthcare. Because RE is a versatile brief therapy, it works well within a managed care framework.

Managed care has increasingly taken over healthcare (including mental health) since the HMO Act of 1974. From the look of today's healthcare marketplace, all healthcare eventually will be managed in some way. Because of consolidations, mergers, and takeovers, the healthcare marketplace is now so volatile that to accurately predict the result of all these changes is probably impossible. However, it is safe to say that managed care is here to stay.

According to Strosahl (1994), managed care systems of the future will stress cost containment, quality clinical outcomes, and customer satisfaction. These criteria will also apply to psychotherapy; in fact most managed care programs now offer psychotherapy programs that are brief and cost effective. Budman and Armstrong (1992) recommend that therapists involved in managed care have training in brief therapy. Relationship Enhancement, with its structured yet flexible, systematic, and time-designated nature, works well within this managed care framework. The number of sessions for each therapy can be designed to fit client (patient) needs and managed care expectations. After the initial session, clients and therapists agree to work for a specified number of sessions. At the end of this agreed-upon period, they assess the benefit derived from the effort, determine the need for additional sessions, and plan for subsequent effort. If additional sessions are desired, a new time-designated period and specific goals are determined. If client and therapist decide to discontinue sessions, they then plan how to generalize and maintain what the client has already learned. Generalization and maintenance skills (part of the core skills) are particularly useful here (see Tables 2.7 and 2.8). In addition, the use of booster sessions—meetings between client and therapist after the formal course of therapy has been completed, during which core skills are reinforced—and the use of homework assignments also contribute to RE's cost-effectiveness, cutting down on the number of sessions.

Relationship Enhancement also works well within a managed care framework because of its essential collaborative nature. Typically, a managed care program requires that a therapist complete and submit a treatment plan after two or three sessions with a client. To satisfy legal and ethical guidelines, clients must sign a release-of-information form accompanying the treatment plan. Thus, managed care requirements echo the kind of collaboration naturally fostered by RE. Such collaborative efforts help ensure that the treatment is brief and promote trust between client and therapist. It also allows client and therapist to cope together with any frustrations arising from meeting the demands of managed care.

In addition, RE works equally well with preventive and ameliorative programs (B. G. Guerney, Stollak, & Guerney, 1970, 1971; B. G. Guerney, 1979). This is particularly important in light of managed care's increasing emphasis on fostering preventive approaches to therapy (American Psychological Society, 1996). Finally, an important advantage of RE therapy over many other brief therapies is its inclusivity. While most forms of brief therapy are developed for small and circumscribed populations that exclude large numbers of patients (Budman & Armstrong, 1992), RE appeals to many diverse populations.

APPLICATION TO OTHER SETTINGS AND POPULATIONS

Both the skill training methodology and the particular relationship skills that are taught in RE are suitable for broad applications. Relationship Enhancement has been found useful in the treatment of alcoholism (Armenti, 1980; Waldo & Guerney, 1983), in recovery (Matter, McAllister, & Guerney, 1984), in relapse prevention (Ginsberg, 1988), and in drug addiction in rehabilitation (Cadigan, 1980). It has also been applied in work with chronic schizophrenics (Vogelsong, Guerney, & Guerney, 1983) and with borderline personality disorder (Waldo & Harman, 1993).

BRIEF STRUCTURED RE THERAPY GROUPS

Among the most effective ways of providing short-term treatment is to develop therapy groups that are structured and time designated (specifying a certain number of sessions). Relationship Enhancement originated as a group treatment approach, and most of the research about RE has been conducted with RE groups. In this light, RE is very compatible with managed care guidelines.

Many more clients can be helped using group formats than through individual therapy. In addition, B. G. Guerney and Vogelsong (1977) suggest a number of other benefits of group training. In RE groups, clients:

1. Learn by observing one another.
2. Have the opportunity to practice facilitator skills (see Table 2.12) and improve their own skills.
3. Become better prepared for home practice.
4. Observe others who have similar conflicts, which eases their self-judgment and provides reality testing of their own difficulties.

Whether to refer clients to a family group or see them only with family members or significant others is a decision best made collaboratively between client and therapist based on client needs. Multifamily groupings and groups for nonrelated individuals can be formed as well. Among the latter, groups whose purpose is preventive education can be formed in community, school, social agency, business, and industrial settings.

RE GROUPS WITH UNRELATED INDIVIDUALS

A special feature of RE is that it can easily be used with people unrelated to each other (Waldo, 1985, 1988, 1989, 1996; Waldo & Harman, 1996). This application is particularly relevant to managed care and brief treatment. After an initial evaluation, clients (patients) can be referred to an RE group while being followed for additional care (e.g., medical intervention, periodic individual booster sessions, stress management). Relationship Enhancement groups with unrelated individuals can also follow a brief intensive individual treatment program. The benefits derived from groups of unrelated individuals are similar to those found with family group therapy.

An early study (Waldo, 1985) explored improving relations between students living together in college. The objective was to allow the group . dynamics to foster the curative factors proposed by Yalom (1975). Waldo developed a structured format for six group sessions. Although Waldo did not formally train group members in RE skills, the principles and skills in this program closely approximated RE. In a later study, Waldo (1989) used RE to train resident assistants in college residence halls to conduct workshops for students (and roommates) in their living units. The workshops consisted of four 2-hour sessions in which students were trained in the expressive (speaking) and empathic (listening) skills. When the students were assessed on expressive and empathic skills, the researchers found that the experimental (trained) group showed significantly higher levels of expressive and empathic skills than the untrained, delayed-treatment group. He also conducted a study in which RE was used with wife abusers and batterers (Waldo, 1988). The subjects were told that if they participated in the program, attending 11 of 12 sessions, they would not have to face trial and their first offense would be expunged. The treatment consisted of 12 weekly 2-hour group counseling sessions. The group was composed of 8 to 12 men and two group leaders. The groups were trained in the core skills of RE: expressive, receptive, and conversive. In addition to RE skills, the men were trained in identifying and managing their emotions, particularly anger. The results indicated that the men who received counseling had a significantly lower recidivism rate than those who refused counseling and those not referred for counseling (there was no statistical difference in the recidivism rates between these last two groups). However, these results need to be interpreted with caution because the subjects were not randomly assigned. Obviously, further research is needed.

Waldo and Harman (1996) informally evaluated a group therapy program based on RE for state hospital patients and staff. Relationship Enhancement groups were held on the patient units. During 50-minute sessions, the patients were given a handout describing the core skills of RE, and the leaders explained the structure of the sessions and the values and skills of RE. They then demonstrated the skills, after which patients were coached to practice by themselves. Informal outcomes indicated that the patients had a positive attitude to these groups; in addition, there were observable changes in their functioning on the unit (e.g., the patients were less manipulative and more interactive). At the same time, staff members were trained in a series of three 2-hour meetings. In response to an anonymous evaluation, most staff and patients found the workshop worthwhile.

Accordino and Guerney (1993) developed a program to train the staff of a community residential rehabilitation program in RE and to evaluate the effect on the staff and their clients. The training was conducted on two consecutive 8-hour days. The staff demonstrated improvement in the use of RE skills in role-play exercises. Researchers also found that clients' feelings toward staff became significantly more positive: They were more willing to approach staff with concerns and desires; felt better understood by staff, more positive about themselves, and more motivated to work on goals; improved in their interactions with staff; and had less interest in returning to an inpatient facility.

Preston and Guerney (1982) have developed a comprehensive, in-depth RE group skill-training program for unrelated individuals, the Relationship Enhancement Skill Training (REST) program. The skills taught in this program are empathic, expressive, facilitative, conversive, problem-solving, and generalization. The methods used in the skill training are understanding, planning, rehearsal with feedback, real-life practice, feedback on real-life practice, and generalization.

B. G. Guerney and Hatch (1974) designed an RE program for single adults, called Singles Training in Interpersonal Relationship Skills (STIRS), geared toward those who want to improve their ability to establish and develop close relationships with others. The skill practice can be used for generic problems on specific or complex relationship issues. The early sessions concentrate on practicing skills in dyadic interactions. Home assignments in the later sessions emphasize practice and supervision involving individuals not participating in the group.

Ginsberg (1978) developed a pilot structured group therapy program for unrelated individuals based on RE. Its objectives are to better understand oneself and others and to learn skills to improve one's relationships. Potential participants were invited to an interview session with the therapist, who informed them of the approach and its methods; at the same time, the therapist ascertained the appropriateness of each person for this training. Typically, there are six to eight members in the group. The group can be led by one therapist, though two are often more effective. Though the 10-session program is highly structured, it can evolve into a less structured, process-oriented group therapy guided by RE principles and limits. Participants may also choose to continue as a peer group, with the therapist acting as a consultant who can be invited to group meetings when necessary.

In this approach to group therapy, it is important that the leader-therapist take a consultative and educative role toward the group. The leader-therapist assures the safety and security of the group by keeping group discussion within a context in which the rules and boundaries (limits) of RE are maintained. In its emphasis on safety, RE groups echo Winnicott's concept of the "holding environment" (1980) and provide the type of context that is likely to lead to second-order change (Watzlawick, Weakland, & Fisch, 1974).

The central value of RE is that significant therapeutic change occurs between the participants—not between therapist and client. If a group participant requires more therapist involvement, an individual session is scheduled for another time. Most often this occurs when a participant is feeling defensive or threatened by the vulnerability this type of group therapy engenders. In the individual session, the therapist works to ease this threat and return the client to the group process. On occasion, the client may feel too vulnerable and threatened by the group process, and needs to withdraw from the group to seek individual therapy. As in other forms of RE, clients can be in individual therapy and still participate in the group.

Professional and Industrial Training

RE has also been applied to professional training and workshops for industry. Sywulak, Spence, Horner, and Essman (1978) developed a professional staff training for caseworkers in community agencies. This eight-session program teaches speaking and listening skills as well as behavior management, reinforcement limit setting, and consequent skills.

Rathnell (1991), who developed an RE program for work teams, studied the effect of RE training on six work teams of 10 to 13 coworkers ($N = 67$). She used an own-control design with a two-week wait-control period before training (equivalent to the two-week training period), and considered the following dependent variables: trust, closeness, ability, confidence, and initiative in interpersonal work relationships, group cohesion, and peer group leadership. The results largely indicated that work team members improved their relationship skills and interpersonal relationships at work as compared to the wait-control group. There was also evidence that RE training increased peer leadership in work groups.

Cosner (1983a, 1983b) developed two successful programs for supervisors (confronting the troubled employee and conflict resolution) based on RE. Both programs were well received by industry.

School Applications

For the professional interested in children's development and families, the schools offer the best opportunity for access. Within the past 20 years, public education has been asked to perform more and more as parent and family, particularly as increasing numbers of parents work and the number of latchkey children grows. As a result, the need for additional supportive services to schools and families is critical.

Early on, Andronico and Guerney (1967) recognized the potential for applying filial therapy in the schools. Such a program would be efficient, in that there is an inherent economy of time and space; more children can be helped with fewer professional personnel; parents can be readily involved; the skills learned at school can be generalized to the home; and collaboration between home and school will improve. They also recognized the benefit to teachers of applying the principles, skills, and methods of the filial program. Having teachers learn the child-centered play techniques of filial therapy, they hypothesized, would improve their communication and relationship skills with children. Ginsberg (1971) has developed a training program called Sensitivity to Children. Through this program, teachers learn methods for working with children having specific problems in the classroom as well as methods for enhancing classroom relationships and management skills. The Sensitivity to Children program has been used extensively in training staff in early childhood education and preschool settings.

Another filial program in the school (Ginsberg et al., 1978) began as a play therapy group during which parents were invited to observe and evolved into a training program for parents as their children drew them into play. The children chosen for the group were referred by their teachers because they either acted out or were withdrawn in the classroom. The one-hour group session was held in the school library during the school day. During the first half hour, children, parents, and group leaders played together; parents were asked only to acknowledge their child's feelings and set appropriate limits when necessary. At first, the leaders modeled the reflections or limits and asked parents to restate them directly to the child. After a while, parents began doing this spontaneously with some guidance from the leaders. In the second half hour, the play session was discussed and parents were trained to conduct such sessions at home.

The authors identified three benefits of conducting filial therapy in this way:

1. Children reproduced school and home behaviors in the group.
2. The group closely resembled the classroom, which helped to generalize any changes.
3. The parents' presence and their assumption of the therapist's role with their own children facilitated children's growth and speeded change.

The outcomes were positive: The children improved both their interpersonal and social skills and were more able to express their feelings. Concurrently, the parents' parenting skills and self-esteem improved. In the initial, informal trial of this group therapy approach, all participants spoke positively about the benefits of the program.

B. G. Guerney and Flumen (1970) reported on a study in which teachers were trained and supervised in child-centered play therapy and conducted individual weekly play sessions with children identified as withdrawn, a program that closely resembled filial therapy. The children participating in these play sessions were compared to a control group of withdrawn children from the same classes on the following variables: initiating talk in class; raising a hand to initiate talk; initiating talk with another student; and initiating talk privately with the teacher. Based on these variables, the children in the experimental group had significantly improved their assertiveness in class while none of the children in the control group showed such a pattern of improvement. In addition, children in the experimental group were more assertive with peers than with teachers, supporting the notion that they had generalized their improvement. A significant correlation between the degree to which teachers successfully performed the therapeutic role and degree of child improvement was also noted.

In another study, Merriam and Guerney (1973) compared a group of elementary students and their teachers who had been trained in the basic receptive and expressive skills of RE combined with democratic classroom management skills to a control group. The trained teachers elicited more feelings and ideas from students and expressed their views more freely than the untrained teachers.

Several other studies support the finding that RE can prove very useful in schools and has a wide range of applications. A group of female high school students who were trained in filial therapy and then compared to students who underwent a non-skills-oriented practicum and lecture-discussion program (Essman, 1977) significantly improved in expressive and empathic skills and in child management (limit setting and applying appropriate consequences). High school students trained in an abbreviated RE program were better behaved and attended school more regularly than those in the control group (Rocks, 1980). Fifth-grade students trained in RE skills evidenced significantly greater gains in empathy as compared to a control group (Vogelsong, 1978). Haynes and Avery (1979) trained high school students in RE skills and found them to have a higher rate of self-disclosure and more empathy than a nontreatment control group. Avery, Rider, and Haynes-Clements (1981) conducted a follow-up study on the same groups and found that the superiority in empathy and self-disclosure of the trained adolescents was maintained.

RETURNING TO THE ESSENCE OF RE THERAPIES

Although therapeutic techniques are important, the success of RE therapy is ultimately derived from its conceptual underpinnings. According to RE, the primary relationship context of individuals is the focus of change. This is not to ignore the fact that changes in the individual are important, but to recognize that individual changes come about in the context of a relationship and never in isolation. If individual change has any value, it has to be expressed in an interpersonal context. Thus, in RE, the relationship context—not the individual—is, in a way, the "client." However, individuals benefit from being taught skills that allow them to sharpen their insight into themselves, enhance their interpersonal abilities, and create the contexts in their life that foster satisfaction and fulfillment.

Psychotherapy is ultimately a learning process that itself fosters change. Learning is dependent on the efforts of the learner, not on the efforts of the teacher. The teacher must have skills that engender effort on the part of the learner, but it is the learner's own effort to learn and use what is learned that will determine the outcome of the learning experience. The emphasis in RE on collaboration between client and therapist acknowledges the primacy of the client's responsibility for his or her learning and application of this learning to real life. The core RE skills of generalization and maintenance attest to this principle. Treatment is more time effective when clients themselves take responsibility for the outcome. Clients who can learn something in therapy and who possess the tools to continue to learn and apply their learning on their own have less need for a therapist; this allows therapists to use their time more efficiently. Furthermore, RE's emphasis on employing the context to foster change draws in and helps other significant people in the client's life, which allows clients to make more efficient use of their time with their therapist.

Empathy

In his description of "emotional intelligence," which links empathy with emotion, Goleman (1995) specifies knowing one's emotions (self-awareness), managing emotions, motivating oneself, recognizing emotion in others (empathy), and handling relationships. All these skills are taught in RE.

The relevance of empathy, however, is not new. In *Sense and Sensibility,* Jane Austen portrayed empathic responding, one of RE's core skills:

> "It is very true" said Marianne, "that admiration of landscape scenery is a mere jargon. Everybody pretends to feel and tries to describe with the taste and elegance of him who first defined what picturesque beauty was. I detest jargon of every kind, and sometimes I have kept my feelings to myself because I could find no language to describe them in, but what was worn and hackneyed out of all sense and meaning."
>
> "I am convinced," said Edward, "that you really feel all the delight in a fine prospect which you profess to feel." (p. 85)

Here Edward seems to be deliberately attempting to acknowledge Marianne's meaning and feelings. In another passage, Austen again denotes the importance of empathic response. Lucy states,

> "I was sure you was angry with me and have been quarreling with myself ever since for having taken the liberty as to trouble you with my affairs. But I am very glad to find it was only my own fancy and that you do not really blame me."

Elinor responds,

> "Indeed I can easily believe that it was a great *relief* to you to ac-
> knowledge your situation to me and be assured that you shall never
> have reason to repeat it." (p. 123)

Not only does Elinor respond with empathy, but Lucy responds by owning her feelings. Furthermore, Elinor lets Lucy know what it means to
her to understand Lucy's feelings ("be assured" is similar to "I want you
to know," an expression of feeling). This is an excellent example of the use
of the three core skills: empathic responding, assertive expression, and in-
teractive/engagement.

Emotion

Austen is quite insightful in yet another way. In the first passage, she recognizes how inadequate language is to express our feelings, and that the
difficulty of expressing ourselves leads us to keep our feelings to ourselves. Yet by adequately conveying our feelings (to ourselves as well as
others) we give meaning to our words. The emphasis in RE on feeling expression derives from this very difficulty. The more skillful we are in
conveying and understanding our feelings, the more we are able to engage with each other and negotiate our differences. Keeping our feelings
to ourselves only heightens our difficulties, whereas openly expressing
them in an empathic relationship with others enhances our coping. Relationship contexts that are secure and trustworthy dissipate defenses, elicit
openness, and foster constructive intimate engagement.

Acceptance

Acceptance, an important component of RE, is integral to this engagement process and to genuine change. Recently, acceptance has become incorporated into many therapeutic approaches (Hayes, Jacobson,
Follette, & Dougher, 1994). Acceptance involves remaining open to
one's own emotions and to those of others, and owning one's present
experience and the feelings that pertain to that experience. To be accepting, one must develop a nonjudgmental stance (of self and others).
Nonjudgment and acceptance go hand in hand. By taking this stance,
one inevitably relates to others by acknowledging the inherent equivalence of all human beings. Relationship Enhancement programs respect

this concept of equivalence without disregarding the hierarchy that pertains in all social systems.

Language and Relationship

How we understand ourselves and each other is mostly dependent on the relationships we have and have had with others. Relationship Enhancement underscores the importance of relationship and communication in giving meaning to our lives. As Martin Buber states (1958), "all real life is encounter" (p. 11).

> Buber maintained that human wholeness, its vitalizing true reality exists only "in-between" separate persons, other creatures, nature, and God—a connecting mutuality recognizable only in their genuine encounter. "All real living is meeting" he says. He says actualized life resides only in honest, open give-and-take between separate selves, and interflow that surpasses both and augments each. "He who takes his stand in relation shares in a reality . . . a being that neither merely belongs to him nor merely lies outside of him," Buber says. Through unaffected personal engagement in the encounter, participants are lifted out of themselves and their "being made real," he says. "All reality is an activity in which I share without being able to appropriate for myself." Where there is no sharing, there is no reality. He coined a special, almost poetic, terminology to distinguish between common, deadening "I—It" relations—which stereotype and reduce everyone and everything to utilitarian objects—and sensitively attentive "I—Thou" relations which enhance and authenticate the being of both partners. *The person becomes conscious of himself as sharing in being, as co-existing and thus as being," he says.* As a simple example, he notes that in a conversation the *"meaning is to be found in neither of the two partners, nor in both together, but only in their dialog itself, in this 'between which they live together.'"* (Cornell, 1988, C1, C3)

It is in the dialogue itself, "this between which they live together," that RE works. The sequences of two-person dialogues upon which RE is based incorporate acknowledgment, acceptance, love, and intimacy. Such I—Thou relations enhance and authenticate (acknowledge and accept) the being of both partners. The wholeness of each of us is recognizable only in our genuine encounters and our sharing in a mutual reality ("engagement") with others. This is what RE elicits.

Filial Therapy
Parents Manual

WHAT IS THE FILIAL PROGRAM?

The Filial Program is an approach that was developed to help foster optimum development in young children; increase their sense of mastery and self-acceptance; increase openness and trust in the parent-child relationship; and increase parents' sensitivity to their children.

Essentially, parents learn to conduct weekly half-hour play sessions with their own children. Each parent establishes a special time every week to have a play session with each child. Where there are two parents in the home, they alternate playing with each child. With only one parent, a practical arrangement for these sessions is established.

WHY PLAY SESSIONS?

The Filial Program is a developmental approach to helping young children and their families. Young children do not have the physical, intellectual, and emotional development and experience that adults have. Their ability to communicate about themselves is as yet immature. Their understanding of their own behavior is also immature, causing them to have difficulty helping others to understand their thoughts, feelings, and behaviors. However, it is through children's play activities that the child learns to deal with those issues. Play is a primary way in which children grow, develop, learn, express their inner

Adapted from L. Guerney, Stover, and Guerney, 1972, 1976 with permission.

selves, and work on important emotional aspects and relationship issues of their lives. Parents conduct weekly half-hour one-to-one play sessions with their children to help them do this. These weekly half-hour play sessions are drawn from the basic principles and skills that psychotherapists have used with young children over many years (see Virginia Axline's books *Dibs* [1947] and *Play Therapy* [1961] for further information).

The principles and skills that are at the core of the Filial Program represent basic parenting principles and once learned can be applied in everyday life (see L. Guerney, 1995, *Parenting: A Skills Training Manual*).

Filial therapy is recommended for families with infants through 12-year-old children. (For teenagers, a comparable program, PARD, Parent-Adolescent Relationship Development [Ginsberg, 1977], is used.) The use of special structured play sessions can be the best way to help young children.

One purpose of a play session is to create a situation in which children may become aware of feelings they have not allowed themselves to recognize. In the presence of the parents, the children have an opportunity to communicate their feelings through play. The parents' acceptance of the children's feelings is essential and helps the children come to a better understanding of how to cope with their feelings as they experience or re-experience difficulties in the session.

Another purpose of the session is to build the children's feeling of trust and confidence in the parents. If parents respond to children in the manner prescribed in the play session, it will increase the children's feeling that they can communicate with the parents more fully and honestly about their experiences and feelings. They will feel more trusting of the parents. This should eventually lead to more moderate and mature ways of expression and less use of extreme and immature forms of emotional expression. Children will have less fear that being open with parents will lose parental respect or affection.

A third purpose is to build the children's confidence in themselves. Just as we expect you will eventually experience a greater feeling that your children trust you, your children should experience your sense of trust in them. One goal is for them to feel more secure in making their own decisions where that is appropriate. They need to learn to be less fearful of making mistakes. It is important for them to learn that they have choices and are themselves responsible for much of what befalls them. This is very important for any child who has a problem to overcome. This means being free to make choices (including many mistakes) and experiencing the consequences, good or bad. By allowing them freedom of choice in the play session and by allowing them to experience the consequence of free choice, you build their sense of confidence. The opportunity to make choices and assume responsibility for those choices ultimately reinforces their ability to make more realistic and appropriate choices for themselves. You build their confidence in themselves also by giving them your complete and exclusive attention in the session. This leads to their experience of themselves as more worthwhile and likable people, which is a key ingredient in self-confidence and good adjustment to and relations with you and other people.

Setting Up a Play Session

The following specific recommendations are essential for obtaining the desired results of closer understanding between parent and child.

1. *Set aside a time* (to begin with, a half hour) every week for a session with your child. This should be at a time and place where you are isolated from the rest of the family and can guarantee no interruptions. If the phone rings, let it ring (or take it off the hook). Try to have arrangements for other children so they will not interrupt this session. Your uninterrupted attention is one of the most important conditions for fruitful play sessions. Do not impede your progress by changing the time each week or canceling a session. Such changes have undesirable effects; continuity is important. Whether they say so or not, children tend to feel that cancellations and changes reflect disapproval of their behavior in the previous play session. Change also breeds a lack of confidence and trust—the very things we are trying to promote. If a change is absolutely necessary, it should be discussed in advance with the child. Once you begin play sessions, you should consider their availability to the child a form of contract you cannot break. It is helpful to establish an alternative date ahead of time in case a cancellation is absolutely unavoidable.

2. *Select a room* for play where there will be least concern if things get spoiled or broken. Least preferred is the child's own room, where other toys might be distracting. Water may be spilled, clay smeared, or toys dropped and broken, so a basement or kitchen floor would be best. Many parents select the area and then spread out a large plastic tablecloth or shower curtain. In this way, parents can feel more at ease and can more genuinely create an atmosphere that is free from restraint for the child.

3. *The choice of toys* is important to the success of the play session. Primarily, the toys should be plastic, inexpensive, or unbreakable. The following will be most useful for a beginning:
   - Inflated plastic bop bag (at least 4 feet high)
   - Dart gun with soft darts
   - Plastic figures
   - Family of puppets
   - Doll family (mother, father, brother, sister, baby)

- Doll furniture
- Baby bottle
- Bowl for water
- Crayons, paints
- House box for doll furniture and family
- Cups and saucers
- One deck of playing cards
- Checkers set
- Ring-toss or similar game
- Drawing paper
- Tinker Toys or similar construction toy
- Blackboard, chalk, and eraser
- Nerf balls
- Basketball hoop for Nerf balls, if convenient

These toys are reserved for use in the play session only. They should not be used by another child at all, except in that child's own play session when you are having sessions with him or her. The children may not take or use toys out of the session (their own drawing or painting is an exception). Ordinarily, they may not add any of their own toys. The toys have been especially selected in order to help the children release their aggressions and to reenact their feelings in relation to family members in a safe and accepted place.

4. *What to tell the child.* It is not recommended to go into a long explanation with the children. You may simply say you want to spend more time with them. Older children may insist on further details. In this case, place the emphasis on your wanting to spend time alone with your children in a special play setting. Not that you want to help them, but that you want to be together, have fun, and improve your relationship. There is usually very little difficulty in getting the child to participate.

   Some children, of course, take more time than others to feel comfortable enough to express themselves freely. On some occasions, children object to having sessions. But most of the time they enjoy the sessions and look forward to them.

5. *What the parent does.* The role of the parent in a play session is to establish an atmosphere of free play and acceptance for the child. This means that the parent has to take a very unusual attitude toward the child—very different from the usual way of relating to people. The stage is set by stating the following: "This is our special playtime. You can do almost anything you like, and you can say anything you like. If there is something that you can't do, I'll tell you." What the children do with the toys and what they say in the session are strictly up to them. Children may use the toys to express things they have not been able to express adequately before or express things they often express in a more

extreme manner. They want to use the time to be very aggressive; they may want to sit and stare at the wall, unwilling to involve themselves at all. They may wish to leave after a few moments. The parent has to have an open mind and be willing to follow the child's lead, whatever form it takes (including not staying). Therefore, it is important that the parent engage in:

- NO criticism.
- NO praise, approval, encouragement, or reassurance.
- NO questions, leads, or invitations.
- NO suggestions, advice, or persuasion.
- NO interruptions or interference.
- NO information given, unless directly requested by child.
- NO teaching, preaching, or moralizing.
- NO initiating a new activity.

In short, it is important for the parent to establish a setting in which the child, and the child alone, sets the values and judgments. If the child wants you to participate in the play, it is the child's job to ask you. The child is in charge of the session.

Equally important, the parent must be fully involved with the child, giving full attention to everything the child says and does and feels. It is most important to be attentive to the child's mood and to note very carefully all the feelings the child is willing to reveal. This will give children the go-ahead to begin to uncover more of their deeper feelings. If parents are asked to participate in an activity, they should engage in it fully. But attention should be focused primarily on how the child *wants* the parent to participate, on following the child's direction, and on reflecting the child's feelings. The child's play in the session need not be conventional. For example, a child may like to cheat at cards or make new rules. In such instances, the parent should reflect only the strong need to win or the child's desire to having things go his or her way, and the means the child uses to accomplish this, in an uncritical, warm, and supporting tone.

The child's actions are also accepted by verbal comment from the parent, for example, "You're really beating up that doll"; "You're going to kick him around"; "It's hard to make up your mind what to do"; "You love to sit on my lap"; "They're all going to be killed"; "You're aiming very slowly so it will be sure to hit." Acknowledging a child's feelings is also important, for example, saying "You like that"; "You're frustrated"; "You're pleased"; "You're disappointed."

These are the only type of appropriate comments from the parent. Complete silence or merely sociable conversation are discouraged. Regarding the first, children may fear disapproval when a parent is silent, so it is important to comment, letting them know that your attitude is continually accepting. With respect to the second, social conversation leads most children to feel that they should answer questions or talk about what the parent wants to, rather than take the initiative themselves.

PUT YOURSELF IN THE CHILD'S PLACE

More important than any technique is the spirit under which the play session is undertaken. It is important that you try not to be mechanical, stilted, or artificial. You can avoid this best by bending all your efforts toward trying to put yourself in the children's place and understand the world as they see it, not as you see it or wish them to see it. Try to understand the children's feelings through what they are doing and saying. Also, leave your own worries or reactions out of it as much as you can. Sometimes it will be difficult. Simply try to understand what the children are trying to express, and communicate to them that you understand: that you know what they are feeling, and it's all right with you. You will find that some of the things the child does are distasteful or worrisome. You need not permit such behavior outside of the play session, during any other time. However, it is crucial to be very giving and accepting of any and all behavior in the play session (except those things mentioned below). Children quickly pick up the idea that what goes on in the play session may or may not be allowed out of the play session; outside the session you can continue to be very firm about prohibiting some of the activities that are permitted in the session.

LIMITS

There are few restrictions on the child's activity in the play session. These "limits" must be adhered to rigidly. If the child should "break a limit," you should point out that this particular behavior is not allowed. If the statement does not suffice and the behavior occurs a second time, warn the child that the play session will end if it occurs a third time. Make sure the child understands. Thereafter, the next occurrence ends the session. This is the one and only consequence of breaking the limit. The session ends without the parent's getting angry. The limits are:

CHILD MAY NOT HIT OR HURT OR ENDANGER PARENT IN ANY WAY (e.g., pointing the dart gun with a dart in it at the parent). A similar limit on dirtying or wetting the parent may also be imposed if the parent wishes. It is important that these limits are expressed in a way that the child can take control of them (e.g., rather than "I can't be *hurt*" be specific: "I can't be *hit*, pinched, wet, etc.").

IF THE CHILD LEAVES THE PLAY SESSION, THE SESSION ENDS (except for one bathroom trip), but child and parent can play the next time.

THE BOP BAG MAY NOT BE POKED WITH A SHARP IMPLEMENT OR BITTEN.

One of the most effective ways to set limits is to state, "The rule is . . .," rather than "One of the things you can't do is . . ." A child will feel less directed and may be able to handle the limit better.

Tell children at the beginning of the early sessions that they may do almost anything they want and that they can say anything they want. If there is something they shouldn't do, you will tell him. And do not try to prevent or discourage a child from breaking a limit. Your task, when prohibited behavior first occurs or is about to occur, is to let them know the rule. If they fail to adhere to the rule, let them know the consequence. The ultimate consequence is termination of the session.

There are three steps in setting limits: (a) statement of rule; (b) warning regarding the consequence (ending the session); (c) imposition of the consequence. In essence this helps the children, through trial and error, learn to control their impulses and adhere to the rules. Remember, the objective is to help children learn to be responsible for the limits, not to punish them. It is useful to allow them to experience the three steps for several sessions before imposing the consequence at the first violation. After a couple of sessions, use two steps (warning of consequence, imposing consequence), thereafter ending the session at the first violation. If they choose to violate a rule anyway during a future session: (a) acknowledge and accept their strong desire to do what they did, and (b) always, without exception, impose the consequences immediately. Remember that your purpose is not to prevent the behavior, but to allow them to make the choice and to experience the consequences.

There may be one or two additional limits used at the discretion of the parent, if necessary, such as not shooting at windows or ceiling, dumping only one bowl of water on the floor (some should be allowed), and not smearing the walls. There should be no limits on what the child says, including swearing, hostile comments toward the parents, or other people.

TIME LIMITS

Part of the structure of the play therapy session includes the amount of play session time (usually a half hour). It is important to periodically let the child know how much time remains in the session. For a half-hour session, it is useful to state warnings at 15 minutes, 5 minutes, and 1 minute. It is best to state the time remaining in the following way; "Johnny, we have (15, 5, or 1) minutes left for the play session." If the child says something (e.g., "I just want to finish this") in response to the time limit, make sure to reflect it (e.g., "You're worried about the time").

CLOSING THE SESSION

When the time is up, state, "Johnny, our time is up for today, our play session is over!" Immediately, get up and look to see if the child is coming. If not, state, "You'd like to stay longer, but our time is up and we have to leave." If the child still doesn't come with you, go to the child and help him or her leave, stating, "You'd like to stay, but our time is up and we have to leave, but we can come back next time."

Bibliography

Accordino, M. P., & Guerney, B. G., Jr. (1993). Effects of the Relationship Enhancement Program on community residential rehabilitation staff and clients. *Psychosocial Rehabilitation Journal, 17,* 131–144.

Ackerman, N. W. (1966). Family psychotherapy, theory and practice. *American Journal of Psychotherapy, 20,* 405–414.

Allen, J. P., Hauser, S. T., Bell, K. L., & O'Connor, T. G. (1994). Longitudinal assessment of autonomy and relatedness in adolescent-family interactions as predictions of adolescent ego development and self-esteem. *Child Development, 65,* 179–194.

American Psychological Society. (1996, April). Doing the right thing: A research plan for healthy living (HCI Report 4—Healthy Living) [Special issue]. *APS Observer,* Washington, DC.

Anderson, H., & Goolishian, H. (1988). Human systems as linguistic systems: Some preliminary and evolving ideas about the implications for clinical theory. *Family Process, 27,* 371–393.

Anderson, W. T., Anderson, R. A., & Hovestadt, A. J. (1988). Intergenerational family therapy: A practical primer. In P. A. Veller & S. R. Hegman (Eds.), *Innovations in clinical practice: A source book* (Vol. 7, pp. 175–187). Sarasota, FL: Professional Resource Exchange.

Andronico, M. P. (1983). Filial therapy: A group of parents of children with emotional problems. In A. L. Rosenbaum (Ed.), *Handbook of short term therapy groups* (pp. 3–21). New York: McGraw-Hill.

Andronico, M. P., Fidler, J., Guerney, B. G., Jr., & Guerney, L. (1967). The combination of didactic and dynamic elements in filial therapy. *International Journal of Group Psychotherapy, 17,* 10–17.

Aponte, H. J. (1985). The negotiation of values in therapy. *Family Process, 24,* 323–338.

Ashby, W. R. (1956). *An introduction to cybernetics.* London: Methuen.

Austen, J. (1995). *Sense and sensibility.* New York: Penguin Books USA Inc.

Authier, J., Gustafson, K., Guerney, B. G., Jr., & Kasdorf, J. A. (1975). The psychological practitioner as a teacher: A theoretical-historical practical review. *Counseling Psychologist, 5*(2), 31–50.

Avery, A. W., Rider, K., & Haynes-Clements, L. A. (1981). Communication skills training for adolescents: A five month follow-up. *Adolescence, 16,* 289–298.

Axline, V. (1947). *Play therapy.* Cambridge, MA: Houghton Mifflin.

Axline, V. (1969). *Play therapy* (Rev. ed.). New York: Ballantine Books.

Azar, B. (1995). *Nursing marriage from sickness to health. APA Monitor,* pp. 10–11.

Bateson, G. (1972). *Steps to an ecology of mind.* New York: Ballantine Books.

Bateson, G. (1979). *Mind and nature: A necessary unity.* New York: E.P. Dutton.

Baumrind, D. (1971). Current patterns of parental authority. *Developmental Psychology Monograph, 491*(Pt. 2.).

Baumrind, D. (1991a). Effective parenting during the early adolescent transition. In P. A. Cowan & M. Hetherington (Eds.), *Family transitions* (pp. 111–163). Hillsdale, NJ: Erlbaum.

Baumrind, D. (1991b). The influence of parenting style on adolescent competence and substance use. *Journal of Early Adolescence, 11,* 56–95.

Beavers, W. R. (1985). *Successful marriage.* New York: W.S. Norton.

Beck, A. T., Emery, G., & Greenberg, R. L. (1985). *Anxiety disorders and phobias: A cognitive perspective.* New York: Basic Books.

Bloch, D., & Simon, R. (1982). *The strength of family therapy: Selected papers of Nathan W. Ackerman.* New York: Brunner/Mazel.

Bloomfield, H. (1983). *Making peace with your parents.* New York: Ballantine Books.

Boardman, W. K. (1962). Rusty: A brief behavior disorder. *Journal of Consulting Psychology, 26,* 293–297.

Boszormenyi-Nagy, I. (1966). From family therapy to a psychology of relationships: Fictions of the individual and fictions of the family. *Comprehensive Psychiatry, 7,* 408–423.

Boszormenyi-Nagy, I. (1972). Loyalty implications of the transference model in psychotherapy. *AMA Archives of General Psychiatry, 27,* 374–380.

Boszormenyi-Nagy, I., Grunebaum, J., & Ulrich, D. (1991). Contextual therapy. In A. S. Gurman & D. P. Kniskern (Eds.), *Handbook of family therapy* (Vol. 2, pp. 200–238). New York: Brunner/Mazel.

Boszormenyi-Nagy, I., & Krasner, B. R. (1986). *Between give and take: A clinical guide to contextual therapy.* New York: Brunner/Mazel.

Boszormenyi-Nagy, I., & Spark, G. M. (1973). *Invisible loyalties: Reciprocity in intergenerational family therapy.* New York: Harper & Row.

Bowen, M. (Anonymous). (1972). Differentiation of self in one's family. In J. Framo (Ed.), *Family interaction* (pp. 111–113). New York: Springer.

Bowen, M. (1976). Theory in the practice of psychotherapy. In P. G. Guerin, Jr. (Ed.), *Family therapy: Theory and practice* (pp. 42–90). New York: Gardner Press.

Bowen, M. (1978a). *Family therapy in clinical practice.* New York: Aronson.

Bowen, M. (1978b). On the differentiation of self. In M. Bowen (Ed.), *Family therapy in clinical practice* (pp. 467–528). New York: Aronson.

Bowen, M. (1978c). Toward the differentiation of self in one's family-of-origin. In M. Bowen (Ed.), *Family therapy in clinical practice* (pp. 529–547). New York: Aronson.

Bray, J. H., & Williamson, D. S. (1987). Assessment of intergenerational family relationships. In A. J. Hovestadt & M. Fine (Eds.), *Family of Origin Therapy: Application in clinical practice* (pp. 31–44). Rockville, MD: Aspen Press.

Bray, J. H., Williamson, D. S., & Malone, P. E. (1984). Personal authority in the family system: Development of a questionnaire to measure personal authority in intergenerational family processes. *Journal of Marital and Family Therapy, 10,* 167–178.

Bray, J. H., Williamson, D. S., & Malone, P. E. (1986). An evaluation of an intergenerational consultation process to increase personal authority in the family system. *Family Process, 25,* 423–436.

Bretherton, I., Fritz, J., Zahn-Walker, C., & Ridgeway, D. (1986). Learning to talk about emotions: A functional perspective. *Child Development, 57,* 529–548.

Brock, G. W., & Joanning, H. (1983). A comparison of the Relationship Enhancement Program and the Minnesota Couple Communication Program. *Journal of Marital and Family Therapy, 9*(4), 413–421.

Brown, T. (1991, June). *Affective dimensions of meaning.* Paper presented at the 21st Symposium of the Jean Piaget Society, Philadelphia.

Brown, T., & Weiss, L. (1987). Structures, procedures, heuristics and affectivity. *Archives de Psychologie, 55,* 59–94.

Buber, M. (1958). *I and thou* (2nd ed., R. Gregor Smith, Trans.). New York: Scribner, T & T Clark.

Budman, S. H., & Armstrong, E. (1992). Training for managed care settings: How to make it happen. *Psychotherapy, 29,* 416–421.

Budman, S. H., & Gurman, A. S. (1988). *Theory and practice of brief psychotherapy.* New York: Guilford.

Cadigan, J. D. (1980). *RETEACH Program and Project: Relationship Enhancement in a therapeutic environment as clients head out.* Unpublished doctoral dissertation, Pennsylvania State University, University Park.

Campos, J. J., Mumme, D. L., Vermoian, R., & Campos, R. G. (1994). A functionalist perspective on the nature of emotion. In N. A. Fox (Ed.), The development of emotion regulation, biological and behavioral considerations. *Monographs of the Society for Research in Child Development, 59,* 284–303.

Caplan, F., & Caplan, T. (1974). *The power of play.* Garden City, NY: Anchor Books.

Carter, B., & McGoldrick, M. (1988). Overview: The changing family life cycle—A framework for family therapy. In B. Carter & M. McGoldrick (Eds.), *The changing family life cycle: A framework for family therapy* (2nd ed., pp. 3–28). New York: Gardner Press.

Carter, E. A., & McGoldrick, M. (Eds.). (1980). *The family life cycle. A framework for family therapy.* New York: Gardner Press.

Collier, A. (1987). The language of objectivity and the ethics of reframing. In S. Walrond-Skinner & D. Watson (Eds.), *Ethical issues in family therapy.* New York: Routledge & Kegan Paul.

Collins, J. D. (1977). Experimental evaluation of a six-month conjugal therapy and relationship enhancement program. In B. G. Guerney, Jr. (Ed.), *Relationship Enhancement: Skill training programs for therapy problem prevention and enrichment* (pp. 192–226). San Francisco: Jossey-Bass.

Cooper, C. R., Grotevant, H. D., & Condon, S. M. (1983). Individuality and connectedness in the family as a context for adolescent identity formation and role taking skill. In H. D. Grotevant & C. R. Cooper (Eds.), *Adolescent development in the family: New directions for child development.* San Francisco: Jossey-Bass.

Cornell, G. W. (1988, December 22). Living is meaning, says Buber. *Daily Intelligencer,* Doylestown, PA, pp. C1, C3.

Cosner, R. (1983a). *Confronting the troubled employee: A guide for supervisors.* Lansdale, PA: The Valley Center.

Cosner, R. (1983b). *Conflict resolution.* Lansdale, PA: The Valley Center.

Coufal, J. D., & Brock, G. W. (1983). *Parent-child relationship enhancement: A 10-week education program.* Menomonie, WI: Department of Human Development and Family Living.

Council on Families in America. (1995). *Marriage in America: A report to the nation.* New York: Institute for American Values.

Dail, J. (1984, March). *Effects of intergenerational contact: A report of recent research.* Paper presented at the 50th Annual Groves Conference on Marriage and the Family, Pinehurst, NC.

D'Augelli, A. R., Deyss, C. S., Guerney, B. G., Jr., Hershenberg, B., & Sborofsky, S. (1974). Interpersonal skill training for dating couples: An evaluation of an educational mental health service. *Journal of Counseling Psychology, 21*(5), 385–389.

Dicks, H. V. (1967). *Marital tensions.* New York: Basic Books.

Doherty, W. J., & Boss, P. G. (1991). Values and ethics in family therapy. In A. S. Gurman & D. P. Kniskern (Eds.), *Handbook of family therapy* (Vol. 2, pp. 606–637). New York: Brunner/Mazel.

Dougher, M. M. (1993). On the advantage and implications of a radical behavioral treatment of private events. *The Behavior Therapist, 16,* 204–206.

Dougher, M. M. (1994a). More on the radical behavioral treatment of private events and acceptance: A reply to Ellis and Miller. *The Behavior Therapist, 17,* 223–224.

Dougher, M. M. (1994b). More on the differences between radical behavioral and rational emotive approaches to acceptance: A response to Roff. *The Behavior Therapist, 23,* 493–506.

Duck, S. (1994). *Meaningful relationships: Talking sense and relating.* Thousand Oaks, CA: Sage.

Duhl, F., Kanton, D., & Duhl, B. (1973). Learning space and action in family therapy: A primer of sculpture. *Seminars in Psychiatry, 5,* 167–183.

Efran, J. S., Lukens, M. D., & Lukens, R. J. (1990). *Language structure and change.* New York: Norton.

Ely, A., Guerney, B. G., Jr., & Stover, L. (1973). Efficacy of the training phase of conjugal therapy. *Psychotherapy: Theory, Research and Practice, 10,* 201–207.

Emmelkamp, P., Van der Helm, J., MacGillavary, D., & Van Zanten, B. (1984). Marital therapy with clinically distressed couples: A comparative evaluation of systemic-theoretic, contingency contracting, and communication skills approaches. In K. Halweg & N. S. Jacobson (Eds.), *Marital interaction: Analysis and modification* (pp. 36–52). New York: Guilford.

Essman, C. S. (1977). *Preparental education: The impact of a short-term, skills-training course on female adolescents* [Summary segment]. Unpublished doctoral dissertation, Pennsylvania State University, University Park.

Fairbairn, W. R. D. (1954). *An object relations theory of the personality.* New York: Basic Books.

Falloon, I. R. H. (1991). Behavioral family therapy. In A. S. Gurman & D. P. Kniskern (Eds.), *Handbook of family therapy* (pp. 65–95). New York: Brunner/Mazel.

Feldman, S. S., & Elliott, G. R. (1990). *At the threshold: The developing adolescent.* Cambridge, MA: Harvard University Press.

Feldman, S. S., & Gehring, T. M. (1988). Changing perceptions of family cohesion and power across adolescence. *Child Development, 59,* 1034–1045.

Fine, M., & Hovestadt, A. J. (1987). What is Family-of-Origin Therapy? In A. J. Hovestadt & M. Fine (Eds.), *Family-of-Origin Therapy* (pp. 11–19). Rockville, MD: Aspen.

Fitzpatrick, M. A. (1988). *Between husbands and wives: Communication in marriage.* Newbury Park, CA: Sage.

Fox, N. A. (1994). Preface. In N. A. Fox (Ed.), The development of emotion regulation: Biological and behavioral considerations. *Monographs of the Society for Research in Child Development, 59,* Nos. 2–3, Vii–VII.

Framo, J. L. (1976). Family-of-Origin as a resource for adults in marital and family therapy: You can and should go home again. *Family Process, 15,* 193–210.

Framo, J. L. (1980). Marriage and marital therapy: Issues and initial interview techniques. In M. Andolfi & I. Zwerling (Eds.), *Dimensions of family therapy* (pp. 123–140). New York: Guilford.

Framo, J. L. (1981). The integration of marital therapy with sessions with family-of-origin. In A. S. Gurman & D. P. Kniskern (Eds.), *Handbook of family therapy* (pp. 133–158). New York: Brunner/Mazel.

Framo, J. L. (1991, February). Memories of Murray Bowen. *Family Therapy News: Newspaper of the American Association for Marriage and Family Therapy, 22*(1).

Framo, J. L. (1992). *Family-of-Origin Therapy: An intergenerational approach.* New York: Brunner/Mazel.

Garcia-Preto, N., & Travis, N. (1985). The adolescent phase of the family life cycle. In M. P. Mirkin & S. L. Koman (Eds.), *Handbook of adolescence and family therapy* (pp. 21–38). New York: Gardner Press.

Garvey, C. (1990). *Play.* Cambridge, MA: Harvard University Press.

Giblin, P., Sprenkle, D. H., & Sheehan, R. (1985). Enrichment outcome research: A meta-analysis of premarital, marital, and family interventions. *Journal of Marital and Family Therapy, 11,* 257–271.

Gilligan, C. (1982). *A different voice.* Cambridge, MA: Harvard University Press.

Ginsberg, B. G. (1971). *Training in sensitivity to children.* Unpublished manuscript.

Ginsberg, B. G. (1976). Parents as therapeutic agents: The usefulness of filial therapy in a community mental health center. *American Journal of Community Psychology, 4*(1), 47–54.

Ginsberg, B. G. (1977). Parent-adolescent relationship development program. In B. G. Guerney, Jr. (Ed.), *Relationship enhancement: Skill training for therapy problem prevention and enrichment* (pp. 227–267). San Francisco: Jossey-Bass.

Ginsberg, B. G. (1978). *Communication and relationship. Skills training program.* Unpublished manuscript.

Ginsberg, B. G. (1982). *Productive communication.* Unpublished manuscript.

Ginsberg, B. G. (1984a, November). Beyond behavior modification: Client-centered play therapy with the retarded. *American Psychology Bulletin, 6,* 321–324.

Ginsberg, B. G. (1984b). Filial therapy with retarded children and their families. *American Psychology Bulletin, 6,* 332–334.

Ginsberg, B. G. (1988, September). *Keeping people engaged: Relapse prevention using relationship enhancement therapy.* Paper presented at the National Conference of the Alcohol and Drug Problems Association of America, Charlotte, NC.

Ginsberg, B. G. (1989). Training parents as therapeutic agents with foster/adoptive children using the filial approach. In C. E. Schaefer & J. M. Breismeister (Eds.), *Handbook of parent training: Parents as co-therapists for children's behavior problems* (pp. 442–478). New York: Wiley.

Ginsberg, B. G. (1990). *Play and filial therapy with the abused.* Paper presented at the annual meeting of the American Psychological Association, Boston, MA.

Ginsberg, B. G. (1995). Parent-Adolescent Relationship Program (PARD): Relationship Enhancement Therapy with adolescents and their families (fathers and sons). *Psychotherapy, 32,* 108–112.

Ginsberg, B. G. (1996). Together in group therapy: Fathers and their adolescent sons. In M. P. Andronico (Ed.), *Men in groups* (pp. 269–282). Washington, DC: American Psychological Association.

Ginsberg, B. G., Stutman, S. S., & Hummel, J. (1978). Notes for practice: Group filial therapy. *Social Work, 23*(2), 154–156.

Ginsberg, B. G., & Vogelsong, E. L. (1977). Premarital relationship improvement by maximizing empathy and self-disclosure: The PRIMES Program. In B. G. Guerney, Jr. (Ed.), *Relationship Enhancement: Skill-training programs for therapy, problem prevention, and enrichment* (pp. 268–288). San Francisco: Jossey-Bass.

Gleick, J. (1987). *Chaos: Making a new science.* New York: Viking Penguin.

Goldberg, J. R. (1993). What is normal adolescence? *Family Therapy News, 24,* 1–20.

Goleman, D. (1995). *Emotional intelligence.* New York: Bantam Books.

Gottman, J. M. (1979). *Marital interaction: Experimental investigations.* San Diego, CA: Academic Press.

Gottman, J. M. (1993). The role of conflict engagement, escalation and avoidance in marital interaction: A longitudinal view of five types of couples. *Journal of Consulting and Clinical Psychology, 61,* 6–15.

Gottman, J. M., & Krokoff, L. J. (1989). Marital interaction and marital satisfaction: A longitudinal view. *Journal of Consulting and Clinical Psychology, 57,* 47–52.

Gottman, J. M., Notarius, C., Gonso, J., & Markman, H. (1976). *A couple's guide to communication.* Champaign, IL: Research Press.

Grando, R., & Ginsberg, B. G. (1976). Communication in the father-son relationship: The parent-adolescent development program. *The Family Coordinator,* 465–473.

Greenberg, I. A. (Ed.). (1974). *Psychodrama: Theory and therapy.* New York: Behavioral Publications.

Greenberg, L. S., Ford, C. L., Alden, L. S., & Johnson, S. M. (1993). In-session change in emotionally focused therapy. *Journal of Consulting and Clinical Psychology, 61,* 78–84.

Greenberg, L. S., James, P. S., & Conroy, R. F. (1988). Perceived change in couples therapy. *Journal of Family Psychology, 2,* 5–23.

Greenberg, L. S., & Johnson, S. M. (1986a). Affect in marital therapy. *Journal of Marital and Family Therapy, 12,* 1–10.

Greenberg, L. S., & Johnson, S. M. (1986b). Emotionally focused couples therapy. In N. S. Jacobson & A. S. Gurman (Eds.), *Clinical handbook of marital therapy* (pp. 253–278). New York: Guilford.

Greenberg, L. S., & Johnson, S. M. (1988). *Emotionally focused therapy for couples.* New York: Guilford.

Greenberg, L. S., Rice, L. N., & Elliott, R. (1993). *Facilitating emotional change: The moment by moment process.* New York: Guilford.

Greenberg, L. S., & Safran, J. D. (1987). *Emotion in psychotherapy: Affect, cognition, and the process of change.* New York: Guilford.

Greenberg, L. S., & Safran, J. D. (1989). Emotion in psychotherapy. *American Psychologist, 44,* 19–29.

Griffin, J. M., Jr., & Apostal, R. A. (1993). The influence of Relationship Enhancement training on differentiation of self. *Journal of Marital and Family Therapy, 19,* 267–272.

Guerin, P., & Gordon, E. (1983). Trees, triangle and temperament. In *The child-centered family, the best of the family 1978–1983* (Vol. 2, pp. 131–145). New Rochelle, NY: Center for Family Learning.

Guerney, B. G., Jr. (1964). Filial therapy: Description and rationale. *Journal of Consulting Psychology, 28*(4), 303–310.

Guerney, B. G., Jr. (Ed.). (1969). *Psychotherapeutic agents: New roles for nonprofessionals, parents, and teachers.* New York: Holt, Rinehart and Winston.

Guerney, B. G., Jr. (1977). Should teachers treat illiteracy, hypocalligraphy, and dysmathematica? *Canadian Counselor, 12*(1), 9–14.

Guerney, B. G., Jr. (1979). The great potential of an educational skill-training model in problem prevention. *Journal of Clinical Child Psychology, 3*(2), 84–86.

Guerney, B. G., Jr. (1982a). The delivery of mental health services: Spiritual vs medical vs educational models. In T. R. Vallance & R. M. Sabre (Eds.), *Mental health services in transition* (pp. 239–255). New York: Human-Sciences Press.

Guerney, B. G., Jr. (1982b). Relationship Enhancement. In E. K. Marshall & P. D. Kurtz (Eds.), *Interpersonal helping skills* (pp. 482–518). San Francisco: Jossey-Bass.

Guerney, B. G., Jr. (1984). Relationship Enhancement Therapy and training. In D. Larson (Ed.), *Teaching psychological skills: Models for giving psychology away* (pp. 171–206). Monterey, CA: Brooks/Cole.

Guerney, B. G., Jr. (1987a). *Relationship Enhancement: Marital/family therapists manual.* State College, PA: IDEALS.

Guerney, B. G., Jr. (1987b). *Relationship Enhancement: Marital/family therapists manual* (2nd ed.). State College, PA: IDEALS.

Guerney, B. G., Jr. (1988). Family relationship enhancement: A skill training approach. In L. A. Bond & B. M. Wagner (Eds.), *Families in transition: Primary prevention programs that work* (pp. 99–134). Beverly Hills, CA: Sage.

Guerney, B. G., Jr. (1989). *Relationship Enhancement manual.* State College, PA: IDEALS.

Guerney, B. G., Jr. (1992). *Relationship Enhancement individual therapy.* Manuscript submitted for publication.

Guerney, B. G., Jr. (1994a). *Relationship Enhancement skills.* Unpublished manuscript.

Guerney, B. G., Jr. (1994b). *Relationship Enhancement therapist responses.* Unpublished manuscript.

Guerney, B. G., Jr., Coufal, J., & Vogelsong, E. (1981). Relationship Enhancement versus a traditional approach to therapeutic/preventative/enrichment parent-adolescent program. *Journal of Consulting and Clinical Psychology, 49,* 927–939.

Guerney, B. G., Jr., & Flumen, A. B. (1970). Teachers as psychotherapeutic agents for withdrawn children. *Mental Health Digest, 2,* 7–11.

Guerney, B. G., Jr., & Guerney, L. (1961). Analysis of interpersonal relationships as an aid to understanding family dynamics: A case report. *Journal of Clinical Psychology, 7*(3), 225–228.

Guerney, B. G., Jr., Guerney, L., & Andronico, M. (1966). Filial therapy: Description and rationale. *Yale Scientific Magazine, 40,* 6–14.

Guerney, B. G., Jr., Guerney, L., & Stollak, G. (1971). The potential advantages of changing from a medical to an educational model in practicing psychology. *Interpersonal Development, 2*(4), 238–245.

Guerney, B. G., Jr., & Hatch, E. J. (1974). *Singles training in interpersonal relations.* Unpublished manuscript, Pennsylvania State University, University Park, PA.

Guerney, B. G., Jr., Stollak, G. E., & Guerney, L. (1970). A format for a new model of psychological practice: Or, how to escape a zombie. *The Counseling Psychologist, 2*(3), 267–282.

Guerney, B. G., Jr., Stollak, G., & Guerney, L. (1971). The practicing psychologist as educator—An alternative to the medical practitioner model. *Professional Psychology, 2*(3), 276–282.

Guerney, B. G., Jr., & Stover, L. (1971). *Filial therapy: Final report on Grant MH182640* [Mimeograph] State College, PA: National Institute of Mental Health.

Guerney, B. G., Jr., & Vogelsong, E. L. (1977). Relationship Enhancement administration and formats. In B. G. Guerney, Jr. (Ed.), *Relationship Enhancement* (pp. 167–191). San Francisco: Jossey-Bass.

Guerney, B. G., Jr., Vogelsong, E., & Coufal, J. (1982). Relationship Enhancement versus a traditional treatment: Follow-up and booster effects. In D. Olson & B. Miller (Eds.), *Family studies review yearbook* (Vol. 1, pp. 738–756). Beverly Hills, CA: Sage.

Guerney, L. (1976). Filial therapy program. In D. H. Olson (Ed.), *Treating relationships* (pp. 67–92). Lake Mills, Iowa: Graphic.

Guerney, L. (1979, Fall). Play therapy with learning disabled children. *Journal of Clinical Child Psychology, 8,* 242–244.

Guerney, L. (1980). *Parenting: A skills training manual* (Adolescent supplement). State College, PA: IDEALS.

Guerney, L. (1983). Play therapy with learning disabled children. In C. E. Schaefer & K. J. O'Connor (Eds.), *Handbook of play therapy* (pp. 419–435). New York: Wiley.

Guerney, L. (1995). *Parenting: A skills training manual* (5th ed.). State College, PA: IDEALS.

Guerney, L., Stover, L., & Guerney, B. G., Jr. (1972). *Training manual for parents: Instruction in filial therapy* [Mimeograph]. University Park: Pennsylvania State University.

Guerney, L., Stover, L., & Guerney, B. G., Jr. (1976). Play therapy: A training manual for parents. In C. E. Schaeffer (Ed.), *Therapeutic use of child's play* (pp. 219–226). New York: Aronson.

Haley, J. (1969). *The power tactics of Jesus Christ and other essays.* New York: Grossman.

Haley, J. (1980). *Leaving home: The therapy of disturbed young people.* New York: McGraw-Hill.

Halford, W. K., Sanders, M. R., & Behrens, B. C. (1994). Self regulation in behavioral couples therapy. *Behavior Therapy, 25,* 431–452.

Halweg, K., Revenstorf, D., & Schindler, L. (1984). Effects of behavioral marital therapy on couples' communication and problem solving skills. *Journal of Consulting and Clinical Psychology, 52,* 553–566.

Halweg, K., Schindler, L., & Revenstorf, D. (1982). Treatment of marital distress: Comparing formats and modalities. *Advances in Behavior Research and Therapy, 4,* 57–74.

Hayes, S. C. (1987). A contextual approach to therapeutic change. In N. S. Jacobson (Ed.), *Psychotherapists in clinical practice: Cognitive and behavioral perspectives* (pp. 327–387). New York: Guilford.

Hayes, S. C., Jacobson, N. S., Follette, V. M., & Dougher, M. J. (Eds.). (1994). *Acceptance and change: Content and context in psychotherapy.* Reno, NV: Context Press.

Haynes, L. A., & Avery, A. W. (1979). Training adolescents in self-disclosure and empathy skills. *Journal of Counseling Psychology, 26*(6), 526–530.

Headley, L. (1977). *Adults and their parents in family therapy: A new direction in treatment.* New York: Plenum Press.

Hoffman, L. (1981). *Foundations of family therapy: A conceptual framework for systems change.* New York: Basic Books.

Holtzworth-Munroe, A., & Jacobson, N. S. (1991). Behavioral marital therapy. In A. S. Gurman & D. P. Kniskern (Eds.), *Handbook of Family Therapy* (pp. 65–95). New York: Brunner/Mazel.

Hovestadt, A., Anderson, W., Percy, F., Cochran, S., & Fine, M. (1985). A family-of-origin scale. *Journal of Marital and Family Therapy, 11,* 287–298.

Hovestadt, A. J., & Fine, M. (Eds.). (1987). *Family of origin therapy.* Rockville, MD: Aspen Publishers.

Jacobson, N. S. (1989). The politics of intimacy. *The Behavior Therapist, 12,* 29–32.

Jacobson, N. S. (1992). Behavioral couple therapy: A new beginning. *Behavior Therapy, 23,* 493–506.

Jacobson, N. S., & Addis, M. E., (1993). Research on couples and couple therapy: What do we know? Where are we going? *Journal of Consulting and Clinical Psychology, 61,* 85–93.

Jacobson, N. S., & Holtzworth-Munroe, A. (1986). Marital therapy: A social learning—Cognitive perspective. In N. S. Jacobson & A. S. Gurman (Eds.), *Clinical handbook of marital therapy* (pp. 29–70). New York: Guilford.

Jessee, R., & Guerney, B. G., Jr. (1981). A comparison of Gestalt and Relationship Enhancement treatments with married couples. *The American Journal of Family Therapy, 9,* 31–41.

Johnson, S. M., & Greenberg, L. S. (1988). Relating process to outcome in marital therapy. *Journal of Marital and Family Therapy, 14,* 175–183.

Jordan, J. V., Kaplan, A. G., Miller, J. B., Stiver, I. P., & Surrey, J. L. (1991). *Women's growth in connection: Writings from the Stone Center.* New York: Guilford.

Kagan, J. (1994). In N. A. Fox (Ed.), The development of emotion regulation: Biological and behavioral considerations. *Monographs of the Society for Research in Child Development, 59,* 7–24.

Kaplan, A. G. (1991). The self-in-relation; Implication for depression in women. In J. V. Jordan, A. G. Kaplan, J. B. Miller, I. P. Stiver, & J. L. Surrey (Eds.), *Women's growth in connection: Writings from the Stone Center* (pp. 206–222). New York: Guilford.

Kazdin, A. E. (1993). Adolescent mental health: Prevention and treatment programs. *American Psychologist, 48,* 127–141.

Kazdin, A. E. (1995). Scope of child and adolescent psychotherapy research: Limited sampling of dysfunction, treatments and client characteristics. *Journal of Clinical Child Psychology, 24,* 125–140.

Kazdin, A. E., & Kagan, J. (1994). Models of dysfunction in developmental psychopathology. *Clinical Psychology: Science and Practice, 1,* 35–50.

Koerner, K., Prince, S., & Jacobson, N. S. (1994). Enhancing the treatment and prevention of depression in women: The role of integrative behavioral couple therapy. *Behavior Therapy, 25,* 373–390.

Kramer, J. R. (1985). *Family interfaces: Transgenerational patterns.* New York: Brunner/Mazel.

Lang, P. J. (1985). The cognitive psycho-physiology of emotion: Fear and anxiety. In A. H. Tuma & J. D. Maser (Eds.), *Anxiety and the anxiety disorders* (pp. 130–170). Hillsdale, NJ: Erlbaum.

Lazarus, R. S. (1993). From psychological stress to the emotions: A history of changing outlooks. *Annual Review of Psychology, 44,* 1–21.

Leary, T. (1957). *Interpersonal diagnosis of personality.* New York: Ronald.

Lederer, W. J., & Jackson, D. D. (1968). *The mirages of marriage.* New York: Norton.

Levant, R. F. (1990). Psychological services designed for men: A psychoeducational approach. *Psychotherapy, 27,* 309–315.

Levant, R. F., & Doyle, G. F. (1983). An evaluation of a parent education program for fathers of school-aged children. *Family Relations, 32,* 29–37.

Levenson, R. W., & Gottman, J. M. (1985). Physiological and affective predictors of change in relationship satisfaction. *Journal of Personality and Social Psychology, 49,* 85–94.

Liberman, R. P. (1970). Behavioral approaches to couple and family therapy. *American Journal of Orthopsychiatry, 40,* 106–118.

Liddle, H. A. (1995). Conceptual and clinical dimensions of a multidimensional, multisystems engagement strategy in family-based adolescent treatment. *Psychotherapy, 32,* 39–58.

Lindahl, K., & Markman, A. J. (1990). Communication and negative affect regulation in the family. In E. Beechman (Ed.), *Emotions and families* (pp. 99–116). New York: Plenum Press.

Lindley, R. (1987). Family therapy and respect for people. In S. Waldron-Skinner & D. Watson (Eds.), *Ethical issues in family therapy.* New York: Routledge & Kegan Paul.

Littwin, S. (1986). *The postponed generation.* New York: William Morrow.

Mahoney, M. J. (1985). Psychotherapy and human change processes. In M. J. Mahoney & A. Freeman (Eds.), *Cognition and psychotherapy* (pp. 3–48). New York: Plenum Press.

Markman, H. J. (1981). Prediction of marital distress: A 5-year follow-up. *Journal of Consulting and Clinical Psychology, 49,* 760–762.

Markman, H. J. (1991). Constructive marital conflict is not an oxymoron. *Behavioral Assessment, 13,* 83–96.

Markman, H., & Notarius, C. (1993). *We can work it out.* New York: G.L. Putnam's Sons.

Matter, M., McAllister, W., & Guerney, B. G., Jr. (1984). Relationship Enhancement for the recovering couple: Working with the intangible. *Focus on Family and Chemical Dependency, 7*(5), 21–23, 40.

Maturana, H. R. (1992). The search of objectivity, on the quest for a compelling argument. In R. Donaldson (Chair), *Language, emotion, the social and the ethical* [Conference workbook]. Seabeck, WA: The American Society for Cybernetics.

Maturana, H. R., & Varela, F. J. (1987). *The tree of knowledge.* Boston: New Science Library, Shambala.

McGoldrick, M., & Gerson, R. (1985). *Genograms in family assessment.* New York: W.W. Norton.

Merriam, M. L., & Guerney, B. G., Jr. (1973). Creating a democratic elementary school classroom: A pilot training program involving teachers, administrators and parents. *Contemporary Education, 45,* 34–42.

Minuchin, S. (1974). *Families and family therapy.* Cambridge, MA: Harvard University Press.

Minuchin, S., & Fishman, H. C. (1981). *Family therapy techniques*. Cambridge, MA: Harvard University Press.

Moreno, Z. T. (1959). A survey of psychodramatic techniques. *Group Psychotherapy, 12,* 5–14.

Murphy, E. B., Silber, E., Coelko, G. V., Hamburg, D. H., & Greenberg, I. (1963). Development of autonomy and parent-child interaction in late adolescence. *American Journal of Orthopsychiatry, 33,* 643–652.

Notarius, C. I., & Johnson, J. (1982). Emotional expression in husbands and wives. *Journal of Marriage and the Family, 44,* 483–487.

Olson, D. H., Russell, C. S., & Sprenkle, D. H. (1983). Circumplex model of marital and family systems. VI. Theoretical update. *Family Process, 22,* 69–83.

Oxman, L. (1971). *The effectiveness of filial therapy: A controlled study.* Unpublished doctoral dissertation, Rutgers University, New Brunswick, NJ.

Paikoff, R. L., & Brooks-Gunn, J. (1991). Do parent-child relationships change during puberty? *Psychological Bulletin, 110,* 47–66.

Pascual-Leone, J. (1991). Emotions, development and psychotherapy: A dialectical-constructivist perspective. In J. D. Safran & L. S. Greenberg (Eds.), *Emotion, psychotherapy and change* (pp. 302–335). New York: Guilford.

Patterson, G. R. (1971). *Families: Applications of social learning to family life.* Champaign, IL: Research Press.

Patterson, G. R., & Brodsky, M. (1966). Behavior modification for a child with multiple problem behaviors. *Journal of Child Psychology and Psychiatry, 7,* 277–295.

Patterson, G. R., Chamberlain, P., & Reid, J. B. (1982). A comparative evaluation of a parent training program. *Behavior Therapy, 13,* 638–650.

Paul, N. L. (1967). The role of mourning and empathy in co-joint marital therapy. In G. Zuk & I. Boszormenyi-Nagy (Eds.), *Family therapy and disturbed families.* Palo Alto, CA: Science Behavior Books.

Paul, N. L., & Paul, B. (1990). Enhancing empathy in couples: A transgenerational approach. In Chasin, H. Grunebaum, & M. Herzig (Eds.), *Working with couples.* New York: Guilford.

Piaget, J. (1981). *Intelligence and affectivity: Their relationship during child development* (T. A. Brown & C. E. Kaegi, Eds. and Trans.). Palo Alto, CA: Annual Reviews.

Pitta, P. (1995). Adolescent-centered family integrated philosophy and treatment. *Psychotherapy, 32,* 99–107.

Preston, J. C., & Guerney, B. G., Jr. (1982). *Relationship Enhancement skill training.* State College, PA: IDEALS.

Prigogine, I., & Stengers, I. (1984). *Order out of chaos: Man's new dialogue with nature.* New York: Bantam Books.

Rappaport, A. F. (1976). Conjugal Relationship Enhancement Program. In David H. L. Olson (Ed.), *Treating relationships* (pp. 41–66). Lake Mills, IA: Graphic.

Rathnell, C. G. (1991). *The effects of Relationship Enhancement Program with industrial work teams.* Unpublished doctoral dissertation, Pennsylvania State University, University Park.

Ridley, C. A., Avery, A. W., Dent, J., & Harrell, J. E. (1981). The effects of relationship enhancement and problem solving on perceived heterosexual competence. *Family Therapy, 8,* 60–66.

Ridley, C. A., Avery, A. W., Harrell, J. E., Leslie, L., & Dent, J. A. (1981). Conflict management: A premarital training program in mutual problem solving. *American Journal of Family Therapy, 9,* 23–32.

Risley, T. R., & Wolf, M. M. (1967). Experimental manipulation of autistic behaviors and generalization into the home. In S. W. Bijou & D. M. Baer (Eds.), *Child development: Reading in experimental analysis.* New York: Appleton.

Ritterman, M. (1995, January/February). Stopping the clock. *Family Therapy Networker,* 44–51.

Rocks, T. (1980). *The effectiveness of communication skills training with underachieving, low-communicating secondary school students and their teachers* [Summary segment]. Unpublished doctoral dissertation, Pennsylvania State University, University Park.

Rogers, C. R. (1951). *Client-centered therapy.* Boston: Houghton Mifflin.

Rogers, C. R. (1957). The necessary and sufficient conditions of therapeutic personality change. *Journal of Consulting Psychology, 21,* 95–103.

Rogers, C. R. (1959). A theory of therapy, personality and interpersonal relations as developed in the client-centered framework. In S. Koch (Ed.), *Psychology: A study of a science* (Vol. 3, pp. 185–256). New York: McGraw-Hill.

Rogers, C. R. (1990). The process of therapy. *Journal of Consulting and Clinical Psychology, 58,* 161–164.

Ross, E. R., Baker, S. B., & Guerney, B. G., Jr. (1985). Effectiveness of Relationship Enhancement therapy versus therapist's preferred therapy. *American Journal of Family Therapy, 13*(1), 11–21.

Sams, W. P. (1983). *Marriage preparation: An experimental comparison of the Premarital Relationship Enhancement (PRE) and the Engaged Encounter (EE) Programs* [Summary segment]. Unpublished doctoral dissertation, Pennsylvania State University, University Park.

Satir, V. (1967). *Conjoint family therapy* (Rev. ed.). Palo Alto, CA: Science & Behavior Books.

Sayers, S. L., Baucom, D. H., Sher, T. G., Weiss, R. L., & Heyman, R. E. (1991). Constructive engagement, behavioral marital therapy and changes in marital satisfaction. *Behavioral Assessment, 13,* 25–49.

Scarf, M. (1986, November). Intimate partners: Patterns in love and marriage. *The Atlantic Monthly,* 45–93.

Scarf, M. (1995). *Intimate worlds.* New York: Random House.

Schlien, S. P. (1971). *Training dating couples in empathic and open communication: An experimental evaluation of a potential mental health program.* Unpublished doctoral dissertation, Pennsylvania State University, University Park.

Sensue, M. E. (1981). *Filial therapy follow-up study. Effects on parental acceptance and child adjustment.* Unpublished doctoral dissertation, Pennsylvania State University, University Park.

Shannon, J., & Guerney, B. G., Jr. (1973). Interpersonal effects of interpersonal behavior. *Journal of Personality and Social Psychology, 26,* 142–150.

Simon, F. B., Stielin, H., & Wynne, L. C. (1985). *The language of family therapy: A systematic vocabulary and source book.* New York: Process Press.

Singer, J. L. (1994). The scientific foundations of play therapy. In J. Hellendoorn, R. van der Kooij, & B. Sutton-Smith (Eds.), *Play and intervention* (pp. 27–38). Albany, NY: State University of New York Press.

Smetana, J. G. (1989). Adolescents' and parents' reasoning about actual family conflict. *Child Development, 60,* 1052–1067.

Snyder, D. K., Mangrum, L. F., & Wills, R. M. (1993). Predicting couples' response to marital therapy: A comparison of short and long-term predictors. *Journal of Consulting and Clinical Psychology, 38,* 61–29.

Snyder, M. (1995). "Becoming": A method for expanding systemic thinking and deepening empathic accuracy. *Family Process, 34,* 241–252.

Snyder, M., & Guerney, B. G., Jr. (1993). Brief couple/family therapy: The Relationship Enhancement approach. In R. A. Wells & V. J. Granetti (Eds.), *Casebook of brief psychotherapies* (pp. 132–148). New York: Plenum Press.

Spiegel, J. (1971). *Transactions: The interplay between individual, family, and society.* New York: Science House.

Stover, L., & Guerney, B. G., Jr. (1967). The efficacy of training procedures for mothers in filial therapy. *Psychotherapy: Theory Research and Practice, 4*(3), 110–115.

Strosahl, K. (1994). Entering the new frontier of managed mental healthcare: Gold mines and land mines. *Cognitive and Behavioral Practice, 1,* 5–23.

Sullivan, H. S. (1947). *Conceptions of modern psychiatry.* Washington, DC: William Alanson White Psychiatric Foundation.

Sutton-Smith, B. (1994). Paradigms of intervention. In J. Hellendorf, R. vanderKooij, & B. Sutton-Smith (Eds.), *Play and intervention* (pp. 3–22). Albany, NY: State University of New York Press.

Sywulak, A. E. (1977). *The effect of filial therapy on parental acceptance and child adjustment* [Summary segment]. Unpublished doctoral dissertation, Pennsylvania State University, University Park.

Sywulak, A. E., Spence, I. O., Horner, P. L., & Essman, C. S. (1978). *Trainer's manual for professional staff training workshop.* Harrisburg, PA: Child Care Systems.

Turkewitz, H., & O'Leary, K. D. (1981). A comparative outcome study of behavioral marital therapy and communication therapy. *Journal of Marital and Family Therapy, 7,* 159–170.

VanFleet, R. (1994). *Filial therapy: Strengthening parent-child relationships through play.* Sarasota, FL: Professional Resource Press.

VanFleet, R. (1992). Using filial therapy to strengthen families with chronically ill children. In L. VandeCreek, S. Knapp, & T. L. Jackson (Eds.), *Innovations in clinical practice: A source book* (Vol. 2, pp. 87–97). Sarasota, FL: Professional Resource Press.

Ventura, M. (1995, January/February). The age of interruption. *Family Therapy Networker,* 18–31.

Vogelsong, E. L. (1975). *Preventive-therapeutic program for mothers and adolescent daughters; A follow-up of Relationship Enhancement versus discussion and booster versus no-booster methods.* Unpublished doctoral dissertation, Pennsylvania State University, University Park.

Vogelsong, E. L. (1978). Relationship Enhancement training for children. *Elementary School Guidance and Counseling, 12*(4), 272–279.

Vogelsong, E. L., & Guerney, B. G., Jr. (1977). Range of application of relationship enhancement programs. In B. G. Guerney, Jr. (Ed.), *Relationship Enhancement.* San Francisco: Jossey-Bass.

Vogelsong, E. L., Guerney, B. G., Jr., & Guerney, L. (1983). Relationship Enhancement Therapy with inpatients and their families. In R. Luber & C. Anderson (Eds.), *Family intervention with psychiatric patients.* New York: Human Sciences Press.

Wakshul, B. (1973). *Application of the conjugal model: The family group.* Unpublished manuscript, Pennsylvania State University, University Park.

Waldo, M. (1985). A curative factor framework for conceptualizing group counseling. *Journal of Counseling and Development, 64,* 52–58.

Waldo, M. (1988). Relationship Enhancement counseling groups for wife abusers. *Journal of Mental Health Counseling, 10*(1), 37–45.

Waldo, M. (1989). Primary prevention in university residence halls: Paraprofessional-led relationship enhancement groups for college roommates. *Journal of Counseling and Development, 67,* 465–471.

Waldo, M., & Guerney, B. G., Jr. (1983). Marital Relationship Enhancement Therapy in the treatment of alcoholism. *Journal of Marital and Family Therapy, 9*(3), 321–323.

Waldo, M., & Harman, M. J. (1993). Relationship Enhancement Therapy with borderline personality. *The Family Journal, 1*(1), 25–30.

Waldo, M., & Harman, M. J. (1996, April). *Relationship Enhancement groups with state hospital patients and staff.* Paper presented at the American Counseling Association World Conference, Pittsburgh, PA.

Watzlawick, P., Weakland, J. H., & Fisch, R. (1974). *Change: Principles of problem formation and problem resolution.* New York: W.W. Norton.

Weingarten, K. (1991). The discourses of intimacy: Adding a social constructionist and feminist view. *Family Process, 30,* 285–305.

Weingarten, K. (1992). A consideration of intimate and nonintimate interactions in therapy. *Family Process, 31,* 45–59.

Whitaker, C. A. (1976). The family is a four dimensional relationship. In P. J. Guerin (Ed.), *Family therapy.* New York: Gardner Press.

Whitaker, C. A. (1989). *Midnight musings of a family therapist.* New York: Norton.

Whitaker, C. A., & Keith, D. V. (1981). *Symbolic-experiential family therapy* (pp. 187–225). New York: Brunner/Mazel.

Wieman, R. J. (1973). *Conjugal relationship modification and reciprocal reinforcement: A comparison of treatments of marital discord.* Unpublished doctoral dissertation, Pennsylvania State University, University Park.

Wile, D. B. (1981). *Couples therapy: A non-traditional approach.* New York: Wiley.

Williams, C. D. (1959). The elimination of tantrum behavior: extinction procedures. *Journal of Abnormal and Social Psychology, 59,* 269.

Williamson, D. S. (1982a). Personal authority via the termination of the intergenerational hierarchical boundary: Part 2. The consultation process and the therapeutic method. *Journal of Marital and Family Therapy, 8,* 23–37.

Williamson, D. S. (1982b). Personal authority in family experience via the termination of the intergenerational hierarchical boundary: Part 3. Personal authority defined and the power of play in the change process. *Journal of Marital and Family Therapy, 8,* 309–323.

Williamson, D. S. (1991). *The intimacy paradox.* New York: Guilford.

Winnicott, D. W. (1980). *Playing and reality.* London: Penguin Books.

Winnicott, D. W. (1982). *Playing and reality.* Hammondsworth, Middlesex, England: Penguin Books.

Wolpe, J. (1958). *Psychotherapy by reciprocal inhibition.* Palo Alto, CA: Stanford University Press.

Wynne, L. C., Ryckoff, I., Day, D., & Hirsch, S. (1958). Pseudomutuality in the family relations of schizophrenics. *Psychiatry, 21,* 205–220.

Wynne, L. C., & Wynne, A. R. (1986). The quest for intimacy. *Journal of Marital and Family Therapy, 12,* 383–394.

Yalom, I. D. (1975). *The theory and practice of group psychotherapy* (2nd ed.). New York: Basic Books.

Author Index

271

Subject Index

Acceptance:
   conflict resolution and, 24–25
   conversive skill and, 29
   in couple relationship, 161
   engagement skill and, 33
   impact of, generally, 240–241
   in initial stage of therapy, 166
   in receptive skill, 28–29
   significance of, 15–17, 50
Acknowledging skill, defined, 70
Acknowledgment:
   in family-of-origin therapy, 194
   impact of, generally, 16, 33
   in initial stage of therapy, 166
   young adulthood, 144
Active listening, 177
Adaptability:
   emotions and, 14
   of family, 7
Adaptation, in children, 104–105
Adjustment, marital, 178
Administering skills, of therapist, 52
Adolescent:
   defined, 107
   developmental objectives, 108
   parent-adolescent development
      program (PARD), 61,
      109–110, 112–113

RE family therapy approaches:
   process-oriented, 134–139
   structured multiple-family
      group, 111–117
   structured single-family,
      117–134
Adult children, *see* Young
   adulthood
Affect:
   negative, 22
   role of, 159
Affiliation, 161
Affirmation, significance of, 11
Ambivalence, 141–142
Anger, 189
Anthropological expeditions, 184
Anxiety management, 49, 177, 179
Assertive expression, 161
Assessment scales,
   intergenerational family
   therapy, 184
Attitude, significance of, 3, 27, 122
Audiotapes:
   in family-of-origin therapy, 188,
      190
   of home practice sessions, 4, 21,
      35–36, 54, 59–60, 172
Autobiography, 190
Autonomous-relatedness, 108